LIFE OUTSIDE
THE LAW FIRM

*Non-Traditional Careers
for Paralegals*

OTHER TITLES IN THE SERIES

Ransford C. Pyle, *Foundations of Law for Paralegals: Cases, Commentary, and Ethics*, 1992.

Peggy N. Kerley, Paul A. Sukys, Joanne Banker Hames, *Civil Litigation for the Paralegal*, 1992.

Jonathan Lynton, Donna Masinter, Terri Mick Lyndall, *Law Office Management for Paralegals*, 1992.

Daniel Hall, *Criminal Law and Procedure*, 1992.

Daniel Hall, *Survey of Criminal Law*, 1993.

Jonathan Lynton, Terri Mick Lyndall, *Legal Ethics and Professional Responsibility*, 1994.

Michael Kearns, *The Law of Real Property*, 1994.

Angela Schneeman, *The Law of Corporations, Partnerships, and Sole Proprietorships*, 1993.

William Buckley, *Torts and Personal Injury Law*, 1993.

Gordon W. Brown, *Administration of Wills, Trusts, and Estates*, 1993.

Richard Stim, *Intellectual Property: Patents, Copyrights, and Trademarks*, 1994.

Ransford C. Pyle, *Family Law*, 1994.

Jack Handler, *Ballentine's Law Dictionary: Legal Assistant Edition*, 1994.

Jonathan Lynton, *Ballentine's Thesaurus for Legal Research & Writing*, 1994.

Danial Hall, *Administrative Law*, 1994.

Angela Schneeman, *Paralegals in American Law*, 1994.

Eric M. Gansberg, *Paralegals in New York Law*, 1994.

Pamela Tepper, *The Law of Contracts and the Uniform Commercial Code*, 1995.

Jonathan Lynton, *Ballentine's Legal Dictionary and Thesaurus*, 1995.

Susan Covins, *Federal Taxation*, 1995.

C. B. Estrin, *Everything You Need to Know about Being a Legal Assistant*, 1995.

Cathy Okrent, *Legal Terminology with Flash Cards*, 1995.

Carol Bast, *Legal Research and Writing*, 1995.

R

LIFE OUTSIDE THE LAW FIRM

Non-Traditional Careers for Paralegals

Karen Treffinger

Delmar Publishers

I(T)P An International Thomson Publishing Company

Albany • Bonn • Boston • Cincinnati • Detroit • London • Madrid • Melbourne
Mexico City • New York • Pacific Grove • Paris • San Francisco • Singapore • Tokyo
Toronto • Washington

Treffinger, Karen.

Life outside the law firm

:s described herein or perform any independent
n contained herein. Publisher does not assume,
de information other than that provided to it by

ll safety precautions that might be indicated by
azards. By following the instructions contained
n with such instructions.

Cover background: Jennifer McGlaughlin
Cover Design: Doug Hyldelund

Delmar Staff

Acquisitions Editor: Jay Whitney
Developmental Editor: Christopher Anzalone
Project Editor: Eugenia L. Orlandi
Production Coordinator: Jennifer Gaines
Art & Design Coordinator: Douglas Hyldelund

COPYRIGHT © 1995

By Delmar Publishers
a division of International Thomson Publishing Inc.

I(T)P˚ The ITP logo is a trademark under license
Printed in the United States of America

For more information, contact:

Delmar Publishers
3 Columbia Circle, Box 15015
Albany, NY 12212-5015

International Thomson Publishing Europe
Berkshire House 168-173
High Holborn
London, WC1V7AA
England

Thomas Nelson Australia
102 Dodds Street
South Melbourne, 3205
Victoria, Australia

Nelson Canada
1120 Birchmont Road
Scarborough, Ontario
Canada M1K 5G4

International Thomson Editores
Compos Eliseos 385, Piso 7
Col Polanco
11560 Mexico D F Mexico

International Thomson Publishing Gmbh
Königswinterer Strasse 418
53227 Bonn
Germany

International Thomson Publishing Asia
221 Henderson Road #05-10
Henderson Building
Singapore 0315

International Thomson Publishing – Japan
Hirakawacho Kyowa Building, 3F
2-2-1 Hirakawacho
Chiyoda-ku, 102 Tokyo
Japan

1 2 3 4 5 6 7 8 9 10 XXX 01 00 99 98 97 96 95

Library of Congress Cataloging-in-Publication Data

Treffinger, Karen
    Life outside the law firm : non-traditional careers for paralegals / Karen Treffinger. — 1st ed.
      p. cm.
    Includes index.
    ISBN 0-8273-6718-X
    1. Legal assistants—Vocational guidance—United States. 2. Job hunting—United States.
3. Career changes—United States.
KF320.L4T68   1995
340'.023'73—dc20
                                                                                94-29379
                                                                                CIP

CONTENTS

PREFACE

PURPOSE

The objective in writing this book grew from feelings of both excitement and frustration: excitement that so many doors are opening to paralegals in non-traditional areas and frustration that so few people know what those paralegals are doing or where they are doing it.

The primary purposes of this book are (1) to explore some opportunities and (2) to provide the reader selected "day-in-the-lives" profiles of non-traditional paralegals. Interviews with sixteen paralegals working in a wide range of settings give the reader the opportunity to hear what non-traditional paralegals have to say.

The book can be used as a textbook or as a career reference book for working paralegals interested in non-traditional alternatives as well as for people exploring the paralegal field. Prospective employers will also find it helpful in determining paralegal utilization.

STRUCTURE OF THE BOOK

Chapter 1 defines the non-traditional paralegal, showing differences in job duties and locations, and factors influencing paralegals to chose or remain in non-traditional employment.

Six chapters of interviews follow: Chapter 2—paralegals in corporate legal departments; Chapter 3—paralegals in corporations but outside the legal departments; Chapter 4—paralegals in local, state, and federal government; Chapter 5—paralegals working for non-profit organizations; and Chapter 6—paralegals as entrepreneurs.

There are three appendices. Appendix A includes resumes of the interviewees. Appendix B comprises three lists of paralegal job titles: The first list is job titles which are based on the type of law a paralegal might practice; the second is law-related job titles found within the federal government; and the third is typical job titles of non-traditional paralegals. Appendix C lists professional paralegal associations. This list is organized by state, with affiliations to the National Association of Legal Assistants Inc., and the National Federation of Paralegal Associations Inc., indicated.

CHAPTER FEATURES

Chapter 1 includes statistics, charts, and graphs from various surveys regarding non-traditional paralegals. The interview chapters (Chapters 2–6) begin with a short discussion of the common themes of the chapter interviews. Job statistics—salary range, benefits, and job descriptions—are included in a chart in each interview. "Hot" topics mentioned by interviewees are discussed in boxes throughout the chapters, with supporting charts and statistics.

INSTRUCTOR'S MANUAL

An instructor's manual is available, with ideas for how the book can be incorporated into the classroom through discussion questions and student projects.

ACKNOWLEDGMENTS

The paralegal profession has been extremely good to me—only because of it was I able to write this book. Along the same lines, Delmar Publishers, and particularly Jay Whitney, deserve my deep gratitude for giving me the opportunity (and the headache!). All sixteen paralegals interviewed for the book were kind enough to give me their time, energy, and thoughts, even under tight deadlines. Thanks!

I would like to say a special thank you to my mom, dad, sister, brother, and brother-in-law, because having a great family makes everything easier; to my wonderful boss, Les Moroye, for having a sense of humor about this, even when I was obnoxious at work; and to Charlie Marlowe for giving me her WordPerfect expertise, patience, and encouragement, even when working with me by camping lantern into the wee hours.

And finally, from the bottom of my heart, thank you to Mark Kronauer, for being there all the time.

For Mark

Who believed I could do it

CHAPTER 1

Traditional versus Non-Traditional Paralegals

INTRODUCTION

*B*etween 70 and 80 percent of paralegals are employed by law firms. This is also where most lawyers are employed. But if 70 to 80 percent of paralegals work in law firms, where are the other 20 to 30 percent? Where do they work? What do they do? How are they different from traditional paralegals? And what are their daily lives like?

This book attempts to answer these questions. The answers are important because, although there are many doors opening for paralegals, few paralegals (not to mention the general public) realize just how many opportunities there are. Paralegals are hired for their legal skills and understanding of the legal system. Non-traditional jobs using legal skills are a whole new world of opportunities for both the new and the experienced paralegal.

Innovation in the job is demonstrated repeatedly by the sixteen non-traditional paralegals interviewed for this book. Each works outside a law firm, as follows:

Interviewee	Employer
Yvonne Barlow	Gaylord Entertainment Company
Donna Barr	Archdiocese of Denver
Jo Barrett	Freelance Paralegal
Scott Collister	DataTrace Mortgage Investment Services, Inc.
Mary Kelly Finegan	Philadelphia VIP
David L. Hay	Dallas County Community College District
Janis Jones	Toyota Motor Sales, U.S.A., Inc.
Kathy Klima	The Money Store Investment Corp.
Marian Miller	City & Borough of Juneau
Rosie Odum	Federal Express Corporation
Lyndi Reed	Diebold, Inc.
Kathy Gedeon Scott	The Philadelphia Institute
Lori Thompson	FDIC
Kathleen Weir	Attorney General's Office
Janis Whisman	The Nature Conservancy
Shelley Widoff	Paralegal Resource Center, Inc.

The interviews represent thousands of paralegals across the nation who have found employment in corporations, government agencies, non-profit organizations, and educational institutions, or as entrepreneurs. Each shares his or her insights and experiences as a non-traditional paralegal.

DEFINITION OF A TRADITIONAL PARALEGAL

To understand the difference between a traditional and a non-traditional paralegal, it is first necessary to define the terms. This is more difficult than it sounds. In an emerging profession without mandatory entrance requirements, there is no single definition of a paralegal. However, most definitions share some common components, although none currently acknowledge the existence of the non-traditional paralegal.

Perhaps the simplest definition can be found in a legal dictionary. For example, *Ballentine's Law Dictionary: Legal Assistant Edition* (Delmar/LCP, 1994) defines a paralegal as

> A person who, although not an attorney, performs many of the functions of an attorney under an attorney's supervision.

The National Association of Legal Assistants (NALA) takes its definition further:

> Legal assistants are a distinguishable group of persons who assist attorneys in the delivery of legal services. Through formal education, training, and experience, legal assistants have knowledge and expertise regarding the legal system and substantive and procedural law which qualify them to do work of a legal nature under the supervision of an attorney. Within this occupational category, individuals are also known as "paralegals."

The American Bar Association (ABA) definition contains many of the same components as the NALA definition, but expands on *where* a paralegal may work:

> A legal assistant is a person, qualified through education, training, or work experience, who is employed or retained by a lawyer, law office, governmental agency, or other entity in a capacity or function which involves the performance, under the ultimate direction and supervision of an attorney, of specifically delegated substantive legal work, which work, for the most part, requires a sufficient knowledge of legal concepts that, absent such assistant, the attorney would perform the task.

However, this definition, too, states that a paralegal works ultimately *only* under the direction and supervision of an attorney.

The National Federation of Paralegal Associations (NFPA) definition is the only one that allows the possibility that paralegals may at times *not* work under a lawyer. Indeed, this is the circumstance in which many non-traditional paralegals find themselves.

> A paralegal/legal assistant is a person qualified through education, training or work experience to perform substantive legal work that requires knowledge of legal concepts and is customarily, but not exclusively, performed by a lawyer. This person may be retained or employed by a lawyer, law office, governmental agency, or other entity, or may be authorized by administrative, statutory, or court authority to perform this work.

Nowhere does this definition state that a paralegal must be supervised by an attorney. Therefore, although it never outwardly discusses non-traditional paralegals, it does allow the existence of paralegals who may not be directly, or even indirectly, under attorney supervision.

What a Traditional Paralegal Does

A traditional paralegal can "perform substantive legal work that requires knowledge of legal concepts." But the question then becomes "What does a traditional paralegal do?" This question is nearly as difficult as the question "What is a traditional paralegal?" simply because there is no single answer.

The reason there is no single answer is that there are so many things paralegals do, and what they do depends largely on where they work. A paralegal working in a law firm which specializes in criminal law performs far different tasks than a paralegal employed by a real estate law firm. Both paralegals perform highly different daily tasks than a third counterpart employed by a nonprofit organization such as Legal Aid.

The complexity of tasks a paralegal may perform increases as his or her level of experience increases. Common tasks that many paralegals perform include drafting legal documents, collecting and organizing information and documents, maintaining records, monitoring cases, interviewing clients, performing legal research, and conducting investigations.

Where a Traditional Paralegal Works

The final question is, "Where does a traditional paralegal work?" The answer is quite simple: in law firms. NALA's 1993 National Utilization and Compensation Survey Report of 3,000 paralegals, found that the average paralegal works in a law firm staffed by twenty-five lawyers and seven paralegals. This paralegal is female, about 39 years old, and lives in a city with an average population of 500,000.

DEFINITION OF A NON-TRADITIONAL PARALEGAL

Now that the traditional paralegal is defined, how does the non-traditional paralegal differ from the traditional?

A non-traditional paralegal is defined as any person with paralegal training or experience who is *not* employed by a law firm, whose position may or may not be titled "paralegal" but requires typical paralegal skills. In some cases, paralegal experience or training is required for the position by an employer. In other cases, paralegals themselves have translated the skills they have gained over time into new positions.

What a Non-Traditional Paralegal Does

As stated above, what a traditional paralegal does is largely defined by where he or she works. This holds true for non-traditional paralegals as well. A non-traditional paralegal performs many of the same tasks the traditional paralegal performs, such as drafting legal documents and collecting and organizing information and documents. So the difference between the two does not lie in the duties which they perform, because the duties are substantially the same. (However, many non-traditional paralegals feel that they have a far higher level of challenging tasks and responsibility than traditional paralegals have).

Where a Non-Traditional Paralegal Works

The place of employment truly defines the difference between a traditional and non-traditional paralegal. Non-traditional paralegals work for corporations (both in legal departments and in a wide range of other departments), in government at all levels (local, state, and federal) in non-profit organizations, and as entrepreneurs. In short, they can work in any environment that uses the legal skills and knowledge that a paralegal brings to the work force.

Current surveys shed some light on the types of places where these paralegals are finding work. The NALA 1993 National Utilization and Compensation Survey Report found that 77 percent of the respondents work in law firms. The other 23 percent, the non-traditional paralegals, are employed in a variety of places. One percent work in banks, 2 percent work in insurance companies, 8 percent work in corporations, 7 percent work for government or in the public sector (the public sector primarily comprising non-profit organizations), 2 percent are self-employed, and 2 percent fall into the category of "other." (See Figure 1–1.)

The NALA survey is conducted every two years. Some small shifts occurred between the 1989 and 1993 surveys. For example, the number of paralegals employed by law firms decreased four percent during the four-year period—from 81 percent in 1989 to 77 percent in 1993 (see Figure 1–2). This is a small change, perhaps, but it does indicate a trend. One can specu-

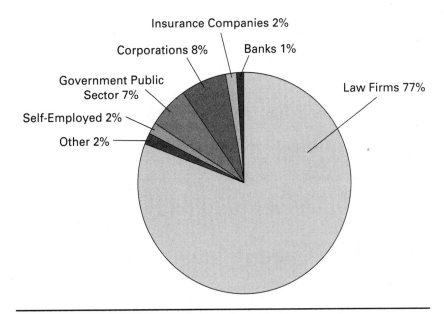

Figure 1-1   Paralegal Employment Sources (*Courtesy NALA 1993 National Utilization and Compensation Survey*)

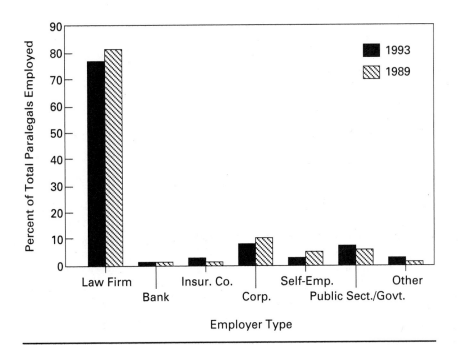

Figure 1-2   Employers of Paralegals (*Courtesy National Association of Legal Assistants*)

late that many paralegals employed outside of law firms may not have the title "paralegal," may not, therefore, identify themselves as paralegals, and consequently may not participate in paralegal surveys. Thus, there may actually be more non-traditional paralegals than any survey indicates.

WHY BE A NON-TRADITIONAL PARALEGAL

There are as many reasons to be a non-traditional paralegal as there are types of non-traditional jobs. The paralegals interviewed for this book cited a wide range of reasons for not working in law firms, including money, altruism, working environment, benefits, skill utilization, challenge and independence, career ladders, and competition for traditional paralegal jobs.

Influencing Factors

1. Money

For non-traditional paralegals employed in corporations, a major reason may be money. *Legal Assistant Today's* 1993 Salary Survey, a national poll of their readership, found that paralegals employed in corporations reported an average salary of $32,949. This is 13.3 percent higher than the average salary of $29,071 reported by paralegals in law firms (see Figure 1–3). For some paralegals employed in corporations, the salary range is far better, as Lyndi Reed stated: " . . . the money is so much better in a corporation. In my first shift from private practice to a corporation, I literally doubled my salary." On the other hand, non-traditional paralegals employed in government or the public sector report an average salary of $27,954—3.8 percent lower than their counterparts in law firms.

2. Altruism

Although non-traditional paralegals in government and the public sector typically make less money than other non-traditional paralegals, they cite altruism as a motivator. They derive satisfaction from working for the public. ". . . there are days when I have wonderful things that I bring home in my heart that I know I've done for people. Today, I got a lawyer for a man who was on the verge of becoming homeless. I'll go home tonight knowing that his situation is taken care of." (Mary Kelly Finegan) ". . . you don't work in the government for big money. But when your clients are the people who live in the state you have a sense of doing something important in every case." (Kathleen Weir)

3. Working Environment

Non-traditional paralegals leave law firms in search of a better working environment. Law firms can be stressful places to work. Other locations

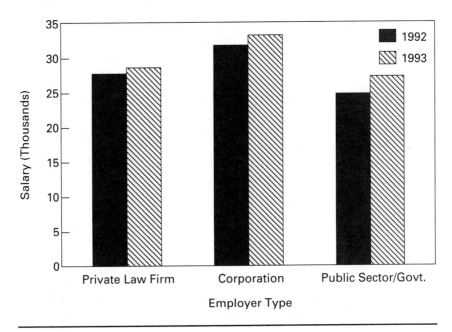

Figure 1-3   Average Paralegal Salaries by Type of Employer
                   (*Courtesy* Legal Assistant Today)

may eliminate some stress. Donna Barr offers the following as a reason for taking a non-traditional position: "I wanted to be in an environment that realized that you had another life outside of work and that there are more important things in life than billable hours and the whole package that comes with that. I was really frustrated with the stress level."

Non-traditional paralegals may also find less hierarchy and more team spirit and camaraderie in work outside a law firm. "... in our office we don't think 'No, I can't do that because it's a secretary's job.' Our attorneys will answer the phone if it's ringing. There's a nice attitude in this office. . . . Things are more informal here. Everybody works together." (Marian Miller) "... the people I work with here are more approachable and team oriented. . . . there's a camaraderie that I never felt at the law firms where I've worked. We're all doing a different part of the job, but the end goal is the same for everybody." (Janis Whisman)

4. Benefits

Benefit packages for non-traditional paralegals are a factor. The 1993 Benefits Survey of 630 paralegals nationwide, conducted by *Legal Assistant Today*, compared benefit packages of paralegals in law firms to those in corporations (see Figure 1–4). Some benefits are actually better for law firm paralegals than for corporate paralegals. For example, 72.5 percent of

	Law Firms		Corporations	
	No. Resp. 473	Percent	No. Resp. 102	Percent
Work Location:				
Metropolitan	270	57.1	52	51.0
Urban	172	36.4	44	43.1
Rural	31	6.6	6	5.9
Sex:				
Male	26	5.5	2	2.0
Female	447	94.5	100	98.0
Office Space:				
Private	343	72.5	60	58.8
Shared	51	10.8	5	4.9
Partitioned	69	14.6	36	35.3
Other	10	2.1	1	1.0
Secretarial Assistance:				
Personal secretary	23	4.9	7	6.9
Shared secretary	247	52.2	54	52.9
Computer terminal	176	37.2	34	33.3
Other	27	5.7	7	6.9
Benefits:				
Retirement plan	390	82.5	99	97.1
Profit sharing	356	75.3	77	75.5
Employer contributions to retirement plan	414	87.5	98	96.1
Health insurance	425	89.9	98	96.1
Life insurance	354	74.8	94	92.2
Dental insurance	173	36.6	90	88.2
Disability insurance	296	62.6	88	86.3
Vision insurance	81	17.1	47	46.1
Maternity benefits	260	55.0	85	83.3
Free legal representation	277	58.6	13	12.7
Business cards	375	79.3	84	82.4
Expense account	78	16.5	51	50.0
Flex time	145	30.7	43	42.2
Mommy track	0	0.0	0	0.0
Parking allowance	186	39.3	28	27.5
Travel allowance	371	78.4	86	84.3
Child care	6	1.3	8	7.8
Credit card	67	14.2	33	32.4
Job sharing	17	3.6	3	2.9
Meal allowance	65	13.7	18	17.6
Professional dues	333	70.4	85	83.3
CLE courses	312	66.0	79	77.5
Retreat	54	11.4	21	20.6
Parental leave	186	39.3	56	54.9
Paid personal days off	272	57.5	70	68.6
Avg. no. vacation days	13.17		12.96	
Avg. no. of sick days	8.48		10.23	
Respondents w/unlimited sick days		24.3		31.4

Figure 1-4   Paralegal Benefits in Law Firms and Corporations (*Courtesy* Legal Assistant Today)

law firm paralegals have private offices, while only 58.8 percent of corporate paralegals enjoy this benefit. Law firm paralegals also receive free legal representation and parking allowances more often than their corporate counterparts do.

Nevertheless, most benefits in corporations are substantially better than in law firms. Health insurance benefits are similar, but other forms of insurance differ. For example corporations are 17 to 51 percent more likely than law firms to offer life, dental, disability, and vision insurance to their paralegal employees. Perhaps even more important for the female paralegal is the fact that maternity benefits are offered in 83.3 percent of the surveyed corporations but in only 55 percent of the law firms. Of concern to both female and male paralegals is that 54.9 percent of the corporations offer parental leave, compared with only 39.3 percent of the surveyed law firms.

None of this takes into consideration the more luxurious benefits that some non-traditional paralegals enjoy. For example, it is not uncommon for non-traditional paralegals employed in government or the public sector to receive four weeks or more of vacation per year. Paralegals working for corporations may have access to company restaurants and health clubs at minimal or no cost. "We have a twenty-four-hour fitness center that is only eight dollars a month. They have aerobics, TV, showers, juice—you don't have to do anything but bring your clothes." (Yvonne Barlow) Other non-traditional paralegals enjoy car or home-computer lease and purchase plans, company stores, and stock investment plans.

5. Skill Utilization

Many paralegals feel that their skills are underutilized in law firms—one more factor for leaving the traditional world. "I quit that job because I didn't think that my paralegal skills were being utilized very well." (Whisman) Fortunately, paralegalism is a career with a wide variety of skills that can be translated into a multitude of positions. "It's very valuable training. . . . you can take the paralegal skills and apply them to something that, although different, is very closely related to being a paralegal." (Scott Collister) "Really, I think the skills paralegals have . . . the basic skills, the organizational skills, and analytical ability are the same wherever you go. . . . You can take your fundamental knowledge and your basic skills and go anywhere with them if you want to." (Barlow)

Non-traditional paralegals successfully parlay their skills into new positions. Their skills are so transferrable that they find a great deal of similarity between their former, traditional positions and their new, non-traditional ones. "Once I got into it, I thought, "Oh, wow, this is exactly what I've been doing for years." (Reed)

Additionally, some non-traditional paralegals have never worked in a traditional law firm, but they, too, find that their past work skills translate well into a non-traditional paralegal position. For example, nurse-paralegals are working for pharmaceutical companies, hospitals, and insurance companies. Their nursing background combined with their paralegal training is invaluable for evaluating medical malpractice claims.

Nevertheless, even non-traditional paralegals sometimes find that their abilities are not well understood. ". . . not many people have a good understanding of what skills a paralegal has. So in order to move from this job into another, I'd first have a big task in educating those around me about what I can do. If I could accomplish that, then I think similarities between jobs and required skills would surface and more avenues would be open to me." (Whisman)

6. Challenge and Independence

Many non-traditional paralegals wanted more independence and challenge than they were able to find in traditional jobs. "[I have] an appetite for challenge. In the private sector, it's almost like working for a factory. . . . I'm not satisfied to do that." (David L. Hay) Non-traditional paralegals thrive on challenge and enjoy their freedom at work. "The job I have now gives me a lot of freedom. I feel like I have a lot of responsibility, and I don't have a lot of people looking over my shoulder. I have a lot of control over what I do." (Finegan)

With freedom comes responsibility. Non-traditional paralegals often work with a high level of autonomy, being primarily responsible for many decisions and cases. "I think that I have more responsibility, more sole responsibility for projects that I do." (Reed) "The challenge for us . . . is that we're the ones who actually . . . make all those decisions. Our supervising attorney is available if we seek guidance, but basically . . . we make most of those decisions on our own." (Janis Jones) The ability to work independently is a large factor in these paralegals' success. "You're not going to be successful in a paralegal position unless you are able to work independently. If you have to have somebody over you all the time telling you how to do it, when to do it, and what to do, you're not going to be successful." (Reed)

7. Career Ladders

An additional reason for leaving the traditional paralegal world is the availability of career tracks or ladders in the non-traditional world. Although some law firms do have career tracks for paralegals, opportunities for advancement are usually better elsewhere. Non-traditional employers such as government and corporations often have a specific path on which paralegals can move up, increasing their pay and responsibilities with each move. Employees can start as associate paralegals, for example, and eventually become senior paralegals. Paralegals employed by government agencies have additional opportunities to advance because they can transfer into other government agencies in their system that have higher positions open.

Non-traditional paralegals also have other advancement opportunities. Their employers may have many positions available that are not law-related, which a paralegal can perform. For example, a paralegal employed in a corporate legal department may advance to a position in the advertising department—an opportunity rarely available in any but the large law firms. Non-traditional employment widens paralegals' skills, making them more prepared for the workplace of the future, in *or* out of a law-related position. "I wanted something that would move me along a career path either here or someplace else, so that I could not only use my legal skills but also get more involved in the business side . . ." (Barr)

8. Competition for Traditional Paralegal Jobs

A final reason that paralegals may end up pursuing non-traditional positions is that competition for law firm jobs is keen. Other employers who need employees with legal skills can open up an enormous number of possibilities for a creative job seeker. Because of the number of applications they receive for paralegal positions, law firms can afford to be picky and hire only those with previous experience. Corporations and non-profit agencies may be more willing to consider a paralegal straight out of school. ". . . I was running into a dead end as far as the traditional paralegal positions went because I lacked experience. . . . [this company] didn't care that I didn't have experience." (Kathy Klima)

More new graduates of paralegal training programs are finding positions outside law firms. Placement figures from paralegal schools demonstrate this nontraditional growth (see Figure 1–5). The Denver Paralegal Institute found an enormous increase in the percentage of its graduates placed in government and corporate jobs between 1987 and 1991. In 1987, 5 percent of new institute graduates accepted positions with government entities, and by 1991 this figure had increased to 14 percent, or nearly triple the original figure. During the same period, graduates going to work for corporations almost doubled—from 9 percent to 19 percent.

If the competition for traditional paralegal jobs is what initially pushes some paralegals away from traditional positions, ultimately it is not what keeps them away. Life is so good outside of law firms that non-traditional paralegals have very little reason to consider going back. ". . . [Non-traditional paralegals] may never want to go to a traditional job because the opportunities are so good outside of the law firms!" (Klima)

Job Satisfaction of the Non-Traditional Paralegal

Non-traditional paralegals are happy with their jobs. As with any job, there are good and bad days, as one interviewee points out: "Now, this job is not perfect; no job is. . . . There are days when things go wrong and everything feels like it's tumbling down, but by and large, I love it." (Barlow)

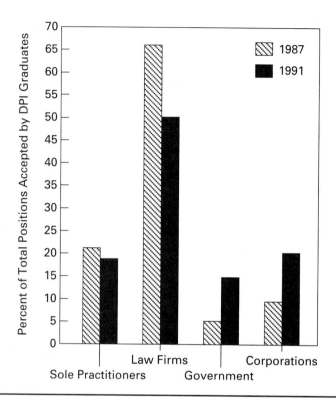

Figure 1-5   Employers of Entry-Level Paralegals (*Courtesy Denver Paralegal Institute*)

Not one of the sixteen paralegals interviewed for this book expressed any plans to leave his or her current position for a law firm job. There are too many benefits stated to return to traditional employment. These paralegals express a high level of job satisfaction and fulfillment. "My job is extremely fulfilling. It's wonderful. . . . I've been blessed." (Kathy Gedeon Scott)

Taking a traditional law firm paralegal job would be a step backward. These paralegals are obviously going to move forward. And if stepping forward means going out of the paralegal field, they have the skills and confidence to move on. They will have reached their peaks as paralegals and will seek new challenges. "Where I am now is very comfortable and I feel very satisfied and successful . . . [but] I'm looking to start a second career because I feel my first career has almost reached a pinnacle, in a certain sense . . ." (Shelley Widoff)

CHAPTER 2

Corporate Legal Departments

aralegals working in a corporate legal department have numerous reasons for pursuing a non-traditional career. One of the most obvious is the opportunity to work for only one client (the corporation) rather than for the multiple clients of a law firm. "When you work in a law firm you have to divide your loyalty and time among your clients and projects. Whereas when you work for the client, as I do, you don't have that division in your interest. All my energies can be given to my one client . . ." (Janis Jones)

Like other non-traditional paralegals, these paralegals enjoy a higher level of freedom and responsibility than they would have in a law firm. "I think I probably have more responsibilities and less supervision than the paralegal friends I have in law firms. . . . I have more freedom and less supervision, sometimes to the point of it being a little scary." (Yvonne Barlow) "I work with a high level of responsibility, with a low level of supervision, which makes it challenging." (Jones)

Sometimes paralegals in corporate legal departments have such a high level of responsibility that they actually perform many tasks that traditionally were the corporate attorney's. "What makes my job so interesting and challenging is that until about three years ago the job that I currently do, along with two other paralegals, was performed by an attorney. At that time management decided that these cases could be managed and administered by paralegals with attorney supervision." (Jones)

Other reasons for pursuing a paralegal career within a corporation are the pay, hours, benefits, and physical environment a corporation can offer. "It's a great company, there are good benefits . . . we have insurance . . . paid vacation and holidays . . . a tuition refund program . . . profit sharing, stock investment, retirement savings, credit union . . . a company store . . . an employee discount . . ." (Rosie Odum) "Also it's beautiful out here. This is just a really nice environment to work in. . . . I got the same pay, I negotiated my extra week of vacation, and have similar benefits. So I felt that all in all I came out ahead." (Barlow)

Some of these paralegals also reap the benefits of a structured career ladder. ". . . the best benefit is the opportunity to advance . . . You have to work for two years as an associate paralegal before you can move up to the paralegal level. . . . An associate paralegal is a level 19, a paralegal is level 21, and a senior paralegal is level 23." (Odum) "When I started I was called legal assistant. After about two years I was promoted to senior legal assistant." (Jones)

However, many enjoy their jobs so much that they aren't particularly concerned about moving up a career ladder. "I'm content to do what I do now. I'm not looking for 'advancement' in terms of changing positions and moving up." (Barlow) "That's what it really comes down to in my mind—that you're fairly compensated for doing your job well day in and day out. So the fact that there's not upward mobility where I am now is not necessarily a negative." (Jones)

Happiness in their work is expressed by this group of paralegals. "I think you should go for what you want and always be happy at what you're doing. If you're not happy, you won't do the job well. If you're happy and willing to step out and learn more, opportunities will come." (Odum) ". . . you should be happy in your job. That's the most important thing of all. The money's not important, the vacation's not important because if all of those hours that you spend on the job are not fulfilling, you're missing the boat. That's my plan—just to enjoy it as long as it's fun. When it's not fun anymore, *if* it becomes not fun anymore, I will look elsewhere. I tell people 'Life is too short not to enjoy what you're doing.'" (Barlow)

INTERVIEW A

Most of the work that I do is in the area of consumer litigation, and most of the claims are brought under breach of warranty statutes or lemon laws. What makes my job so interesting and challenging is that until about three years ago, the job that I currently do, along with two other paralegals, was performed by an attorney. At that time management decided that these cases could be managed and administered by paralegals with attorney supervision.

Janis Lewis Jones

Company: Toyota Motor Sales, U.S.A., Inc.
City: Torrance, CA
Department: Legal Department
Title: Senior Legal Administrator
Salary Range: $38,000–$54,000
Benefits:
    Insurance: medical, dental, vision, life, disability
    Financial: savings and pension plan, credit union
    Vacation: 15 days (after 5 years)
    Sick time: 7 days
    Misc.:   2 days personal time, 12 paid holidays. On-campus facilities: fitness center, 3 restaurants, store, dry cleaner. Vehicle lease/purchase/rental program, tuition aid, holiday party, service awards, family picnic, dependent care reimbursement, etc.

Previous Work Experience:
Three years as a litigation paralegal for a large law firm. Three years as an entertainment transactional and litigation paralegal for a small law

firm. One and a half years as an entertainment litigation paralegal for a small law firm.

JOB DESCRIPTION:

General Summary

Administer consumer lawsuits, provide paralegal support to business litigators and other departments in the company.

Principal Duties:

- Manage litigation on fifty to sixty "Lemon Law" and breach of warranty lawsuits from complaint through resolution, including trial.
- Respond to all third-party subpoenas for company documents.
- Conduct legal and factual research.
- Obtain for outside counsel documents and company information needed in business litigation.
- Review all garnishments and advise payroll department on any resulting legal issues.

KZ: Janis, you work for Toyota, in California, at the company's national headquarters, and you're in a legal department.
JJ: It is *the* legal department, for the whole country.

KZ: So, a big job.
JJ: Right. My duties cover the entire country, which makes it interesting. I have forty-nine states worth of civil procedure to contend with.

KZ: Minus what?
JJ: Hawaii. Since we're the importer of the vehicles from Japan, it makes sense just to drop them off in Hawaii directly rather than bring them to the U.S. and then send them back. The company's been in the U.S. about thirty years.

KZ: You are senior legal administrator. Can you tell me a little about how the department is structured?
JJ: There were actually two legal departments until recently. One was called Business Law, and one was called Product Law. The Product Law group's main emphasis was product liability litigation.

The Business Law group basically did everything else for the company: corporate maintenance, finance issues, dealer relations, dealer litigation, labor and employment, and it handled all non-injury consumer litigation. That's the group that I work in. The Department recently combined under one vice-president and general counsel, but there's still these different aspects. I believe we have about seventy people in our department.

KZ: How many attorneys and paralegals?

JJ: Approximately twenty attorneys and nine paralegals. We have one professional staff person, which is how the paralegals are categorized and one manager, or attorney. So that's a pretty good ratio for support.

Most of the work that I do is in the area of consumer litigation, and most of the claims are brought under breach of warranty statutes or lemon laws. What makes my job so interesting and challenging is that until about three years ago, the job that I currently do, along with two other paralegals, was performed by an attorney. At that time management decided that these cases could be managed and administered by paralegals with attorney supervision.

KZ: That's wonderful, because you must have a large amount of autonomous responsibility.

JJ: Yes. From the day the complaint is served through the day the settlement agreement is signed or the case dismissed, it is the responsibility of the paralegal to handle the case. It is never assigned to an attorney. But we work with attorney supervision. The attorneys have trained us to be aware of the legal issues and legal strategies involved in handling the cases, and they are available to discuss issues of law that come up or strategies with motions or discovery that we want to address. Also, for certain dollar amounts we have to go to the attorneys for our authority.

KZ: Do the attorneys have to sign off on legal documents for you, or do you have the authority to do that?

JJ: By legal documents do you mean documents filed with the court?

KZ: Yes, generally.

JJ: No. On each of our consumer litigation cases, if we decide to answer the complaint and go forward with the litigation, we retain local counsel with a law firm in the state where the case was brought. Usually, it's just one plaintiff, and the cases are fairly straightforward as to the facts. So we do some discovery, take the deposition of the plaintiff and, maybe, his expert, such as his mechanic, and during the whole time we try to evaluate whether it's something we want to defend or settle.

The challenge for us, as paralegals, is that we're the ones who are the client contact with the local counsel, and we make all those decisions. Our supervising attorney is available if we seek guidance, but basically, after having done these for years now, we make most of those decisions on our own.

KZ: You have a high level of independence.

JJ: Yes, we do. The country is divided up among the three paralegals by state. We each have a third of the states, and for variety, I guess, we each have states on the East Coast, in the Midwest, in the South, and in the West. I spend probably fifty percent of my time on the phone, and on any given day I might talk to people from North Carolina, Illinois, Wyoming, and Southern California.

It's quite interesting. The challenge is really in the volume. Toyota has very few cases in comparison to other manufacturers, but I probably have about fifty open cases at any one time.

KZ: Which is a fairly high case load.
JJ: Yes. That's a pretty heavy case load, and it takes up about fifty percent of my time.

KZ: What do you do with the other fifty percent? Your title is senior legal administrator. Does that mean the other fifty percent of your time is spent in a supervisory capacity? Or does every paralegal there have the same title?
JJ: No. When I started I was called legal assistant. After two years, I was promoted to senior legal assistant. But in our company, people who are at our grade level, in the professional category, are called administrators, which is where the title derives. "Administrator" is a word which correlates with other job titles, so those outside the legal department can tell from your title what level you are.

KZ: I expect that, in the corporate world, that's important.
JJ: Yes. In corporate politics, that's important. The title is also a form of recognition that I've worked for Toyota for six years. Especially with times being a little financially tight, the raises are not as frequent as they used to be, so you take things like title upgrades as a reflection of your value to the company.

The "administrator" part of my title doesn't mean that I supervise anyone. I don't actually have anyone working under me, although I have helped the newer paralegals. What it does refer to is the fact that we paralegals administer the cases.

KZ: Back to the other fifty percent of your time—what do you do with it?
JJ: I'm available to provide paralegal support for business litigation, which is something that at one time I was much more involved in than I am now. By paralegal support I mean coordinating with our outside law firms to provide them with all of the documents that we have to help them respond to discovery requests or to evaluate or defend the case. The company [Toyota] is the client, and in order to properly represent the client they need quite a bit of information. Providing that information and being the communication channel is my role.

KZ: That must put you into contact with an enormous number of people.
JJ: That's one of the great things about my job. I not only have contact with attorneys all over the country, but I also have contact with all types of people within Toyota. I work with accountants, marketing people, distribution people, technical people, and operations people. That makes the job very interesting. These are very knowledgeable people who have a lot to share, and that expands my own knowledge base. Many times in these lawsuits, I learn so much that I become sort of a lay expert on aspects of the company, and I find that very enjoyable.

A related comment to that is that it is always very clear whom I work for. When you work in a law firm you have to divide your loyalty and time among your clients and projects, whereas when you work for the client, as I do, you don't have that division in your interest. All my energies can be given to my one client, Toyota.

However, we don't think of Toyota itself as being just one client. We view the different departments in Toyota as individual clients. My particular clients are the customer relations department for both Toyota and Lexus, and the payroll department. For example, I advise the payroll department on all wage garnishments for all of Toyota's companies all over the country, so I have to review them to see that they're valid. I have to do the research for the state that the garnishment is in, so I can answer their questions properly.

An area which has kept me very busy this week is vehicle safety complaints. Periodically, the National Highway Traffic and Safety Administration, which is an arm of the Department of Transportation, gets enough safety-related complaints about a type of vehicle that they will do an investigation. It's my job to respond on behalf of my department. This means that I have to review all of the files, which, fortunately, are on a computer database, to determine which might be responsive, and then I pull them, review them, make the copies (my secretary would make the copies), and put them into memo form.

I also review and respond to all third-party subpoenas for company records. With this job, again, I get to meet and work with people from other departments.

I think your observation is correct. I work with a high level of responsibility and a low level of supervision, which makes it challenging. But I never feel like I'm floundering in terms of not having attorney support, because there are attorneys available who have experience in all the areas I work in.

KZ: As you said, in your current job, Toyota is your client. Working for that one client is different from working for a law firm, where you typically have many clients. Did you come out of a law firm environment where that was the case?
JJ: Yes.

KT: What was your background?

JJ: To begin with, I worked in a large, downtown Los Angeles law firm with hundreds of attorneys for about three years. I spent most of my time summarizing documents and depositions and indexing and Bates stamping.

KT: All the fun stuff!

JJ: Right. Fortunately, I did sometimes get involved with trial work, which *was* exciting. After I decided that the hurry-up-and-wait pace of litigation was not for me, I was fortunate to find a very old, prestigious entertainment law firm with about sixteen attorneys in Hollywood that was looking for a litigation paralegal to train in entertainment. That just sounded so great to me. I went to work for this law firm, and they paid me to train in music publishing, some television production, corporate maintenance for entertainment clients, contracts and licensing, and copyright registration for music clients on new albums and new songs. I was the only paralegal there. The firm had many high profile music clients, performers, and directors.

But, believe it or not, after about a year and a half, I started to miss litigation. I'm someone who's always looking ahead for my next career move, even if I have no plans on changing jobs.

KT: You want to keep the doors open, even if you don't ever go through them.

JJ: Right. What I found was that the work I was doing in the entertainment section was not very marketable—it's a very specialized niche. The studios and record companies did have people in similar positions, but they didn't pay them beans. So I thought "You know, I really need to keep my finger in the litigation pie."

KT: What did you do then?

JJ: I approached the litigators in the firm and told them I'd like to provide them with litigation support. Of course, they snapped me up right away. I did that for about three years. Then I took a position in an entertainment litigation law firm. It was perfect because it combined the excitement of being in the entertainment area with the skills that I wanted to continue to build in the litigation area.

That was a very small firm. It had five attorneys, and again I was the only paralegal. I was at that job until I moved. A headhunter called me out of the blue about a month before I was planning to move to my home down here by the beach. She had an entertainment job up in Beverly Hills. I said "Sorry. I'm moving in the other direction, but if you hear of anything that comes up down toward Long Beach, please let me know." She said "As a matter of fact, Toyota is looking for a paralegal and you would be perfect."

KT: It's nice to be in demand!

JJ: I hadn't planned on interviewing in a corporation and hadn't paid a lot of attention to what goes on in one. I had *never* dreamed I would work for an automotive company. What probably attracted me most was the geographic desirability and the reasonable hours, because at that time I had a young child. I thought "This is coming along at the right time for me."

So I accepted the job and started out doing a different kind of work than I do now—prelitigation claims. I did that for a couple of years before I started doing the litigation.

KT: Now that you've been in both the law firm and the corporate world, which do you like better?

JJ: The corporate.

KT: Why?

JJ: The answer is probably what appears to be obvious to me—the reasonable hours and the benefits package, combined with a competitive salary. Having only one client, Toyota, is a plus because it enables you to develop an ongoing working relationship with the client. You can become familiar with the client's products, personnel, and philosophy. You have the luxury of developing a really deep knowledge. Another great benefit is that we don't do time sheets.

KT: The infamous billing requirements!

JJ: Yes. Working for one client eliminates that problem. I also very much enjoy the opportunity to work with other people daily who are not legal types. When I worked in a law firm, it was very easy to develop a certain mindset and attitude. Here we have a philosophy I'm proud of, even though it increases our workload, and that is that we try to be proactive. We try to get involved in things on the front end—when a contract is being drafted, when a license is being entered into, when legislation is being drafted—so that Toyota can continue to be a responsible citizen and contributor to the country, rather than be seen as cleaning up the mess after something falls apart.

KT: Unlike a law firm, where, although through no fault of the law firm perhaps, you often spend much of your time fixing problems that have already developed.

JJ: It's a whole different ball game. We walk a fine line between the economics of managing a case and the bigger economic picture of knowing you can't pay the plaintiff on every frivolous lawsuit filed, because it could open a floodgate of people who think all you have to do is file a complaint against Toyota and they'll send you a check.

KT: Any drawbacks to the job?

JJ: There's not a lot of upward mobility in our company.

The Dreaded Billing Requirement

Very few, if any, paralegals are neutral on the topic of billing. Most hate it. In a billing system, paralegals are expected to work a certain number of hours per day which can be billed out to a client. Many firms have a minimum billing requirement. For example, paralegals in a particular firm may be expected to bill out seven and a half hours a day. Obviously, this can be difficult, especially if the paralegal is also expected to perform daily tasks which are not billable to any client, such as training new paralegals or attending a company workshop.

There is a correlation, although perhaps a weak one, between billable hours and a paralegal's compensation. Supposedly, if a paralegal is producing more hours of work which can be billed to a client, more money is coming in to the firm and the paralegal's salary may be higher. But working more hours, and thus billing out more hours, may not, in reality, have much effect on a paralegal's actual salary. For example, the Legal Assistant Management Association (LAMA) 1993 National Compensation Survey found that, in the previous year, paralegals who billed from 1,251 to 1,500 hours made $31,917 a year; from 1,501 to 1,750 hours, $32,167; from 1,751 to 2,000 hours, $33,103; and more than 2,000 hours, $35,247 (see Figure 2–1). There wasn't a huge difference in the salaries of the bottom and the top billers, yet the top billers were working far more hours. In other words, even though a top-billing paralegal may make more money, he or she may actually make less money per hour than a bottom biller. Of course, some firms base annual bonuses on how many hours a paralegal has billed throughout the year, which may more than make up for the inequity in pay.

HINT:

One thing almost all non-traditional paralegals love is not having to deal with billing requirements. They like not having to track every minute of their time on the job, and they like not having the stress of meeting a billing minimum. There are a few non-traditional paralegals who still have billing requirements. If this is an important consideration to you, ask about it when interviewing for a non-traditional job.

KT: Then what do you see as your future?
JJ: Well, I never perceived that much upward mobility in a law firm, either. I think you just continue to do your best job and hope that you're recognized in terms of interesting work, attorneys coming back to you—

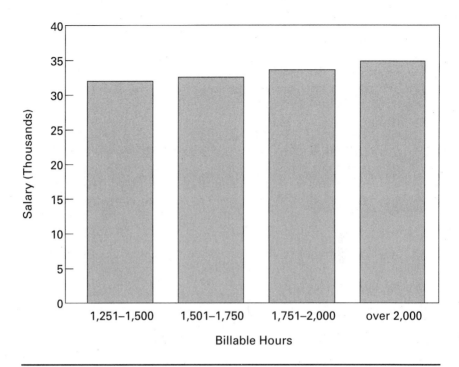

Figure 2-1   Paralegal Salaries versus Billable Hours (*Courtesy Legal Assistant Management Association*)

attorneys you like—and your raises. That's what it really comes down to in my mind—that you're compensated for doing your job well day in and day out. So the fact that there's no upward mobility where I am now is not necessarily a negative.

I think that when I feel my ambition rearing its head (I won't say its ugly head), what I would like to try, and what I'm starting this fall, is teaching. I might like to freelance, too—not as a working paralegal but perhaps as a consultant to law firms on setting up paralegal programs and hiring paralegals, especially by hooking up with placement departments in paralegal schools. I think that's a good source of trained, professional paralegals.

I don't know about Denver, but in Los Angeles, you see a lot of people passing themselves off as paralegals who have no background whatsoever. They come and go. Many of them are want-to-be actors who are just passing their time doing paralegal work, and it really disparages those of us who are trained in the profession and have deliberately chosen it as what we want to do.

I don't see any change for me in the near future because I'm still finding out if I like teaching and if teaching likes me and if I can be successful with it. I am on the advisory board of a local junior college, and I'm learning a lot about the education process. Although I never perceived myself as a teacher, it's something that I'm very excited about.

KZ: It sounds like much of your motivation to teach stems from your wanting to pass on your knowledge and also hoping that you can help train paralegals better than they have been in the past, if they've been trained at all.

JJ: Yes. Another thing I don't think is being done nearly enough is the training of attorneys in the use of paralegals. We work very hard to network and educate ourselves, legislators, and people who want to come into the profession, but we forget to educate the attorneys. After all, we're still mainly hired by attorneys. We need to let them know that there are trained, professional, committed paralegals out there.

KZ: Any final words of wisdom?

JJ: I guess my thoughts for new and currently working paralegals is to encourage them to continue to grow in the profession and in the direction that the profession and market demand. That includes getting involved with a local professional organization as well as continuing their education. I think that's very important. Some paralegals say, "Well, I've been doing it for twenty years," as though there's nothing else they can learn. But I think there are always new areas of law opening up where paralegal support is needed.

INTERVIEW B

I think that in today's employment market, you've got to be well-rounded. If you specialize too heavily, it's going to limit you when you go to look for another job. I think that's what got me the job here. There were several candidates, but I believe I had a broader knowledge than they did.

Carla Yvonne Barlow
(Yvonne)

Company:	Gaylord Entertainment Company
City:	Nashville
Department:	Legal Department
Title:	Paralegal
Salary Range:	$34,000–$40,000
Benefits:	
Insurance:	medical, dental
Financial:	pension plan, credit union, 401(k), stock purchase plan
Vacation:	21 days
Sick time:	6 days
Misc.:	2 personal days, fitness center

Previous Work Experience:
Sixteen years with a bank as a legal secretary, paralegal, and legal administrator.

JOB DESCRIPTION:

General Summary

Assists attorneys in all legal services provided to Opryland USA, Inc., and related companies, including the Broadmoor Hotel and Fiesta Texas, through investigation, research, drafting of legal documents, monitoring of court proceedings, and the organization and computerization of records and department information.

Job Duties

- Prepare contracts for corporate sponsors, concessionaires, and performers (singers, dancers, etc.)
- Prepare various releases and indemnities; prepare various corporate documents, including but not limited to written consent actions, resolutions, secretary's certificates, meeting notices, etc. Prepare various corporate filings (i.e., annual reports, foreign qualification, dissolutions, assumed-name filings). Maintain current list of officers and directors for each corporate entity as well as current mailing addresses.
- Accept service for garnishments and wage assignments, forward to appropriate payroll entity, answer to appropriate court, and field any problems related to same.
- Prepare and maintain records for collection of cable and satellite royalties.
- Maintain approximately 250 trademark/service marks. Fill all requests for information regarding date of first use, provide specimens of use, etc.
- Assist with preparation of various SEC filings (i.e., proxy statement, S-8s, 10-K, Forms 3, 4, and 5).
- Review and revise talent contracts.
- Assist attorneys with investigation and accumulation of information and supporting evidence, scheduling, responses, etc., for litigation.
- Assist outside counsel with lawsuits.

Education/Experience:

Formal Education: College degree
  and/or
  Specific Experience Required: two years with a law firm or corporate legal department, including assistance in litigation, legal research, drafting legal documents, and maintaining corporate books and records.
  Licenses or certifications required: paralegal certification from an ABA-approved school.

YB: I work for Gaylord Entertainment Company, which went public about two years ago. It's a conglomeration of entertainment and hospitality services, including the amusement park Opryland USA, the Grand Old Opry, radio and television stations, a production company, a hotel with convention facilities, and a really nice golf course.

I came here about a year and a half ago. I had been a paralegal with First American National Bank in Nashville for sixteen years.

KT: Sixteen years! A long time.

YB: Yes. I was ready to make a change. I was supervising at the bank as well as doing paralegal work. I was the office administrator. I didn't like that at all.

KT: Office administrator of the legal department?

YB: Yes. I wanted to go back to doing just plain, cut and dried, paralegal work. And this opening came up. It's outside of the city; in fact it's at the amusement park, and it's very pretty. It's a great job. There are currently three paralegals and I just like dealing with all the entertainment services that we provide.

KT: Other than not having the administrative duties that you had in your other job, how is it different from that job?

YB: Oh, it's very different! Banking and the entertainment industry? It's like night and day. Banking is very, very restricted, structured, regulated, conservative. It is very cut and dried as to how you do things. I did a lot of SEC work there, budgeting, and a lot of administrative and supervisory tasks.

Here my work runs the gamut. One day I may do a license agreement for a trademark; today I did one for a character called Patchy Panda. We're entering into a license agreement to allow a woman who is writing a children's book to incorporate Opryland USA into her book. So it's very different.

KT: If the areas are so different, how were you able to take your skills from banking to entertainment? Did they translate at all, or did you have to completely retrain?

YB: I think that organizational skills and analytical ability can move with a paralegal no matter where you go. Also, I had experience with contracts— not a lot, but I knew the basic parts of a contract, what was legal and what was not. What was hard was transition from banking terminology to entertainment terminology. They kept talking about a venue. And I finally asked, "What is a venue? I don't know what you're talking about."

KT: I thought it was a legal term, a place of trial.

YB: Not in the context they were using it. They told me it's the theater where a performance will take place.

Clearly, the organizational skills that I brought with me serve me well. I may be in the middle of something, have to drop it to move on to something else, and then two hours later come back to what I was doing. There are a lot of dates to keep track of here, seeing that the contracts get out, get signed, and get back.

KT: What is a typical day like for you?
YB: Very busy. I have lots of contracts. The amusement park is seasonal. It's usually open from the spring until late fall. We're constantly redoing the contracts for the upcoming year or for special events the park may be doing, or for a concert that's coming up. I do a lot of corporate work here also, as we have many corporate entities. There are always written consents to be done, banking resolutions, minutes . . . In any one day I may work on corporate matters for an hour, go to trademarks, then go to contracts, and then go back to corporate. I do some or all of it every day. I never do one thing all day long.

KT: Are there attorneys in your department?
YB: Yes. There are six.

KT: Did you start out in a law firm before you worked for the bank?
YB: No, I started out at the bank. I went from secretary to legal secretary to paralegal.

KT: Did you have any formal training as a paralegal, or did you work into it?
YB: No. I have formal training. I went to a paralegal school for six months and received a certificate. Most of my training, I must admit, came on the job, but the paralegal certificate was a way for me to say, "I have formal training." If I had stayed at the bank, I don't think it would have made any difference, but it does when you get ready to change jobs. I do think that with almost any job, most of the skills you use every day are going to come from on-the-job training regardless of how much formal education you have.

KT: What do you like best about your job?
YB: One of the things I like best is that it's less stressful than my old job because I'm not in an administrative capacity. Another thing is the variety—the contracts are all the same, but they're different. You do an artist contract, then you do a corporate sponsorship contract, then you do a concession contract.

Also, it's beautiful out here. This is a very nice environment to work in. There's a 2000-room hotel/convention facility located on the complex, which is beautiful inside. It has a conservatory and a large inside waterfall called the Cascades. They're planning to build an addition to the hotel with a river delta through it. We can walk out into the amusement park at lunch, or we can go to matinee performances at the Grand Old Opry. We currently share the building with a TV station (TNN). When I went downstairs yesterday to get a drink, they were doing a cooking show.

KT: It sounds exciting.
YB: It's fun. Nashville is famous for country music, so there are always interesting artists coming in town. Our office isn't downtown, and I really like being out of the downtown area.

I don't have the hassles with budgeting and staff here. That was one of the things I had wanted to do at the bank. I had wanted to be an office manager for a while to see if that was something I could take my skills to and move on. I did, but it was not what I wanted after I got there. I really enjoy paralegal work.

KT: The substantive work.
YB: Yes. At the bank I ended up not doing that much of it, and when I did it was usually after hours and at home because the day just wasn't long enough.

KT: What kind of hours do you work now?
YB: Basically, I work eight or nine hours a day.

KT: So it's reasonable.
YB: Very reasonable. Now, there are periods of time, such as right before the park opens for the spring season, when I have to work quite a bit of overtime to get all the contracts ready.

KT: What do you think it was that got you this job, as opposed to some other candidate?
YB: I think my all-around experience. Working at the bank, I had done some trademark work, contracts, and corporate and SEC work. They would allow you to do anything you had an interest in. Consequently, I tried to learn a little bit about everything because I assumed that eventually I would move on and I wanted to be well-rounded.

I think that in today's employment market, you've got to be well-rounded. If you specialize too heavily, it's going to limit you when you go to look for another job. I think that's what got me the job here. There were several candidates, but I believe I had a broader knowledge than they did. I also think that my willingness to take continuing-education classes and to do whatever it took to better my contract skills is what got me the job.

KT: Did you end up taking some CLE classes?
YB: I haven't had time, but they have trained me. I'm still learning as I go, but I've been told that I put together a very good contract.

KT: I assume that you don't bill hours.
YB: That's right. When I was at First American, we did bill hours for a while, but we found that for an in-house department it did not work very well. You do too many little things, so that at the end of the day, your day's gone but you

may not have spent more than ten minutes on any one billable cost center. A consulting firm survey on time and efficiency showed that in-house billing was not conducive to using our time in the most efficient manner.

My current employer has not done any in-house billing up to this point. I think that in the future, they'll give it a try, just for the sake of saying that they've tried it. Most in-house legal departments I have talked with have tried in-house billing or plan to do it on a limited basis. I love not having to bill time.

KT: Do you have your own office? Or do you share an office with paralegals?
YB: I have an office, but it's a cubicle with a door. When we move to the new corporate offices next year, that's the kind of office we will have.

KT: Are there any benefits to your job other than being in a beautiful setting?
YB: We have good health care and retirement packages. We have a twenty-four-hour a day fitness center that is only eight dollars a month. They have aerobics, TV, showers, juice—you don't have to do anything but bring your clothes. I work out almost every day.

Another thing I like is that they have security guards. To get in at any entrance to the complex you have to go through a ranger station. I feel safe out here, and that is something you do not have in downtown Nashville. Also, we park right outside our offices, which is not something you have downtown. Downtown, you pay dearly for any kind of parking.

It's a wonderful group of people. The people in the entertainment industry have fun.

KT: How big is this company?
YB: Someone told me that we have over four thousand full-time employees and over four thousand seasonal and temporary employees.

KT: Do you have thoughts as far as your future career goes?
YB: Not really. I'm content to do what I do now. I'm not looking for "advancement" in terms of changing positions and moving up. I did the administrative thing, and I was not particularly happy with it. I like doing the substantive legal work. I like to be given an assignment and left alone until I complete it. I hope to stay here until I retire, but after having been in one position for sixteen years, I take it a day at a time, a week at a time.

I do not regret one moment of working for First American, but I also don't regret leaving, because I have a wonderful job. I think you should be happy in your job. That's the most important thing of all. The money's not important, the vacation's not important, because if all of those hours that you spend on the job are not fulfilling, you're missing the boat. That's my plan—just to enjoy it as long as it's fun. When it's not fun anymore, *if* it becomes not fun anymore, I will look elsewhere. I tell people "Life is too short not to enjoy what you're doing."

Now, this job is not perfect; no job is. I told someone recently about a bad day I was having, and I added "But overall I love it." She said to me, "It wouldn't be called work if it was fun every single moment of the day." She's right. There are days when things go wrong and everything feels like it's tumbling down, but by and large, I love it.

When I was looking to change jobs, I was scared about the money because I had been at the bank so long and had received a couple of promotions that had boosted my pay up. I thought, "There is no way I'm going to go out and find a job making what I make, with my limited banking experience." But you can take your fundamental knowledge and your basic skills and go anywhere with them if you're determined to be flexible and learn new things.

KT: Did you end up having to take a cut in pay?
YB: No.

KT: So all your fears were for nothing.
YB: Yes. I also negotiated for an extra week of vacation beyond what was originally offered. At the bank I had to work so much overtime in order to take a vacation that the vacation really wasn't very much fun because I dreaded coming back to work. My current job is not that way. I have a week less of vacation here than I did at the bank, but I feel more free to take my vacation time. I also have about the same benefits here; in fact, they may be a little better. All in all, I came out ahead.

The only thing that I can tell paralegals out there, whether they're young and just starting their career, or whether they've been in the work force for awhile and are changing careers, is this: You've got to go with the flow and be flexible for that first job. You can't always go in and sit in a private office with a private secretary and get the choice assignments. Some of us who've been doing this for many, many years don't get that.

New paralegals are going to have to look in other places for jobs outside of the law firm setting. There are many jobs that use paralegal skills which are just as much fun. The key is to keep an open mind regarding the minimum you will accept. The job market in Nashville is getting a little better, and I think the people coming out of the paralegal schools here are looking in places they wouldn't have looked for jobs three or four years ago. They've been forced to do that because of hard economic times, and now it's become a habit. After all, who would have ever thought that a paralegal could work at a bank for all those years?

I have never considered myself to be a non-traditional paralegal. I think I probably have more responsibilities and less supervision than the paralegal friends I have in law firms, partly because in a corporate setting you basically have one client, so we don't have the malpractice issues to face that law firms

Skyrocketing Malpractice Cases

Something attorneys try hard to avoid is any accusation of malpractice by a client. Basically, malpractice occurs when an attorney (or his or her staff, including paralegals) fails to exercise, for the benefit of the client, the level of knowledge, skill, and ability which an attorney is ordinarily expected to have. If the client is damaged by this failure, the client may have grounds for suing the attorney. Unfortunately, even though attorneys try to avoid malpractice, the number of such lawsuits is steadily increasing. This may be due to several factors: American society has become more and more litigious; juries award higher and higher dollar amounts, making these lawsuits more attractive to plaintiffs (although sometimes states put caps on the amounts juries can award); the public is increasingly conscious of its right to sue; and clients' expectations of their attorneys have generally increased.

Whatever the reasons, there is no dispute that attorneys are being sued more and more and that their insurance companies are paying out higher and higher dollar amounts. Statistics from CNA Insurance Companies, which insures about 40,000 lawyers against malpractice claims through its Lawyer's Protection Plan, show that from 1987 to 1991, malpractice claims increased 28 percent (see Figure 2–4). In 1987, there were only 2.5 malpractice claims against every 100 attorneys; by 1991, that number had increased to 3.2 claims per every 100 attorneys. Not only that, but the cost for each claim increased from $55,000 to $99,500, or 81 percent, during the same period.

There is no sign that malpractice rates will decrease anytime soon, although mediation of malpractice disputes, loss prevention seminars for attorneys and their staffs, and vigorous defense by attorneys being sued for malpractice may help to curb the increase. Most important, of course, attorneys and their staffs, including their paralegals, need to conduct themselves in a professional, ethical manner—the best defense of all against a malpractice suit.

HINT:

Usually in a malpractice suit, the attorney is going to be sued, not the paralegal. However, paralegals can be and have been sued themselves. (See the box entitled "Malpractice Insurance for Paralegals" in Chapter 6 for a further discussion of this.) One of the benefits of being a paralegal in a corporation or non-profit organization is that your client is your boss, which means that you may get fired if you do a poor job, but you probably won't get sued!

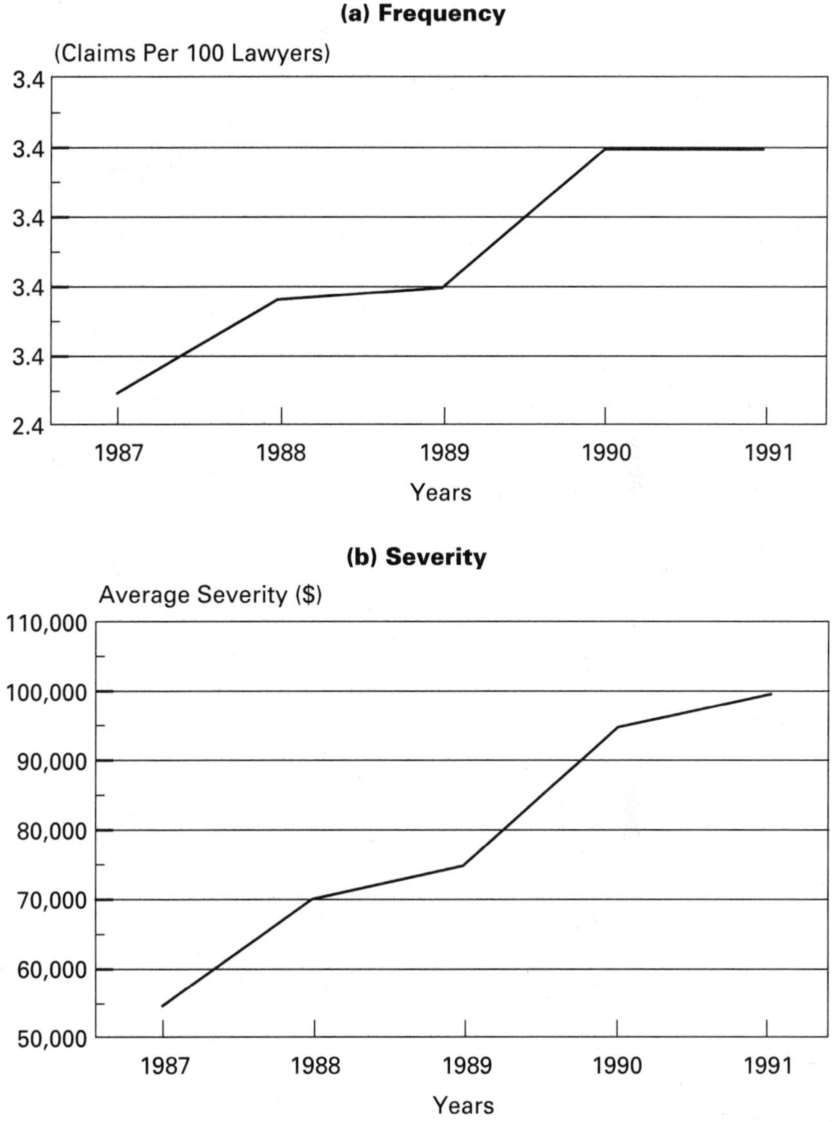

(a) Frequency

(Claims Per 100 Lawyers)

(b) Severity

Average Severity ($)

Figure 2-2   Frequency (a) and Severity (b) of Malpractice Claims Against Attorneys (*Courtesy CNA Insurance Companies*)

have to deal with. I have more freedom and less supervision, sometimes to the point of it being a little scary. Often, I'll do a contract and the attorney will simply ask, "Is there anything unusual I need to know about it?" I'll say "No," and he'll initial it. If there *is* something unusual, I type a memo setting out all the items that he needs to pay particular attention to.

INTERVIEW C

I work in four areas: trademarks, international corporations, bankruptcy, and customer complaints. In the complaint section, we handle customer complaints that come through the vice presidents' offices, or from our CEO Mr. Smith's office. In trademarks, I do anything from filing applications, to infringements, copyrights, and searches. In international corporations, I handle business pertaining to the company's subsidiaries. I also support the international counsel.

Rosie Odum

Company: Federal Express Corporation
City: Memphis, Tennessee
Department: Legal Department
Title: Associate Paralegal
Salary Range: $20,160–$31,440
Benefits:
   Insurance: medical, dental, vision, short- and long-term disability
   Financial: optional profit sharing and retirement savings plan
   Vacation: 2 weeks when hired, 3 weeks after 5 years of employment, 4 weeks after 10 years of employment
   Sick time: up to 5 consecutive days paid sick leave; sick time then switches into short-term disability pay
   Misc.:   2 personal days and 2 floater days per year, 6 major holidays per year; employee discount when using Federal Express, company store

Previous Work Experience:
Five years as a secretary and legal secretary with Federal Express Corporation. Two years of part-time legal experience with DeSoto

County Planning Commission. One year as a clerk and data entry clerk and two years of secretarial experience.

JOB DESCRIPTION

Provide timely assistance to the legal department staff in completing corporate legal mandates in the areas handled by customer support. To assist other departments and management in obtaining legal advice on day-to-day customer support matters:

1. Assist customer support attorneys in planning, organizing, coordinating, and tracking programs and/or projects associated with the legal department and customer support.
2. Prepare and coordinate correspondence between the legal department and others as directed.
3. Provide timely assistance to outside counsel as requested.
4. Assist and coordinate with the overgoods department and as paralegal of the day on department schedule.
5. Provide other departments within the company with necessary information pertaining to copyright and trademark issues, and bankruptcy, international, corporate, and business matters.
6. Assist in preparation and updating of customer support training materials for the legal department.
7. Work with all departments in the company to ensure timely review of advertising and policy and procedures.
8. Collect information to be included in the legal department's monthly activity report.
9. Under the direction of an attorney, prepare filings and applications for trademarks, service marks, etc.
10. Perform non-complex legal research and prepare analyses and summaries of non-complex reports.
11. Perform other duties as assigned.

RO: I work at Federal Express Corporation, in Memphis, as an associate paralegal.

KT: What does "associate paralegal" mean? Are there levels of paralegal positions?
RO: Yes. There's associate paralegal, which is entry-level and requires no experience, then paralegal, which requires two years of experience, and then senior paralegal, which requires four years of experience, two of which must be obtained at Federal Express Corporation.

I work in four areas: trademarks, international corporations, bankruptcy, and customer complaints. In the complaint section, we handle customer complaints that come through the vice presidents' offices, or from our CEO Mr. Smith's office. In trademarks, I do anything from filing applications, to infringements, copyrights, and searches. In international corporations, I handle business pertaining to the company's subsidiaries. I also support the international counsel. We have six or seven regional counsel who can send any type of request to us here in Memphis, as the base office.

KZ: Can you give me an example?

RO: Just now I'm forming a corporation by preparing the articles of incorporation, bylaws, and such, to set up a subsidiary of Federal Express in Belgium. I keep track of all the international subsidiaries. For example, I maintain the corporate minute books on each subsidiary.

KZ: What about the other area you work in, bankruptcy?

RO: Last year, I started working in bankruptcy, but I don't do too much in it now because another paralegal has been hired. Basically, I request invoices on bankruptcies filed by customers of Federal Express.

KZ: Do you mean corporate customers? Big customers?

RO: Fifty-fifty. It wouldn't have to be a big customer. It could be anybody who's filed bankruptcy and owes Federal Express money—perhaps a smaller company.

For example, as a customer of Federal Express, you can apply to use one of our Power Ship units, which is a little computer that produces a shipping label. Oftentimes, when a company files bankruptcy, they don't leave a forwarding address, their building is now locked up, and the landlord won't allow us entry so we can recover the unit. In our department, we might track down who the landlord is and try to get into the building to get the unit back, so that it isn't included in the bankruptcy.

KZ: So that would be a typical thing you might do in bankruptcy. What about customer complaints?

RO: In customer complaints, we write letters to customers who feel that we didn't meet our service commitment in connection with their shipments. If they think we mishandled their package, they may want to file suit against us, and we have to answer those complaints. Primarily, we handle complaints which have reached our CEO's office. Mr. Smith, our CEO, then passes those complaints on to the executive office, which sends them down to the legal department if there are legal issues involved.

KZ: I'd like to go back to your trademark work. That's intellectual property, which is a big, upcoming field these days. Can you give me some examples of what you do in that area?

RO: Sure. We maintain registrations, affidavits, and due dates for filing of, for example, the Federal Express logo. We have a Federal Express and a

Intellectual Property

Intellectual property (IP), as defined by *Ballentine's Law Dictionary: Legal Assistant Edition*, is "property that is the physical or tangible result of original thought." It is also property protected by law, which is where paralegals enter the picture. IP paralegals are employed by corporations, government agencies, and law firms working with copyrights, trademarks, trade names, and patents, which are all part of intellectual property law.

Intellectual property is a booming area. As Richard Stim states in his 1994 book *Intellectual Property: Patents, Trademarks and Copyrights* (Delmar Publishers and Lawyers Cooperative Publishing),

> There is no doubt, within the legal profession, that the leading legal specialty currently desired by legal employers is intellectual property. A recent article in the *American Bar Association Journal* stated, 'Forget the trendy law practice areas of the 1980s . . . intellectual property is where the action will be in the 1990s.' As a case in point, consider one of San Francisco's largest law firms, Morrison Foerster. In 1990, it did not have an intellectual property division. In 1992, it had 75 attorneys and registered agents handling intellectual property divisions" (p. xxviii).

According to the International Trademark Association (INTA), a not-for-profit professional organization committed to the promotion of trademarks throughout the world, job opportunities and advancement abound for paralegals involved in trademark work, both in companies and in law firms. Not only are opportunities good, but there are also corresponding salaries. A recent survey by INTA found that salaries of paralegals working in trademarks range from $29,412 to $42,212 for those employed in companies and from $24,812 to $37,650 for those employed in law firms (see Figure 2–6).

Fed Ex logo in each country where we do business, and they must be protected in each country. Right now, a lot of those marks are up for renewal, so we do forms called "Statement of Use" to show that the mark is active in the particular country.

We have outside counsel, for trademarks in Chicago, for trademarks, who works with us in regard to countries where we do business. She lets us know when a registration is up for renewal, and she basically handles the other countries, whereas we do all of the filing for the United States.

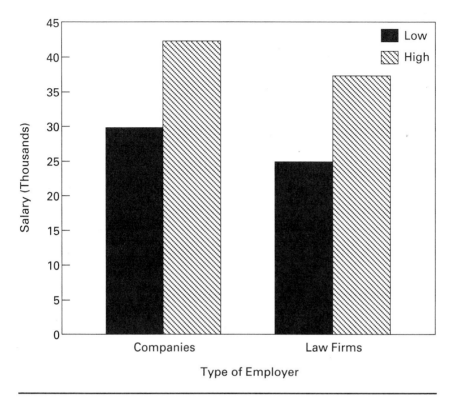

Figure 2-3   Paralegal Salaries—Trademark Work (*Courtesy International Trademark Association*)

KZ: I was wondering about that. Don't the other countries have their own laws regarding trademarks? Are you saying that your counsel in Chicago handles those requirements, but your office handles the United State's requirements?

RO: Yes, exactly. She lets us know if there's something particular we need to do for her, such as a power of attorney. Then she can go ahead and handle everything with that country so that we're on top of things.

One of the other things we do here is called "Paralegal and Lawyer of the Day." Two days out of the month we take all of the customer complaint calls that come into the Legal Department. We answer the phones on those days and assist customers with their problems.

We also have one day out of every, say, three months, when a paralegal has to go to our lost and found department. Any package, especially a package with legal documents, that has torn open or been ripped apart in our hub we try to track who shipped it and who the recipient is. Sometimes that is so hard because you have no idea who was sending the item or who was to receive it.

KT: Changing the subject, how long have you been with Federal Express?
RO: I've been with Federal Express for six and a half years, but I've been a paralegal for only a year and a half.

KT: Great! How did you move in to the paralegal position? Did you have formal schooling, or training on the job?
RO: Oh, I wish it was only training on the job! But no, I had schooling. I took a nine-month paralegal course, and I have a certificate from that school. Working in the legal department as a legal secretary, I was familiar with the job. We bid on jobs here.

KT: What do you mean?
RO: A listing comes out every Friday of all of the openings in Federal Express. If there's a job you want, you can bid for it.

KT: So you bid for your paralegal job.
RO: Right. They post the jobs internally before they're advertised externally.

KT: Tell me a little about the three levels of paralegal positions. You're an associate paralegal—how do you move up the ladder to the next position, or to the senior paralegal position?
RO: You have to work for two years as an associate paralegal before you can move up to the paralegal level. But there are performance reviews, too, which tie into whether you move up a level or not. I'm due for a promotion next fall, but, of course, it's up to my boss. Your boss has to feel that you're qualified to move up to the next level. An associate paralegal is a level-19, a paralegal is level-21, and a senior paralegal is level-23.

KT: Those levels probably have corresponding increases in pay and responsibility.
RO: Right. You get a lot more responsibility as you move up. You get more advanced work and bigger projects to work on. There are always bigger projects to work on.

One thing I haven't really done much of is copyright work. I do trademark searches and infringements. Someone infringes on Federal Express' name in their advertising if they don't clear it with Federal Express. Any use of the Federal Express name must come through us before it is used. We do ad copy—the marketing department brings all their ads over for us to look at before they are sent to print. We make sure that all of our trademarks are being used correctly in the advertisement. For example, we have economy two-day service, and the mark has to be used the exact way it's used in Interstate Commerce. In the case of economy two-day service, the word "two" must be spelled out and not be the number "2".

KT: What do you like best about your job?
RO: As far as intellectual property goes?

KT: As far as your entire job goes.
RO: The international corporations section is exciting and challenging to keep up with, because of all the different countries. I like the trademarks section best. Trademark is very interesting to me. There's always something different each day that I can do to improve my educational scope.

KT: How many paralegals work there?
RO: We have about seventeen or eighteen paralegals, with an attorney staff of forty to fifty.

KT: Did you ever work in a traditional law firm?
RO: Not as a paralegal. I worked in a law firm as a legal secretary.

KT: How does working for Federal Express compare to working in a law firm?
RO: It evens out, I think.

KT: What do you feel some of the pluses are to being in a company?
RO: In a company, you have more flexibility. It's a great company, there are good benefits, and there's flexibility in my position as far as growth goes.

KT: Tell me a little about your benefits.
RO: We have insurance, of course, and paid vacation and holidays. But the best benefit is the opportunity to advance into any area that we would like to. There's also a tuition refund program. I had a chance to use that. We have all the basics such as profit sharing, stock investment, retirement savings, and credit union, the most important, of course, is the St. Jude's Golf Classic Tournament.

KT: Is St. Jude's a hospital?
RO: Yes, a children's hospital and the proceeds from the tournament are given to the children. We can volunteer to work at the golf tournament and meet all the big celebrities like Michael Jordan and Phil Donahue.
　　Also, we have a company store where we can buy Federal Express items.

KT: Do you get to send things for free through Federal Express?
RO: Not for free, but we do get an employee discount.

KT: Are there any primary skills that you use in your job?
RO: I do use my communication skills—written and oral—a lot, I have to; and my research skills. We didn't cover international or trademarks or intellectual property at all in school, and I had to learn all of that on the job. Les,

my boss, is great—he's really up on all of it. We don't have a formal training program on the job; you're paired with an attorney and learn as you go.

KZ: Do you have any words of wisdom for other paralegals out there?
RO: I think you should go for what you want and always be happy at what you're doing. If you're not happy, you won't do the job well. If you're happy and willing to step out and learn more, opportunities will come.

CHAPTER 3

Corporate–Outside the Legal Department

A wide variety of corporations and companies have become employers of paralegals in recent years. Typically, a paralegal working for
such an employer works in the legal department, but this is not always the
case. Companies have begun to find that the skills a trained paralegal can
offer them are applicable to a wide variety of positions. "The companies
are starting to value the skills that paralegals have. I think I'm one of the
first ones in our company. . . . I know [a paralegal certificate is] pertinent.
It's something that the company is looking at and for." (Kathy Klima)

Often, the paralegal's job title is not "paralegal" (the titles of the three
paralegals interviewed for this chapter are director, administrator, and loan
secretary), but paralegal schooling or work experience is mandatory for the
position. "They wanted to know what was involved [in my paralegal train-
ing] because they wanted to see how it would pertain to the position I would
be working in. They wanted someone in this position to have paralegal
training." (Klima) ". . . one of the mandatory criteria for this position is that
the person have a paralegal certificate or training." (Lyndi Reed)

The paralegals working in these non-traditional positions have been
able to put to use the skills they've gained through paralegal education or
work experience. "I literally use all the paralegal skills that I received from
paralegal training and my other positions. But the primary skills I use are
negotiation skills, organization skills, communication skills, and writing
skills." (Reed)

This group of paralegals has widely varying reasons for working in non-
traditional paralegal positions. One brand-new paralegal found that the competition for traditional jobs within law firms was too intense. ". . . I was
running into a dead end as far as the traditional paralegal positions went because I lacked experience. . . . [This company] didn't care that I didn't have
experience." (Klima)

Another paralegal spent years working in traditional as well as non-traditional jobs, but finds her greatest satisfaction in her current non-traditional position. ". . . this certainly seems to be the culmination of everything I've done."
(Kathy Gedeon Scott)

The benefits, money, and flexibility that a corporation can offer were
motivating factors for a third paralegal to work in a non-traditional position. "In my first shift from private practice to a corporation, I literally

doubled my salary. . . . The benefits in a corporation are so much better than most law firms can offer. . . . my main motivation for being in a non-traditional position is . . . flexibility." (Reed)

Life outside the law firm is good for these paralegals. They express satisfaction with the prestige and the lack of stress they find there. "I think that in some law firms, they use paralegals to the point of burnout, instead of using them for the talents that they can contribute to the firm . . . what a paralegal can do for a law firm or a corporation is very valuable, and I don't think that a lot of law firms treat their paralegals that way, as though they are a valuable asset to the firm. . . . [Now I have] less stress, and I think that there's more prestige in my position now than being in a law firm." (Reed)

In conclusion, this group of paralegals wouldn't abandon their positions to return to the traditional paralegal world. "My job is extremely fulfilling. . . . It is exciting. It's wonderful. It's been a lot of hard work and determination, too! But I've been blessed." (Scott) ". . . [paralegals] may never want to go to a traditional job because the opportunities are so good outside of the law firms!" (Klima)

INTERVIEW D

I provide all of the one-on-one counseling for every student, in all six specialty areas, on career development. I come into the classroom and present a seminar on resume preparation, a seminar on interviewing techniques, a seminar on job search in the private sector and then another on job search in the public sector. I break the classes up into groups of ten and hold mock interviews. They are encouraged to see me again on a one-on-one basis about their job search. Of course, I tell them to be very agressive in this market.

Kathy Gedeon Scott

Company: The Philadelphia Institute
City: Philadelphia, Pennsylvania
Department: Career Development Center
Title: Director, Career Development Center
Salary Range: $35,000
Benefits:
    Insurance: medical (HMO)
    Financial: none
    Vacation:
    Sick time: 10 days
    Misc.:   4 personal days

Previous Work Experience:
Paralegal in wills, estates, zoning and labor law. Assistant to the disciplinary board chairman of the Supreme Court of Pennsylvania for one year. Tax and corporate paralegal for a large law firm for five years. Executive director of the Philadelphia Association of Paralegals for one year. One year as manager of a paralegal placement company.

JOB DESCRIPTION:

General Summary

Responsible for management of entire department and staff.

Principle Duties

- Create and conduct career instruction seminars for all students on a tri-mester basis.
- Perform one-on-one career counseling with all students.
- Promote and market the institute through public relations activities, including attendance at various legal association and civic organization functions, and various speaking engagements.
- Publish articles and press releases, and edit institute newsletter.
- Coordinate special projects with executive director and dean.

KZ: You work for The Philadelphia Institute. Tell me a little about what you do there, or how you got there, or both, in whatever order you like.
KS: I'll start with how I got here, and with the fact that I was interested in politics and law from a very early age. I was raised outside of Washington, D.C., and my mother was involved in Maryland politics. I was quite comfortable with attorneys and political figures early on. I was a Junior Democrat for John Kennedy. My father was a government worker, but ultimately was hired by a British firm, and I traveled around the world with my father and mother.

We settled, after traveling for a long time, on Long Island, New York. After graduating from high school, I was accepted at a local community college, and at the same time I received a flyer from a business college nearby that offered something called a legal course.

KZ: A legal course?
KS: A legal course. And I thought "I don't know if I want to become an attorney, so why not do this?" It was a ten-month course. Of course, in those days, it was not as in depth as any of the courses that you can get now at ABA-approved schools.

KZ: Even though it was ten months long?
KS: Yes. It was ten months long, but we took trips over to the courthouse and were told "The green books are this, and the red ones are that." I felt it was very clerical, and it wasn't structured very well. But it was enough of an exposure. They didn't know what to do with paralegals in those days, and we weren't called paralegals. We were going to be legal secretary/ assistant, and there was always a clerical edge to it. Nonetheless, we graduated, armed with legal terminology and a familiarity with the law.

Choosing a Paralegal School

Finding a paralegal school to attend is not much of a problem; there are about 700 paralegal programs across the country. Finding the right program is more of a problem. There are several factors to consider when weighing the merits of various programs. One consideration is length. Programs can vary from several weeks to four years, depending on whether a certificate or a degree is offered. Whether a prospective student qualifies to study for a certificate or a degree (and the degree may include an attached certificate) will probably depend on whether the student has any previous college experience.

Other factors to consider are cost and type of program. There is an enormous difference in program costs, which range from around $1,500 to over $8,000 for a certificate alone. Programs in private and proprietary schools generally cost the most, while programs in state colleges, universities, and community colleges cost the least. There are different types of programs, too. Some schools offer a general paralegal program covering many different areas of law, while others offer specialty programs, which focus on specific areas of law such as corporate or probate. In either case, a good school will spend the bulk of its time teaching its students by a hands-on method, rather than by a lecture method, so that the students will have some developed skills when they enter the work force.

The most important factor, however, is the reputation and quality of the program. If a school has American Bar Association (ABA) approval of its paralegal program, there is assurance that it has a good reputation for quality education. In early 1994, approximately 175 programs across the United States, or about 25 percent of the total number of available programs, had approval. ABA approval is voluntary, however, so the fact that a particular school is not approved does not necessarily mean it is not a good school. But if a school does have ABA approval, a prospective student knows that it meets exacting guidelines regarding curriculum, instructors, placement, and facilities.

HINT:

Here are two resources that can aid a prospective student:

How to Choose a Paralegal Education Program. This inexpensive brochure is published by the Conclave, an assembly of six national paralegal and law-related organizations: the American Association for Paralegal Educators (AAfPE), the American Bar Association (ABA), the Association of Legal Administrators (ALA), the Legal Assistant Management Association (LAMA), the National Association of Legal

Assistants (NALA), and the National Federation of Paralegal Associations (NFPA). The brochure includes such topics as curricula, types of programs available, and ABA approval. It can be ordered through any of the Conclave members. (NALA's phone number is (918) 587-6828; NFPA's is (816) 941-4000.)

General Legal Assistant Information Packet. This $6 packet is published by the American Bar Association and contains information on what a paralegal is and does, what types of programs exist, and which programs are ABA-approved. It can be obtained by calling the ABA at (312) 988-5000.

After getting out I thought "Well, I'll go to college now." However, my father was transferred yet again, to the Philadelphia area. And this is where my career really started. In a neighboring town, the president of the bar association of the county was looking for an assistant, and when I went for the interview, here I was all of twenty years old, and I'm telling him "I do not want to be a secretary, I want to be an assistant." Well, it just so happened that he had a general practice, which was great. He was a zoning expert. He was president of the historical society. If you lived in Pennsylvania, you would know how important historical activities are. I became his assistant. I did all the critical matters, and at that juncture, I started to draft wills, had a couple of estates that I was responsible for, drafted zoning proposals, and attended township board meetings that concentrated on zoning.

Well, he was an extremely conservative fellow, and being very young and having been a product of the sixties, I was not happy with this. Nor was the suburban location for me. Meanwhile, through this firm, I met a man who was in labor law. He was a member of a firm that was a satellite of a New York firm. They were organizing all the hospitals in the Philadelphia area at that time. He needed an assistant.

KZ: So you took the position?
KS: Yes. The beauty of that position was that he traveled to Washington and all along the East Coast while they were organizing, so I was the liaison between New York and him, piecing together these briefs to take up to the National Labor Relations Board. He served as a mediator for the American Arbitration Association as well and involved me in all aspects of labor law.

KZ: It sounds like exciting work.
KS: Right. In addition, I continued to work in political campaigns, which

was my main interest. From there, I did a stint with the disciplinary board chairman of the Supreme Court of Pennsylvania. He only needed someone for a year, but he needed someone to keep him organized. That's what I did, and I helped work on the disciplinary cases. It was very confidential, a real eye opener.

From there, I went to a major law firm in Philadelphia, where I did tax and corporate law.

KT: You really bounced around.
KS: I bounced around, yes. But each job was truly a learning experience.

When I went to this firm there were forty paralegals there. After a year I went to the general manager of the firm, and I said to him, "We're on five floors, we never get together, I think we need to organize here."

KT: A unionizer.
KS: While I was there I tried to stress the importance of belonging to your own local paralegal association. As the firm representative to The Philadelphia Association of Paralegals, when I greeted new paralegals in the firm, I brought information on the association. I got one-hundred-percent membership from that firm. I then went on to become the vice president of the Philadelphia association.

While I was there we also developed a firm paralegal handbook. There's always an attorney handbook listing all the attorneys and their backgrounds. We listed all the paralegals with their backgrounds, their specialty areas, and any other areas where they might be valuable.

I dearly love to write, and while I was there an attorney asked me to become co-editor of their international trade publication, so that kept me very busy too. This went out to all our clients and overseas.

KT: How many years into your career are we talking about by now? This sounds like a fairly lengthy career already.
KS: Over ten years. In the meantime, the paralegal association was up to about a thousand members, and they decided that they needed an executive director. I was approached to take this on. It was with great trepidation, believe me, that I was going to leave this cocoon-like structure, this wonderful law firm that had been so good to me, that had given me all this great work to do.

KT: Very substantive work.
KS: I think so, very significant work. But I could see that things were pretty firmly in place there, and there wasn't a paralegal manager's track. They do have one now, but that didn't come until probably two or three years after I left. So I took the job with the paralegal association. I went into non-profit, and that was a whole new experience.

KT: This was a paid position?

KS: Yes, with an office.

I was also an active participant in the Philadelphia Bar Association, and I still serve on several bar association committees. When I moved into the position as executive director, I worked in tandem with the bar association to try to create a structure for the paralegal association which was similar to the bar association's structure. We had an annual conference of all the paralegals in the country, NFPA, at that time. It was an exciting time and a very good experience for me. It gave me the opportunity to write numerous articles and be very creative. However, my background was the for-profit structure.

KT: So this was a big change.

KS: Absolutely. Billing ceased to be a priority. And it was good to have such an opportunity to meet people across the city. I would venture into law firms and do recruiting for the association. I would hold breakfast meetings and luncheons. That was a joy, to see everyone, or at least many of the paralegals in Philadelphia.

KT: It doesn't surprise me that, with that type of background, you would end up at a school.

KS: I agree. I was recruited from the association to manage a personnel firm that was going to focus exclusively on paralegals. I went into that, but, unfortunately, it was at the time when the legal community seized up, and nobody was hiring. It was a start-up company, very small, and we quickly saw that it was fruitless to even try. That was three years ago.

KT: That was when the economy plummeted back there.

KS: Oh yes, the bottom fell out. And that's when I agreed to manage this new venture!

I was at a paralegal association luncheon, and someone from The Philadelphia Institute asked me what I was doing. I said, "Well, funny you should ask. The bottom is falling out, blah, blah, blah." She said, "I just saw you speak to a group in Jersey (I did and do speaking engagements as well, around the country). You're very motivational, and I have something in mind for you." She said she would check it out and get back to me. I came home the following evening, and the light was flashing on my answering machine. Sure enough, it was the institute. They were restructuring their Career Development Center, and would I be interested in heading it up?

I thought, "Well, this certainly seems to be the culmination of everything I've done." So I came in, and the rest is history.

KT: So now you've been there for three years.

KS: I've been here for two years. I provide all of the one-on-one counseling for every student, in all six specialty areas, on career development. I come into the classroom and present a seminar on resume preparation, a seminar on interviewing techniques, a seminar on job search in the private sector and then another on job search in the public sector. I break the classes up into groups of ten and hold mock interviews. They are encouraged to see me again on a one-on-one basis about their job search. Of course, I tell them to be very agressive in this market. And I encourage them to belong to their local paralegal associations because the institute recruits students from all over the country.

I also set up presentations by paralegals in the specialty areas. We have paralegals here who are teaching the students some hands-on skills and giving them an idea of what people in their field are doing. For the presentations, I bring in paralegals working in that particular field. For example, for an employee benefits presentation, I bring in an institute graduate who has been working in employee benefits for a while and can share those experiences with them.

We also have a newsletter here at the school, and I'm editor of that. We have published one newsletter and have another coming out in November.

KT: And that goes to your alumni?
KS: Yes. I am also responsible for some marketing of the school. I just had the opportunity to have the current chancellor of the bar, our first African American Chancellor, speak at our graduation last week. Our State Representative, Marjorie Margolies Mesvinsky, whom I campaigned for, came to the school and met with us to hear our needs. She was very responsive.

And in my spare time . . .

KT: What spare time?
KS: No kidding. I spend a lot of my time with previous graduates, because career development is a lifetime service here at the school. I help them to redirect their careers.

I try to attend all the paralegal association luncheons and the bar association quarterly meeting. I don't currently serve on any committees with the association, but I do encourage all of our students who will be staying in the Philadelphia area to take out a student membership and get active.

My job is extremely fulfilling. I get thank yous and calls when they get their jobs. It's exciting for me when students come in and tell me they have accepted their first position in the paralegal profession.

One regret—I never did get my college degree.

KT: I was going to ask you about that.
KS: Never did, although I've had many attorneys say to me, "Why don't you just CLEP your courses and get on to law school?"

KT: Any ambitions to do that?
KS: No, actually not. At forty-six years old, this is very fulfilling. I'm ex-

posed to everyone in the legal community. I am truly a non-traditional paralegal. I want to make a point of this—I feel very fortunate that I worked closely with so many attorneys, and it was really their guidance and support and belief in my abilities that brought me to this point. Those attorneys were extremely instrumental in my success. For example, my first boss said to me, "If you don't take yourself seriously, no one else will."

The political figures that I've known have also been very encouraging. I think all of them are a bit frustrated with me that I won't consider law school.

KT: Obviously, you've had some people who've helped you along and influenced you, but what do you think are your own qualities which have led to your success?

KS: Enthusiasm for the profession. Enthusiasm and respect. A genuine love of the law. And I want to involve people in there somewhere because it's people in the profession who have been a real plus for me.

I enjoy a variety of personalities, and I pride myself on my ability to communicate with people on any level. Do you know what I mean?

KT: Maybe to empathize?

KS: Right. Exactly. And I know what it's like to aspire, to be on the bottom rung, and to aspire to move along. I know what it takes to get there, and I think I can, again, empathize with the students and tell them my story. They're probably two legs up from the way I began, and the sky's the limit for them.

KT: It's exciting.

KS: It *is* exciting. It's wonderful. It's been a lot of hard work and determination, too! But I've been blessed.

INTERVIEW E

I started looking through the paper, and I sent resumes to just about anything that looked like it would be a possibility. I always looked at the job description to see what the job entailed and whether the requirements were something that my paralegal skills from school would match. I came across an advertisement for a loan secretary in the mortgage section of the newspaper. I thought, "If I could get in on the bottom, I could at least work my way up somewhere" because I did have the education. I just lacked the experience that everyone was looking for.

Kathy Klima

Company: The Money Store Investment Corp.
City: Aurora, Colorado
Department: Processing
Title: Loan Secretary
Salary Range: $18,000–$20,000
Benefits:
    Insurance: medical, dental, and life
    Financial: 401(k) plan
    Vacation: 1 to 5 years, 10 days; 6 to 10 years, 15 days; more than 10 years, 20 days
    Sick time: 5 paid sick days per year
    Misc.:   personal days at the rate of 1/6th day per month of employment; educational assistance reimbursed up to $1,000 per calendar year after 1 year of employment

Previous Work Experience:
Customer service and temporary positions for two years. Paralegal internship with District Attorney's office.

JOB DESCRIPTION

- As assigned by Central Processing (CP) supervisor or manager, assist in preparation of commitment letters and authorizations, as drafted by loan officer.
- Prepare Small Business Administration (SBA) loan submission packages for local branch and occasionally other "central processing" offices (CPOs), with assistance from loan officer.
- Setup loan files and warehouse loans alter final disbursement.
- Set up and maintain borrower escrow accounts.
- Send out SBA Form #155, Compensation Agreement, to be signed by appraisers, legal firms, and Phase I companies, etc., as applicable.
- Set up and maintain tickler system to ensure these items are signed, returned, and ready to be included in review package sent to legal department for approval prior to closing.
- Type closing documents, with direction from loan processing officer (LPO).
- Send copy of SBA authorization to borrower for review.
- Assist loan processors and loan officers as necessary to expedite loan closings.
- Under direction of CP supervisor, prepare and send wire transfer requests.
- Prepare closed files for audit, to be reviewed by loan processor prior to shipment.
- Prepare "closed loan" report, as directed by CP supervisor.
- As directed by LPO, prepare and send compensation agreement to environmental assessor and to appraiser.
- Prepare commitment letter, and prepare final SBA authorization from CPO draft.
- Prepare borrower checklist of information needed.
- Order, review, and file flood certification.
- Perform miscellaneous administrative duties as requested, including back-up support for front desk.
- Maintain borrower escrow accounts: prepare out-of-pocket expense letter; post charges to individual borrower escrow accounts; prepare monthly escrow report.
- Prepare semimonthly closed and anticipated loan report for Sacramento.
- Maintain adequate supply of SBA documents; order forms as necessary.

KZ: Your job title is loan secretary?
KK: Yes. Within the company, the job is titled either loan secretary or loan facilitator, but it's basically the same job description.

KZ: By the title of the job, a person wouldn't necessarily think that you were a paralegal.

KK: Right. And actually, I don't know if you would really consider me a paralegal. This is new to me. I know that paralegals work in law firms and with legal documents and that a lot of them report to a lawyer. I don't work directly for a lawyer, but all of our loan packets that we put together have to be submitted to our legal office for review to make sure that everything is right.

KT: But you use the same skills as a traditional paralegal.
KK: Right, right. I was looking through some of my syllabi from paralegal school to see how my classes pertain to my job. The legal environment of business class and the business organizations class, where we went through the structure of a corporation and partnership—all of that applies to my job. When I go through a file, I'm viewing documents that have to do with corporations and partnerships.

I don't supervise anyone. I would say my benefits are comparable to a traditional paralegal position. They have health and dental insurance. I get two weeks paid vacation and comp days, and I get personal days off. I get all of the major holidays. The pay scale for my position is $18,000 to $20,000 a year, depending on experience. I don't have billable hours.

KT: Tell me a little bit about how you got your position.
KK: Basically, I was running into a dead end as far as the traditional paralegal positions went because I lacked experience.

KT: And you had never worked before?
KK: I had worked before, but in fast food and for a temporary agency, doing filing and odd jobs, and it wasn't for very long. I think the longest assignment I had was for three months.

KT: Was that recently? Or had you been home with kids?
KK: No, not recently. I'd been home with my kids for years. I worked on and off. I never had any real office or professional experience.

KT: So you had several obstacles to overcome in looking for a job.
KK: The lack of experience was my biggest hurdle. So I started looking through the paper, and I sent resumes to just about anything that looked like it would be a possibility. I always looked at the job description to see what the job entailed and whether the requirements were something that my paralegal skills from school would match. I came across an advertisement for a loan secretary in the mortgage section of the newspaper. I thought, "If I could get in on the bottom, I could at least work my way up somewhere" because I did have the education. I just lacked the experience that everyone was looking for.

When I went for this job interview, the woman was impressed with me and with the fact that I had a paralegal certificate. When I had my second interview, they pinpointed on my paralegal training. They wanted to know what was involved because they wanted to see how it would pertain to the position I would be working in. They wanted someone in this position to have paralegal training.

And I'm not sure, but I'm hoping that my position is going to work into the processor position.

Searching for That Paralegal Job

One of the most difficult challenges a paralegal may face in his or her career is finding a job, especially if he or she has no previous paralegal work experience. Many career counselors and job search experts quote the $10,000/month rule—for each $10,000 a person wishes to earn, the person should anticipate spending a month doing a job search. If the economy where the paralegal is searching is poor, it is not unusual for a job search to take even longer than that. Furthermore, these experts estimate that only 12 percent of jobs are found through classified want ads.

Therefore, it is essential that paralegals view learning job search skills as being as important as learning paralegal skills. Many schools which offer paralegal training also offer classes or seminars in job search skills, such as resume writing, interviewing, informational interviewing, networking, and tapping into the hidden job market. Although some schools make this type of class mandatory for students, others don't, in which case the smart paralegal will be self-motivated and seek out the training anyway.

HINT:

There are a number of excellent job search books in most book stores which can be helpful to paralegals. However, other books are available which are directed specifically at the paralegal and are extremely helpful, such as

1. Bernardo, Barbara, *Paralegal: Insider's Guide to One of the Fastest Growing Occupations of the 1990's*, Peterson's Guides, Princeton, NJ (1993).
2. Estrin, Chere, *Paralegal Career Guide*, Wiley Law Publications, New York (1992).
3. Kisiel, Marie, *How to Find a Job as a Paralegal*, 2nd Edition, West Publishing Company, St. Paul (1991).
4. Wagner, Andrea, *How to Land Your First Paralegal Job*, Estrin Publishing, Santa Monica, CA (1992).

KT: That was going to be my next question. What steps up are there for you in the future?

KK: Well, the processor position, even more than mine, really needs paralegal training, because the processor orders title reports, opens escrow accounts, and orders preliminary title reports.

In my position, I work directly for the processor. I help her to prepare all of the documents that the borrower needs to sign and get together to be solicited to the SBA so that they can approve or disapprove the loan. I also get the documents to submit to our legal department.

KT: What is your company's purpose or business?

KK: We do small-business loans. From $100,000 up to $1 million for small businesses. These loans are guaranteed through the Small Business Administration.

KT: What would you do in a typical day?

KK: It depends on how busy we are. Whenever I get a loan file to work on, I prepare all the documents that need to be submitted to the SBA and put the file together. After the borrowers come in and sign all those documents, like the commitment letter and the authorizations, we prepare it for closing. Then I get all the closing documents prepared—the first payment letter, and so forth. Once the loan has closed I get it ready for servicing. There's so much more that I don't know yet.

KT: Because you haven't been in your job very long?

KK: I've been here for a little over three months. I've just learned a fraction of what goes on.

I don't have any set thing that I do every day. I might have several loans that have already finished and closed, or I might have several loans that I have to start from the beginning. It just depends.

KT: Do you think your job would be harder if you didn't have your paralegal training?

KK: I think so, because without my training I wouldn't have the knowledge of the corporations and partnerships that I have. Just about everything that I learned in real estate law class I use on my job, although the class focused on residential real estate and my job focuses on commercial real estate. But I've been able to transfer what I learned into commercial real estate.

KT: Had they ever hired a paralegal before?

KK: Where I am, no. The one who had my job before me was a legal secretary and she could have moved up to be a loan processor if she had chosen to, but she went back to a law firm.

KT: Is your company's experience with her background what made them think they might want to hire a paralegal?

KK: I don't know. I know that at my second interview, I was asked about my training, and I went blank and said "I don't know! What *did* I learn?" But the supervisors of the woman who interviewed me wanted a paralegal in the loan secretary position. And I know that they do have paralegals who work in their legal department back in California. I'm in the processing department, and everything that I work on has to go through the legal department for review to make sure that everything is right, because all those documents have to be legal. There are contracts and deeds of trust, and everything else. They have to be legal.

KT: You're a good example of the kind of employee companies are hiring for jobs not titled "paralegal."

KK: Yes. Companies are starting to value the skills that paralegals have. I think I'm one of the first ones in our company. I'm definitely the first one in our office. I know that one of our processors is talking about going back to school and getting her paralegal certificate, so I know that it's pertinent. It's something that the company is looking at and for.

KT: I think that's exciting!

KK: I do too. It was good for me, especially since they didn't care that I didn't have experience. When I had my interview, the manager asked me, "Do you have any hands-on experience with title commitments or anything like that?" and I said, "No, I don't. All I know is what I learned through my classes." I know that my grades came into play; they looked at that. And I know they looked at the fact that I did well in my internship. The district attorney's office, where I did my internship, cannot give you a reference, but my supervisor there sent me a copy of my evaluation, and I took that in. They were very impressed with that.

KT: I can't ask you to compare your position to a traditional paralegal job because you haven't been in one, but what do you like about it, or not like about it?

KK: I enjoy the paperwork. I enjoy the fact that I'm learning something new all the time, and I enjoy the people I work with. It's a great work environment; everyone gets along really well. I feel fortunate. And I like the fact that there are advancement opportunities.

I don't know much about traditional paralegal positions, but I know that in a law firm, if you have a paralegal position, you might become a supervisor of paralegals, but that's about as far as you can go unless you want to get your law degree. I have a lot more leeway for advancement opportunities. I'm learning a broader area than I think I would learn in a law firm, too. With the experience that I'm getting, and especially if I decide to further my education and get a bachelor's degree, I have a wide area to go into.

KT: You mean that you're getting some business background, some mortgage background, and some real estate background?

KK: Right. Because of the wide variety of experience I'm getting, it's going to open me up as to where I can go from here. That's something important to me. I'm hoping that I'll be able to stay with this company and grow with it. One of the main things that I emphasized in my interview was that I was looking for a company that I could grow in and have a career with.

KT: Is it a fairly new company?

KK: No. The branch office I'm in has been here for eight years. I don't know when the company started in California. There are branches in eighteen states. We have servicing departments, franchise departments that work with loans to franchises such as Burger King, the processing department, which I'm a part of, and the legal department. There's also the mortgage department, which does second mortgage loans. And in some states they have student loan programs, but not here in Colorado because they're not licensed to do it here.

KT: Since you're right out of school, do you have any advice for somebody who's just graduating?

KK: Be open-minded about the area you want to go into. When I first got out of school I wanted to go into family law. As a matter of fact, when I was in real estate law class, I would have said, "There's no way I will ever go into real estate. This is just not my bag." But it is! So just be open minded.

I know one of the first instructors I had there, for law office administration, told us, "More than likely, the field that you get into is going to be the one that least interests you." I remembered his saying that after I got this job.

Just be persistent. I know I just wanted to give up looking for a job at times. I'd say, "My God, what have I done? I don't really want a job!" It was difficult for me.

KT: But really, finding a job in three months, as you told me before, never having worked in an office situation, is really excellent.

KK: Yes. But nobody ever told me that. The best advice I can give anyone going through school is to learn to look for a job. I had no clue. I knew I should take my resume to some places, and I needed to look through the paper, but I was lost after that. I did take workshops at the school on resume writing and job search techniques, and that really helped. Students should take full advantage of any workshops on job search that their schools offer.

KZ: Anything else that you want to talk about?

KK: I know that I do want to advance. I really feel fortunate with the job that I have. I know I couldn't have obtained it without my paralegal certificate.

KZ: It sounds to me that even though you might have had a different idea of what you wanted when you started job hunting it turned out for the best. It sounds like it's not a dead end for you.

KK: No. It's not. This was the job that I wanted, and this was the job that I pursued. I did all the things that you're supposed to do to get a job—I wrote them letters saying "Thank you for the interview. . . . Looking forward to hearing from you again. . . . really want this position. . . . feel like I can be an asset to your staff. . . ." It paid off for me.

I do have to say that there's a lot of advice regarding how to find a job for people who've been paralegals for a while. But that really didn't help me much because I had no experience. I was running into dead ends because of that.

KZ: It may be that there's a trend of new paralegals with no experience finding that it's easier for them to get their foot in the door in a non-traditional job outside a law firm.

KK: I feel that way here. And then they may never want to go to a traditional job because the opportunities are so good outside of the law firms!

INTERVIEW   F

I have more responsibility, more sole responsibility for projects that I do. I have better benefits and less stress, and I think that there's more prestige in my position now than in a law firm.

Lyndi Reed

Company:	Diebold, Incorporated
City:	Canton, Ohio
Department:	Corporate Real Estate
Title:	Administrator
Salary Range:	$35,000–$48,000
Benefits:	
Insurance:	medical and dental
Financial:	401(k) (Diebold matches up to 6 percent)
Vacation:	80 hours
Sick time:	
Misc.:	stock purchase plans, tuition reimbursement, loans for purchase of home computers

Previous Work Experience:

Freelance paralegal and insurance agent for four years. Vice President of a paralegal education program for half a year. Six years as a paralegal for a corporation. Two and a half years as a general-practice paralegal.

JOB DESCRIPTION

General Summary

Manages and coordinates all corporate real estate activity, including relocation, termination and renewal of existing lease, site selection, lease negotiation and execution, lease administration, including maintenance of real estate database, and approval and payment of rent expenses for all leased locations. Arbitrates all lease provision disputes with landlord and refers to legal counsel if necessary; prepares and distributes all real estate reports both internally and externally; assists field management in budget planning; assists director of corporate facilities in real estate strategic planning and budgets, operations costs projections, cost containment planning, and acquisition and disposition of corporate-owned facilities. Travels to field for site selection when necessary. Plans and coordinates departmental quality projects, training, and participation.

Organizational Relationships

Trains and supervises two paralegal interns per year. Trains and supervises departmental personnel in quality techniques and tools. Supervises shared departmental secretary on a minimal basis. Supervises brokers engaged by Diebold for property searches.

Scope of Responsibility

Responsible for lease administration in approximately 430 cities in the United States, including 84 branch facilities, 250 storage facilities, and 38,000 square feet of office space. Financial responsibility exceeds $8,000,000 annually and includes base rent, real estate tax, insurance costs, operating expense (CAM), maintenance, maintenance contracts, and utilities.

KT: Tell me a little about your company and what you do.
LR: Diebold has been in existence for 134 years. We sell banking security equipment, like ATM machines, vaults, and surveillance equipment.

I'm in the corporate real estate department. The way I got my position is that a group of us got together and started the NorthEastern Ohio Paralegal Association. Through those committees we worked on, I met a lot of people in the area who were paralegals.

A professional friend, Carolyn Furcolow, called me and told me that she had found a new job and her boss had asked her to find somebody to fill her position at Diebold.

At the time, I wasn't looking for a job; I was doing freelance paralegal work and working in a law office for a sole practitioner. Carolyn coerced

Professional Paralegal Organizations

There are two major national professional organizations for paralegals: the National Federation of Paralegal Associations (NFPA) and the National Association of Legal Assistants (NALA).

NALA was formed in 1975 and currently represents over fifteen thousand paralegals. Its membership is made up of individuals and state, local, and metro-area associations. NFPA was also formed in the mid-1970s and now has over seventeen thousand members. Its membership is made up of sixty-four affiliated state, local, and metro-area associations, whose members thereby become members of NFPA.

Both organizations state that promotion of the paralegal profession through education and politics is their major goal. However, the two groups have major philosophical differences, one of which concerns the licensing of paralegals so that they can practice law without the supervision of an attorney. This philosophical difference is discussed in the box entitled "Non-Lawyer Practice of Law" (or Limited Licensure) in Chapter 6.

HINT:

Both organizations provide information to any individual paralegal or association of paralegals. In fact, if your association is contemplating joining either, both NFPA and NALA may send an officer or member to lobby for its organization. The organizations can be reached at

National Association of Legal Assistants
1601 S. Main Street, Suite 300
Tulsa, Oklahoma 74119
(918) 587-6828

National Federation of Paralegal Associations
P.O. Box 33108
Kansas City, Missouri 64114
(816) 941-4000

A listing of the affiliated local paralegal associations, by city and state, is in Appendix C.

---

me by saying, "You know, you should just go interview for this job." So I did, and it turned out to be terrific.

KL: What did you like about it from the interview?
LR: It was more money and more security. The fortunate thing about go-

ing from private practice to a corporation is that the money is so much better in a corporation. In my first shift from private practice to a corporation, I literally doubled my salary. Then, at that corporation, where I worked for six years, we had an attempted takeover and a termination of 204 people, one of which was me. At that time I was making over $25,000 a year, so it was very difficult to go back to private practice. I kept interviewing for all these positions, but they didn't want to start me out at what I'd left at, not to mention the benefits. The benefits in a corporation are so much better than most law firms can offer.

KZ: So then you went freelance.
LR: Yes. And I also got my insurance license, so I was doing estate planning work.

KZ: Freelance estate planning?
LR: Right. Estate planning, selling insurance, disability policies, life, health insurance. Then, when I interviewed with Diebold, my friend gave me a lot of insight into the job. She knew how many hours she put in and how hard she worked to develop the position. It was important to her to find someone who would be as committed as she was. I think that eighty percent of paralegals who are very successful and have the high-paying jobs are people who are willing to work hard and long hours.

KZ: I agree. I think they're willing to do whatever it takes to get the job done.
LR: You sometimes get into this rut where you're working all these hours and you're not being paid what you're worth. And if you like the place where you are, you hesitate to branch out and look at other possibilities. I think that since the 1970s, the profession has grown tremendously, and employers are more aware of what a paralegal is worth.

KZ: Do you feel you're fairly compensated at Diebold for the hours you put in and the time you put in?
LR: Yes.

KZ: What about the benefits? Do you feel they're comparable to what you had before?
LR: They're better than what I had in other places. They offer an excellent health and dental plan; they match up to six percent of whatever you put in for the 401(k) plan. They also offer stock plans and pay for any training that I want to take, including college. They pay 100 percent tuition and books.

KZ: Have you been able to take advantage of that?
LR: Yes. So far, in the first year, I've taken ten different training courses.

KZ: Like workshops and seminars?

LR: Yes, workshops and seminars, and then I went to a technical college and took the real estate courses again. Diebold paid for all of that. Also, you can pick out a computer system; you have to have a certain classification in your job to do it, but if you do, you can buy whatever computer system you want, and they will reimburse you. Then you make a no-interest loan with Diebold to pay them back. The money is taken out of your paycheck.

KZ: So that's a computer for your own home use. What about vacation time or personal time?

LR: When I started, I negotiated two weeks of vacation. I won't get three weeks until I've been here three years.

KZ: How long have you been there now?

LR: Just over a year.

KZ: Tell me a little about what you do in your job.

LR: I manage 400 properties—warehousing and office facilities. My annual budget is over $8 million. This includes acquisition, relocation, expansion and downsizing, and termination of all corporate real estate activities for Diebold, Incorporated.

KZ: All in Ohio?

LR: No, all over the United States and Europe.

We look at prospective sites and negotiate with the landlord for our build-out, rental rate, term, and other amenities. We have a corporate quality team that sets standards and develops specifications as to how we want our offices laid out, what colors we want in the offices, what type of carpeting, what insulation, electrical, and that sort of thing.

KZ: So you know about all of that?

LR: Right. I have assisted in putting these specifications together with the team. Across the United States, we try to standardize all of our offices and warehouse locations so that you could walk into any Diebold office and it would pretty much look the same.

KZ: What about in Europe?

LR: We have branch offices in Europe, but because of the travel time, we do almost everything by phone. We're just developing our market there, so we make sure that our leases are as standard as they can be for the European market. We have offices in Hong Kong, West Germany, London, and Canada.

KZ: In your department, corporate real estate, are there other paralegals? Are there attorneys?

LR: No, it's pretty much a department of one. I'm the administrator of the department. Now there isn't another paralegal working with me. There is a secretary that we all share. I report to the director of corporate facilities.

KT: What typical paralegal skills do you feel that you're using in your position?
LR: I use all the paralegal skills that I received from my paralegal training and my other positions. But the primary skills that I use are negotiation skills, organization skills, communication, and writing skills.

KT: You've been a paralegal for a long time.
LR: I got my first position in 1978.

KT: Did you go to a paralegal school or get a paralegal certificate?
LR: Yes. I went to Ohio Paralegal Institute.

KT: Do you have any further degree, such as a bachelor's degree?
LR: No. Our program was eighteen months long. Other than that, I've taken some college courses in real estate, and I went to The Philadelphia Institute for seminars, things like that.

KT: You've touched on this a little bit already, but how do feel that your position is different than being in a traditional law firm? Better or worse?
LR: I think that I have more responsibility, more sole responsibility for projects that I do. I have better benefits and less stress, and I think that there's more prestige in my position now than in a law firm.

KT: Explain that.
LR: I think that, in a corporation, you're looked on more as a professional.

KT: Is there anything you don't like about it?
LR: Well, I'll never get used to the corporate politics. But they're everywhere, even in law firms. I'd say that's really the only negative. My position's very flexible.

KT: Hour-wise, do you mean?
LR: Well, I spend at least fifty hours on my job per week. At least.

KT: But you can make your own schedule?
LR: Right, I can make my own schedule. I set my own appointments. Sometimes, when the work gets really heavy, I just stay at home and do my work. I have children, and if they have something at school, I'm pretty much free to go to it because my boss trusts me to get the work done. And I'm the one accountable for it, so I will get it done.

KT: What else do you want to tell me?

LR: You asked me about my typical day. I also handle problems in the field, say, with leased properties. If their heating and cooling system goes out, or if they have any type of problem, I'm the person who goes to the landlord or property manager and tries to work those problems out. I go to the property site and review it for maintenance to see what we need to do, such as new paint or carpet. Then I go back to the landlord and try to negotiate that at the end of our term when we renegotiate our lease.

Another thing I do is work on cost-containment projects—for instance, to prepay the rent for a year to receive a discount. I have to do a budget every year for the cost of utilities for what we call common area maintenance, plus our rentals.

KT: Did you have real estate background coming into this?

LR: I had contract background. When I worked at General Tire, I handled all their contracts and did contract review.

KT: So those skills transferred over. Have you found it hard, though, to learn all these new things? It sounds like it's a lot.

LR: That's what I worried about before I interviewed for the position. I thought, "Oh, gosh, I just don't have that strong a background in real estate." But once I got into it and was trained on the procedures the woman before me started, it was just a matter of applying all the skills I used before. Once I got into it, I thought, "Oh, wow, this is exactly what I'd been doing for years. Only then it was handling product liability cases, and now it's real estate. But you still negotiate, just like you did with the litigation side of it. And you use your organization skills, your communication skills. Instead of doing interrogatories, now I'm doing leases and making sure that our associates' needs are met with the landlords. I go in and negotiate with the landlord to see that the needs are met.

KT: It sounds fun.

LR: It is! I didn't think it would be this much fun. And you can be creative because of the decorating in the offices. You can also be creative with the lease provisions.

KT: What about the future—any thoughts?

LR: Diebold is growing so fast. In this position, I'm going to be getting more and more responsibilities. I do see that the department is going to grow. One person can only do so much for so long. I have clerical support, but I think eventually we'll probably have to hire someone else, too.

KT: You seem to have been very successful. Do you think you have any personal quality that has helped you get where you are?

LR: I guess organization and imagination. You have to be willing, no matter what the position, to sit down and look at the problem and use your imagination. If you do, you can figure out almost anything. You're not going to be successful in a paralegal position unless you are able to work independently. If you have to have somebody over you all the time telling you how to do it, when to do it, and what to do, you're not going to be successful.

KZ: Anything we haven't covered or that you'd like to add?
LR: I don't bill hours.

KZ: I'm sure you love that.
LR: Yes, I do! And you wanted to know how I deal with the issue of not being supervised by an attorney. Well, number one, I don't give legal advice, and I don't practice law. If I have a legal question, or if I have any question when I review a lease, I always send it over to the law department to have them bless it.

Also, you wanted to know what my main motivation is for being in a non-traditional position. I would say flexibility. I have more responsibility, and I feel that responsibility is looked at differently here than it is in a lot of law firms.

KZ: How differently?
LR: I think that in some law firms, they use paralegals to the point of burnout. What a paralegal can do for a law firm or a corporation is very valuable, and I don't think that a lot of law firms treat their paralegals that way, as though they are a valuable asset to the firm. Many times in a corporation, on the other hand, the paralegals train the new attorneys who come in. And even though you might not be called "paralegal," all of your paralegal skills are being used. My title is administrator, but one of the mandatory criteria for this position is that the person have a paralegal certificate or training.

CHAPTER 4

Government Paralegals–Local, State, and Federal

aralegals who work for local, state, or federal government share a common characteristic: All of them represent the public, public officials, or public agencies. For example, at the local level, a paralegal may represent a city council or assembly: "We are prosecutors, and we advise the governing body of the Assembly." (Marian Miller) At the state level, ". . . [We] represent the citizens of the state, as well as state officials and all of the state agencies." (Kathleen Weir) And at the federal level, a paralegal may represent a federal agency, such as the Federal Deposit Insurance Corporation (FDIC).

There are benefits and drawbacks to government work. One benefit is the work variety and the responsibility these paralegals have. "The interesting part . . . is that you get to be involved in all aspects of the case. . . . our assigned paralegal staff of three ha[s] tremendous responsibility." (Weir) ". . . what I like about our department is that it's so varied. It's never dull, and it's very busy." (Miller)

Not all government paralegals find the work to be as challenging as they would like, however. "In D.C., there is a lot of work for paralegals, but the work could be more substantive. . . . paralegals in government generally are underutilized. . . . I wish I had more challenging work." (Lori Thompson)

Paralegals employed by the government profit from the career tracks in government employment. "FDIC has a series of positions within the corporation: legal technician . . . legal assistant . . . paralegal or paralegal specialist. . . . Entry-level paralegals begin at Grade 5, and there is a promotion range to Grade 12 as a senior paralegal specialist." (Thompson) As a paralegal progresses upward, duties, pay, and challenge increase commensurately. "It's a mini career path—three levels with increasing responsibility and salary at each level." (Weir)

One advantage to these career tracks is that a non-paralegal working in government can start out at a lower level, transfer into a paralegal position, and then work up the paralegal career track. "I . . . started as a legal secretary here . . ." (Miller) "The first position I was offered was . . . as an administrative assistant. I took it so that I could be employed in government while waiting for a paralegal position to open up." (Weir) "We have many paralegals who have worked their way up from a secretarial position." (Thompson) This is good for a person willing to work up to a paralegal position, but it may be bad for someone who wants to start out as a paralegal. ". . . basically, there weren't any paralegal jobs in the state government unless you started as a secretary. The jobs were coveted, and you got them if you paid your dues." (Miller)

Of course, career tracks are finite, and eventually paralegals reach a point beyond which they cannot progress. "The Grade-12 senior paralegal specialist positions are rare. . . . FDIC views Grade-12 paralegals as not just senior paralegals, as private law firms do, but as supervisory paralegals. Each Grade 12 supervises at least three other paralegals (usually Grade 9 or 11). In my section, there are only two paralegals, so there are no promotion opportunities." (Thompson) Thus, in order to move up, government paralegals often need to take a new position in a different level of government or with a different government agency. "There really isn't any advancement for me within the city government. There would be in the state government." (Miller)

Progress up a career ladder is sometimes stymied by budgetary considerations. ". . . with the current budget trends, pay increases or position upgrades come very slowly, more slowly than in a successful private firm." (Weir) Budget also affects daily workloads for these paralegals. "The number of FTE's [full-time employees] for each section is allotted every biennial budget cycle. If you get caught with a large case and a small FTE count, the workload can be tremendous." (Weir)

Government budgets have one other effect on these paralegals. Contrary to what the general public often believes, government paralegals do not necessarily work the traditional government hours of 8:00 A.M. to 5:00 P.M. They may work as many hours as in a private law firm, and, again because of budgetary considerations, they may not be compensated accordingly. ". . . many divisions work long hours, especially if they litigate, and there are no staff bonuses. . . . It's discouraging when you've worked very hard on a case or several cases with successful results and learn that this budget does not allow any pay increases or promotions." (Weir)

Nevertheless, there are compensating factors, ranging from good benefits packages to altruism, for these paralegals. "The longer I'm here, the harder it is to go. I have seniority, and we have excellent benefits and leave." (Miller) ". . . you don't work in government for big money. But when your clients are the people who live in the state, you have a sense of doing something important in every case." (Weir)

Pride in their profession is evident in these paralegals, tempered with concern for the profession, its future, and those who work in it. ". . . the profession . . . can provide a liveable wage with the potential for big money. And, it's guaranteed to be a challenging exercise, every workday. . ." (Weir) ". . . I worry that the paralegals here, who have never worked elsewhere and who aren't involved in a professional paralegal organization, will think that this is all that paralegals are capable of doing. . . . I feel that many paralegals have no clue to what the job involves. . . . most of the paralegals in government come up through the ranks and don't understand that being a paralegal is a profession. . . . I'm a professional, and I want to be treated as one." (Thompson)

INTERVIEW G

There are paralegal positions within the state government. They might not have the title "paralegal," but quite a few use paralegal skills. I learned of a state position recently that's called associate attorney but is really a paralegal position. The job holder reviews agency regulations for content and form. It sounds like an interesting position.

Marian Miller

Company: City and Borough of Juneau
City: Juneau, Alaska
Department: Law Department
                City Attorney's Office
Title: Legal Administrator
Salary Range: $27,000–$36,000
Benefits:
    Insurance: medical (Blue Cross), life insurance 28% of salary
    Financial:
    Annual leave: combined vacation and sick leave: less than 1 year: 1.75 days per month; 1 to 2 years: 2.00 days per month; 2 to 5 years: 2.25 days per month; 5 to 10 years: 2.50 days per month; 10 + years: 3.00 days per month.
    Misc.:   health and wellness program

Previous Work Experience:
Legal secretary I and II with City and Borough of Juneau Law Department for five years.

JOB DESCRIPTION

Definition

Perform complex administrative, legal secretarial, and paralegal duties as personal assistant to the city-borough attorney and supervisor of two legal secretaries. Duties include more difficult assignments to assist the legal staff and provide routine legal information and advice; such assignments are designed to free the legal staff to devote full time to matters requiring legal expertise. Duties require a high degree of tact, independence, and discretion in dealing with the public, local, state, and federal officials.

Typical Responsibilities

- Assist attorneys with litigation; prepares exhibits and routine pleadings; prepares and answers interrogatories; performs basic legal research and files research.
- Assist in resolving a variety of legal problems. Independently prepares correspondence, legal notices, and forms appropriate to the work of the office; revises drafted correspondence and reports to improve clarity and quality.
- Maintain follow-up records relating to legal matters in process. Ensure that appropriate legal documents are prepared to meet legal requirements and processed to meet deadlines. May answer a wide variety of inquiries concerning the progress of legal actions and give information on the procedures required in handling these actions.
- Set up and maintain files and records for current cases and projects.
- Receive requests from other departments, private or public agencies, and the general public for general and routine legal information, texts of ordinances, proper channels to obtain special legal assistance; research individual requests and prepare replies to individuals in a variety of specialized and professional fields; answer questions on status of current projects.
- Assist city-borough attorney in drafting specific portions of legislation.
- Arrange for transportation and accommodations of traveling staff members; check and process expense claims; keep time and attendance records; make arrangements for meetings and notify conferees.
- Responsible for general management of the office, including maintenance of law library; ordering supplies; maintaining accounting records. Work with city-borough attorney to prepare annual department budget.
- Perform other related duties as required.

Minimum Qualifications

Graduation from high school or the equivalent; six years of office clerical or administrative experience, including not less than one year of legal secretarial/clerical work. Completion of a college-level paralegal program may be substituted for the one-year legal secretarial/clerical work.

MM: It would probably be helpful to describe what type of office I'm in first. The City and Borough of Juneau [CBJ] is the state capital, and the population is about 28,000. We're only accessible by boat or plane. We're surrounded by ice fields.

KZ: Did you grow up in Alaska?
MM: No, I grew up in Michigan.
   We don't have any counties in Alaska. The city and borough is like a county, as far as structure goes. It's a home-rule, charter-based government with a council, which is called the Assembly. There are nine members on the Assembly. The city attorney and the city manager are directly accountable to the Assembly.

KZ: Is the Assembly elected?
MM: Yes, so it's not a strong mayor form of government.
   In our office we have four attorneys: the city attorney and three assistants. There are three support staff: two legal secretaries and myself. I'm considered the legal administrator. It's a small office.

KZ: Do you have a paralegal background?
MM: Yes. I've been in this position for almost eleven years now. When I moved to Alaska from Michigan with my husband, I noticed an ad in the paper for a legal secretary with the city. I had gone to Michigan State and was a sophomore when we moved. I had taken pre-law classes and was very interested in working in that area. I applied for the job and reviewed the code of the city. I got the job and started as a legal secretary in the criminal division of the city law department. Then I took classes at the University of Alaska Southeast. I have a paralegal degree from UAS that I obtained by taking one or two classes at a time for quite a few years.
   I didn't really explain the function of the office. We are prosecutors, and we advise the governing body of the Assembly. We handle misdemeanor cases—DWI, domestic violence, assault.

KZ: Is there much of a market for paralegals in Alaska?
MM: Certain law firms use paralegals, and certain law firms don't. There are paralegal positions within the state government. They might not have the title "paralegal," but quite a few use paralegal skills. I learned of a state position recently that's called associate attorney but is really a paralegal position. The job holder reviews agency regulations for content and form. It sounds like an interesting position.
   In fact, we do some of those things here. The law department advises the Assembly and all the departments. We also review contractual

agreements and other legal documents. Another major function of our office is legislative drafting of ordinances arrd resolutions in addition to our prosecution work.

What I like about our department is that it's so varied. It's never dull, and it's very busy. I work closely with the city attorney. In the legislative work, part of the process is researching prior law so that it can be amended or a new law created. A great deal of my position deals with the tracking of legislation.

KT: What is a typical day like for you?
MM: Well, I come into my office and turn on my computer. The city attorney is very computer-oriented. Each attorney has a PC. They do a lot of their own initial typing, and the support staff reviews it. We have a program that keeps track of our hours. We don't bill hours, but we are starting to track them.

KT: Just for internal management?
MM: So we can know how much time we spend advising each department. Right now, we're not like a private firm where you have billable hours. I haven't worked for a private firm, but I do have friends who do. We don't have that kind of pressure in regard to billable hours, but we do have nine bosses—the Assembly members to whom we are accountable.

This is a very political town. Juneau's main industry is government; we are the state capital, and there is a lot of federal government here, too.

When I get to work, I start up my time sheets. Right now I'm working on the agenda for the next Assembly meeting. I coordinate the legislation for it.

KT: What does that mean?
MM: We initially draft the legislation, and then most of it is sent to committee first, prior to being sent to the Assembly. I check the current CBJ code to make sure that the new legislation amendment and additions are correct. Last week, I worked a couple of hours researching legislation on sales tax exemptions. I had to look at the prior CBJ code to see when the exemptions came into effect and why. I frequently look up CBJ code sections which were previously in effect, such as what was in effect regarding zoning in 1980.

For a research tool, we have a CD-ROM of Alaska case law. It's similar to WESTLAW in that you use a buzz word to narrow your search. We do have a law library, which isn't too extensive, but we have access to the state law library. Sometimes I have to do research in the state library system.

We do not handle a lot of litigation in this office. We do handle administrative appeals, which are then appealed to the superior court. Tort cases, like a slip-and-fall suit, are contracted out to private attorneys. We do prosecution of misdemeanors—both court trials and jury trials. I have prepared jury trial notebooks when necessary.

CD-ROM

A technological advance which may have the most far-reaching effect on the practice of law is CD-ROM, or compact disk–read only memory. CD-ROMs are small storage devices, in the form of laser disks, which are used much like a floppy disk is used in a computer. The disks are about the same size as a floppy disk, but can hold much more information. One disk can hold the equivalent of approximately 100 to 125 average books; it would take about 600 floppy disks to hold the same number.

What this means for the legal field is that law libraries as we know them could eventually become obsolete. A law firm might buy one disk instead of an entire set of law books, which would bestow the added ability of doing a word search on-disk quickly instead of having to search manually through page after page in book after book.

CD-ROM technology is already in use to some extent. For example, some states currently have all of their case law on disk. Lawyers Cooperative Publishing produces American Law Reports (A.L.R.) and U.S.C.S. on CD-ROM. In seconds, a user can search all of A.L.R. third, fourth, and fifth editions on one disk and then jump directly to the needed article or section.

The big issue in our city right now is mining. We have a couple of administrative appeals of conditional-use permits that are headed to superior court and beyond. At the moment, a mining company is trying to reopen two large mines in the CBJ, and it has really split the community. Our office is involved in the conditional-use permit process. One of my earliest projects on the mining issue was to compile a historical resource on mining in the CBJ by researching all our files regarding mining and putting together a notebook on prior ordinances, agreements, and so forth.

KT: Those are pretty big projects.

MM: Yes. I'm trying to learn the table of authorities on our new WordPerfect 5.1 software for the Superior Court appeals. I haven't got it down pat yet.

KT: Was there anyone there to train you when you started your job? Had you gained enough knowledge in your legal secretary position that you were comfortable when you assumed this position?

MM: Actually, I think the position has evolved while I've been in it. I still do some functions that are considered secretarial. I do the bills for the office. I also help with the budget, which is critical.

KZ: Sounds like a smorgasbord of administrative duties and paralegal duties.

MM: The variety is nice. I also like it that, we don't think, "No, I can't do that because it's a secretary's job." Our attorneys will answer the phone if it's ringing. There's a nice attitude in this office.

KZ: Is it an informal atmosphere?

MM: Maybe it's just being in Alaska. Things are more informal here. Everybody works together. We do dress professionally in our office. In comparison with a large city, though, it's much more informal.

KZ: Do you ever feel tempted to go into the private law firms there?

MM: I've had offers a couple of times. I know if I wanted to venture into a private firm, there would be opportunities. I think certain firms appreciate and use paralegals well. I have a friend who works for one firm in town that does a lot of oil and gas work. She says that she's on one case doing discovery—just that one thing. I like the variety of my job more than I would like that. Plus, I've been here for eleven years. The longer I'm here, the harder it is to go. I have seniority, and we have excellent benefits and leave.

KZ: What kind of benefits and leave do you have?

MM: The leave depends on how long you've been here. We don't have sick leave, just annual leave. It accrues by the number of years you've been here. If you've been here a while, it really adds up. The salary range is from $27,000 to $36,000, and the benefits are about $14,000 of that. The City and Borough of Juneau is self-insured. We contract with Blue Cross. We also have a program called Health Yourself, which encourages healthy life-style choices. The employees as a whole were able to reduce their overall health costs, and so we each received a rebate. Health Yourself also gives you discounts on local health club memberships, lunch-hour presentations on cholesterol, free health screenings—things like that.

I'm also on a committee within the city for employees. We have one union, and the city manager wanted to get feedback from people other than union members.

KZ: A union for whom?

MM: For certain groups of CBJ employees. The law department cannot be in the union because we are management and administration. I'm on the committee as a representative of employees in administration, which includes the law department, the manager's office, data processing, land and resources, personnel, and libraries. The employee council presents ideas to the manager to make the CBJ work more efficiently and safely—a total quality management idea.

KT: Are there some main paralegal skills that you use? You've mentioned that you do a fair amount of research, and obviously you're organized, what with all the administrative work that you do, but is there anything else that you think you use a great deal?
MM: I enjoy the research portion. Writing skills are important. I think a very important skill is working with people. That's a human skill, not a paralegal skill, but they go together.

KT: Do you have any plans to move to a different position, or are you content where you are?
MM: Because Juneau is small, there aren't many places to move. There really isn't any advancement for me within the city government. There would be advancement for me in the state government.

KT: You said one of the things you like the best about your job is the variety. Are there any other things that you love about it, or hate about it?
MM: What I really like about it is the people. The attorneys here have diverse backgrounds with their own areas of expertise.
    What do I dislike? I can't think of anything right off the top of my head.

KT: That's good!
    Do you think you've been successful as a paralegal?
MM: I think so. I think the problem in Juneau is lack of appreciation for paralegals. We do have a training program at the university, but they don't have a placement program. I'd like to see more of that. When I went into the training program, it was exciting because much of what I was learning applied to my current job. But for someone who has a real interest in law and who doesn't have the hands-on experience, it's hard. They do have an intern program, but I'd like to see more of a push for placement. More education about paralegals is needed—for example, presentations to the bar association about what paralegals can do.
    The paralegal association here is disbanding. We don't have enough interest. It's very discouraging. There's a core group of us, but we're getting burned out. Someone from the state came to talk to our organization a couple of years ago; she said that there weren't any paralegal jobs in State government unless you started as a secretary. The jobs were coveted, and you got them if you paid your dues. I don't know what can change the job outlook for paralegals here, except for education about what paralegals are and what they can do. I keep hearing it's the fastest-growing profession, but I don't think that's hit Juneau yet. We're a little backward here.

KT: I think you're right about the need for education. There are jobs out there that are ideal for a paralegal, but they might not be titled "paralegal," and the people who are hiring don't always understand that a paralegal would be the perfect person for that position.

MM: Yes, there could be a job in real estate or contract administration.

We've had some hard economic times here. I have a friend who does freelance work. When she first came here, she was competing with attorneys because our economy was so bad that attorneys were taking paralegal jobs. I think the answer is education, especially about the cost-effectiveness of using a paralegal. Speaking of freelance paralegals, one big reason for freelancing is the flexibility that can come with it.

KZ: Is your own position flexible?

MM: I wouldn't say so. We're too busy for that. But maybe some day!

INTERVIEW   H

We promote fair trade in the marketplace by encouraging competition. We are plaintiffs. We look at businesses and industries which we believe are committing antitrust violations.

Kathleen Weir

Company: Washington State Attorney General's Office
City: Seattle, Washington
Department: Solicitor General's Office, Antitrust Section
Title: Paralegal 2
Salary Range: $28,260–$38,880
Benefits:
  Insurance: choice of 18 medical plans, some of which include vision care, choice of 4 dental plans.
  Financial: mandatory pension plan, deferred compensation plan available, state employees credit union available.
  Vacation: graduated scale, beginning with 12 days per year and maximizing at 22 days from 1 year continuous employment through 16 years.
  Sick time: 8 hours per month of continuous employment, cumulative until employment ends.
  Misc.:   10 state holidays and 1 floating personal day, approved education/training tuition discount or reimbursement (this is limited based on current budget and agency policy), commuter van-pool membership available.

Previous Work Experience:

Paralegal in a law firm specializing in tax, bankruptcy, and immigration law. Administrative assistant for Washington State Department of Labor and Industries. Field representative for a building and construction trades council. Market analyst for a food corn and seed company.

JOB DESCRIPTION

Definition

Under the supervision of an assistant attorney general, perform paralegal work (e.g., analyze facts, compose initial drafts of documents and pleadings, interview witnesses, etc.) on assigned cases or projects at an entry level.

Typical Work

Under the supervision of an assistant attorney general, may perform the following legal work:

- Collect, organize, and analyze factual information and documents related to litigation, potential litigation, or legal services to a state agency client.
- Organize and maintain litigation, investigation, and research files; track case status.
- Log and assist with the organization, preparation, and, in certain cases, microfilming of large volumes of documents.
- Compose, organize, and enter information into computer databases
- Select documents from databases and document sets using listing and other indexes.
- Investigate facts of cases and interview potential witnesses.
- Prepare interrogatories, requests for documents, and responses to the same.
- Prepare questions for depositions and summarize deposition contents.
- Identify, compile, and prepare documents for discovery and trial.
- Organize and prepare trial notebooks by selecting relevant pleadings and exhibits to be used at trial.
- Take notes and summaries at depositions and trials.
- Compose legal notices, pleadings, and other legal documents.
- Negotiate, under close supervision, claims with recurring or readily identifiable legal concepts or simple fact patterns, or claims of moderate monetary impact.
- Perform other work as required.

Minimum Qualifications (one of the following)

- Two years experience as a paralegal or legal assistant.
- Graduation from an accredited two-year paralegal or legal assistant course.
- Graduation from an accredited four-year college and completion of a nine-month legal assistant or paralegal program or one year of paralegal or legal assistant experience.
- Three years experience as a legal secretary and thirty quarter or equivalent semester hours in non-secretarial legal courses which are normally part of a paralegal or legal assistant course at a college or community college.

KW: There's a difference in the practice of law in the private and public sector. The public sector deals with enforcement and representation. The attorney general's office represents the citizens of the state, as well as state officials and all of the state agencies. I suppose the main difference is that in government, we write the rules and actually administer the law.

From a personnel perspective, there's a huge difference between the private and public sector. All government employees must adhere to the Department of Personnel code. The code defines everything about our employment. It establishes wages and benefits, hiring, disciplinary actions and dismissal procedures, types of leave, pensions, affirmative action programs, disability programs, job descriptions . . .

KT: Pretty much everything.
KW: Yes. Then there are internal differences between the agencies. So much has to do with how the budget is allotted . . . how much money you have to work with. Moving from one agency to another can be like working at a completely different place, not only in the body of law but also in the resources available, such as staffing, equipment, and even furniture.

KT: You're in the Washington State attorney general's office, in the antitrust section?
KW: Yes.

KT: What is an example of something you do?
KW: We promote fair trade in the marketplace by encouraging competition. We are plaintiffs. We look at businesses and industries which we believe are committing antitrust violations.

KT: What type of industry?
KW: It doesn't matter. It just has to fall within the definition of antitrust activity with harm to the people of the state—for example, price fixing or monopolistic activities. Recently, there was a large bank merger. We

proactively stepped in and reviewed the demographics of the markets to determine the repercussions if the merger proceeded as planned. Our purpose was to ensure that all the money of several counties wouldn't end up in one institution. We were able to define what branches could be taken over and, if a group of banks was purchased, which branches had to remain independent.

Another example is an oil case that began in the 1970s, involving all of the major oil companies in this country. I don't know how old you are, but in the 1970s, there were gas shortages that produced long gas lines.

KT: I remember that.

KW: The case involved allegations by several joint plaintiff states that the oil companies had conspired to create the shortage and were manipulating the pricing in the marketplace. A settlement was reached only last January.

KT: What would you be doing in a case like that? A lot of paperwork, research, investigation?

KW: The interesting part about a case like this is that, as a paralegal, you are involved in all aspects of the case. This was a unique case for many reasons—age, size, multiple plaintiff states, geographic locations of the teams and the court, and the formidable opponents. I worked on the damages document production and on the massive exhibit lists. We had about three weeks to review millions of pages of material to locate our damages documents. We sent people across the country and ran as many as six microfilming cameras simultaneously, per location, to capture approximately 200,000 images. Then we had to organize the data and route documents to each economic expert. At the same time, we were preparing the exhibits. Washington was the central document store for the case, so our assigned paralegal staff of three had tremendous responsibility. We hired many temporary employees for coding, sorting, numbering, and so forth.

KT: That sounds either exciting or nightmarish.

KW: It was both. We worked the equivalent of one and three-quarter years in one calendar year.

KT: We often have the impression that people in government have eight- to -five jobs.

KW: Right, but they don't. There are paralegals with more traditional hours, but many divisions work long hours, especially if they litigate, and there are no staff bonuses.

KT: Do you get paid overtime when you work long hours?

KW: Yes, if the project has overtime approval. If not, no.

KT: How does billing function in a public-sector law firm such as yours?
KW: Billing is almost the same as in the private sector. We calendar our time and bill our client agencies. The legal work of certain sections of the office is statutorily budgeted, but even so, the spending is monitored.

KT: How many paralegals are working there?
KW: In the antitrust section, we have seven, and our agency has about sixty. Two of our paralegals job-share one position, so we have six full-time employee [FTE] positions. The number of FTEs for each section is allotted every biennial budget cycle, so if you get caught with a large case and a small FTE count, the workload can be tremendous.

KT: You can't add more people until the next budget cycle, and by then that case could be over.
KW: Right.

KT: How did you end up at the attorney general's office? Were you ever in the private sector?
KW: I worked in a private firm for about two years, took a break for a year of law school, and then went to work for the government to make a liveable wage to pay back my student loans.

KT: You deliberately looked for a government job?
KW: Yes. I was lucky that I placed high enough to be put on the register.

KT: That was the first position that you had in state government?
KW: No. The first position I was offered was with the Department of Labor and Industries as an administrative assistant. I took it so that I could be employed in government while waiting for a paralegal position to open up.

KT: Do they announce jobs internally first and then externally?
KW: Very often, yes.

KT: So you had a definite advantage in getting the job.
    How many years have you been with the attorney general's office? Or how many years in your current position?
KW: Two years.

KT: And you had told me before that they have three levels of paralegals. Can you explain that?
KW: It's a mini career path—three levels, with increasing responsibility and salary at each level.

KT: How do like your position?

KW: I enjoy my work, but with the current budget trends, pay increases or position upgrades come very slowly, more slowly than in a successful private firm.

KT: There are pros and cons to both private and public sector work. Do you feel a little stymied at times by the structure within which you work?
KW: It's discouraging when you've worked very hard on a case or several cases with successful results and learn that this budget doesn't allow any pay increases or promotions.

KT: You'd like some type of reward based on merit?
KW: Yes. But you don't work in government for big money. When your clients are the people who live in the state, you have a sense of doing something important in every case.

KT: What skills do you use the most on your job?
KW: Knowing where to find information, how to get it, and what it says after you read it, and then how to polish it up for the legal show.

KT: Did you have paralegal schooling?
KW: I have a bachelor's degree in English and have taken all of the courses currently required in this state to obtain a paralegal certificate, but I don't have one. That's another reason I applied for a government position. My qualifications were analyzed based on the courses I took and the length of my work experience rather than on having a certificate alone.

KT: Are you happy with where you are now? What do you see for your future?
KW: I would like to get more information-systems management training because our last investigation was conducted electronically. We used spreadsheet analyses of the respondent's electronic files by transferring fields of numbers rather than by looking at hundreds of pages of figures, coding, and then calculating.

KT: Is there anything else you'd like to mention that we haven't addressed?
KW: The paralegal profession in general, regardless of age, gender, or ethnicity, can provide a liveable wage with the potential for big money. And it's guaranteed to be a challenging exercise, every workday, in almost every city in the western world, for as long as you stay in the game. That's a rare bird.

INTERVIEW I

There is a great deal of litigation out there right now because of the banking crisis of the past. My section monitors court decisions in the various jurisdictions. I am responsible for locating new decisions through WESTLAW and LEXIS searches. These cases are summarized and put into topical sections in the Cumulative Case List which is distributed monthly to our regions and field attorneys. The Cumulative Case List is an excellent research tool.

Lori Thompson

Company:	Federal Deposit Insurance Corporation (FDIC)
City:	Washington D.C.
Department:	Legal Division, Liquidations Branch
	Closed Bank Litigation & Policy Section
Title:	Paralegal Specialist
Salary Range:	$44,00–$58,000
Benefits:	
Insurance:	Medical, dental, life
Financial:	401(k), U.S. government pension plan
Vacation:	1–3 years: 1 day per month, 3–15 years: 1.5 days per month, 15+ years: 2 days per month
Sick time:	one day per month
Misc.:	limited tuition reimbursement

Previous Work Experience:
One year as Paralegal Supervisor for the Federal Savings and Loan Insurance Corporation. Two years as a freelance paralegal. Two years as Paralegal Supervisor in a legal aid society. Six months as a Paralegal

intern in a private law firm and two years as a researcher and guardian ad litem in a private law firm.

JOB DESCRIPTION

Responsibilities

- Assist in the preparation of memoranda which are used to determine appropriate legal advice given by Section attorneys to Regional Field Offices, Consolidated Field Office, the General Counsel, DOL, DOR, the FDIC Board of Directors and Chairman. Usually, the subject of these memoranda is of a highly complex nature.
- Draft legal documents to evaluate and implement closed bank litigation policies for Division of Liquidation and Board Resolution, which are reviewed by the section attorneys.
- Assist in the preparation of responses to congressional inquiries and to inquiries from outside legal counsel.
- Assist in the preparation of internal position papers analyzing novel or unique factual issues and recommending an appropriate policy for the corporation. The memoranda are reviewed by section attorneys, assistant general counsel, or senior counsel, as appropriate.
- Conduct legal research and prepare legal memoranda and directives for review by section attorneys.
- Assist section attorneys in coordinating activity between the Department of Justice, regional field offices, consolidated field offices, other FDIC legal sections, and government officials, as well as the Office of the General Counsel.
- Assist section attorneys in review of pleadings submitted by outside counsel and in-house legal staff in the regional field offices and in the consolidated field offices to ensure that consistency is preserved on the various special issues that affect FDIC in its litigation throughout the country.
- Monitor the decisions rendered by the federal courts in order to alert section attorneys to adverse or inconsistent opinions by the courts and to keep abreast of any changes that might affect the interests of the corporation.
- Prepare case digests which are disseminated to the regional counsel and the section.
- Assist other GS-7 through GS-11 law clerks, paralegals, and legal technicians in preparing memoranda and court documents used in the purchase and assumption transactions and bridge bank transactions.
- Prepare the Reserve for Potential Losses Report, which is furnished to the Government Accounting Office, in order to audit corporate activity within the Bank Insurance Fund and Savings Association Insurance Fund.

LT: I work for the Federal Deposit Insurance Corporation, or FDIC. FDIC has a series of positions: legal technician (this is a secretarial promotion opportunity, but the responsibilities are still clerical), legal assistant (more of a rarity), paralegal, or paralegal specialist. I'm a paralegal specialist. I have a paralegal certificate and an undergraduate degree. Entry-level paralegals begin at Grade 5, and there is a promotion range to Grade 12 as a senior paralegal. I've been with the FDIC in Washington, D.C., for three years.

KT: Have you moved up in the grades?
LT: Yes, I have.

Let me tell you about my background. I worked for a satellite office of the Federal Savings and Loan Insurance Corporation [FSLIC] in Salt Lake City, Utah, which was responsible for regulating and liquidating savings and loan associations ["institutions"]. The Resolution Trust Corporation [RTC] is responsible for liquidating institutions since the new 1989 legislation. The Federal Home Loan Bank Board [FHLBB] would determine when an institution was in serious trouble and appoint FSLIC as liquidator. Eventually, the office in Salt Lake was closed and consolidated with the regional office in Los Angeles. I received an offer to move to the regional office during the Summer of 1989.

I had an opportunity to work with either RTC or FDIC. I was interested in RTC because of the challenge of working in a new agency. I spent a year with RTC in California, preparing the documents for the institution closings. I had a lot of opportunities to travel and organize a variety of closing transactions.

I moved to Washington, D.C., to work for FDIC in The National Bank of Washington [NBW] field office. This office was very small and was assigned only one bank to liquidate because of the size of this one institution. In comparison, the RTC office where I worked has over thirty-five institutions. The NBW field office was consolidated with another field office in Chicago during the Fall of 1991. I accepted an offer to work for the FDIC Corporate Headquarters in Washington, D.C., where I'm currently working.

I began with RTC as a Grade-9 paralegal specialist. Grade is determined by education and experience. Entry-level paralegals begin at Grade 5. Within each grade there are ten steps. When paralegals are first hired and their grade has been determined, the step is chosen that will most closely match their previous salary. Every year, you can progress one step, automatically, until Step 4, and then you can move one step every two years. Paralegals can be given a quality step for work performance, and there are merit awards (bonuses) for special projects or sustained superior performance. I was promoted to a Grade-11 paralegal specialist when I accepted employment at FDIC Corporate.

KT: So you're at almost as high a grade level as you can be.
LT: Yes. There are Grade-12 senior paralegal specialists within the corpo-

ration. FDIC views them not as just paralegals, as private law firms do, but as supervisory paralegals. Each Grade-12 supervises at least three other paralegals (usually Grade 9 or 11). In my section, there are only two paralegals, so there are no promotion opportunities.

KT: You would have to move out of your current section to move up?
LT: Yes. My current job is very similar to being in-house counsel within a corporation. The legal division has four branches (liquidation, supervision, operations, and resolutions). I work in the liquidation branch, which has four sections. I'm in the closed-bank litigation and policy section. The other sections are bankruptcy, special projects, and regional affairs. My section has grown very large during my two years here. We currently have twenty-four attorneys, five legal technicians (secretaries), and two paralegals. We are very top-heavy with attorneys.

KT: Very top-heavy.
LT: We try to tell them that, but they don't believe us!
    The legal technicians are basically given secretarial tasks and don't have time to do much else. It would be great to be able to delegate more "paralegal" work to them. The section is a fun group because once a bank is closed, FDIC acquires special powers through the legislation because of our role as liquidator. We have an obligation to maximize the funds to distribute to creditors and minimize the costs of liquidating an institution.

KT: What do you do, then, in your daily job?
LT: There is a great deal of litigation out there right now because of the banking crisis of the past. My section monitors court decisions in the various jurisdictions. I am responsible for locating new decisions through WESTLAW and LEXIS searches. These cases are summarized and put into topical sections in the Cumulative Case List which is distributed monthly to our regions and field attorneys. The Cumulative Case List is an excellent research tool. FDIC attorneys can easily review all cases that discuss important FDIC topics (say letters of credit and administrative claims procedure). I prepare an annual edition, which is also mailed to law firms that represent FDIC. The case list helps new attorneys to understand FDIC's philosophies. It also saves FDIC money because outside law firms don't have to research case law.
    The FDIC staff attorneys have a choice of handling a case in-house or hiring outside law firms. We now have an agreement with the Department of Justice that they will represent the FDIC.
    I track the cases that are referred to DOJ and keep the attorney responsible for the DOJ referrals up to date on the status of the case.

KT: Do you do this on a computer system?
LT: Yes. I use WordPerfect Tables.

The FDIC is also very involved in alternative dispute resolution [ADR]. Our general counsel has set a goal of having ten percent of our litigation in some type of mediation or arbitration, which is great. FDIC maintains a computerized database of all the disputes. I update the disputes every quarter and prepare a variety of reports. These reports save money for FDIC by

Alternative Dispute Resolution

When Americans have a dispute that needs resolution, they often seek a remedy through the court systems. But such litigation can be extremely costly and lengthy, and because litigating is by nature adversarial, neither party may end up happy. Alternative dispute resolution (ADR) refers to methods of resolving disputes that are speedier, less costly, less formal, and more amiable than litigating.

Arbitration and mediation are two main types of ADR. Both attempt to resolve disputes amicably in a non-adversarial manner. In arbitration, a neutral and impartial third party (who is generally an expert with extensive experience and expertise in the area of the dispute) hears and considers the evidence and testimony provided by the disputing parties, and then issues a decision. The decision is either binding or non-binding, depending on what the parties previously agreed to.

In mediation, a neutral and impartial third party (the mediator) facilitates communication between the disputing parties which may enable them to reach a settlement. The mediator does not render a decision, but simply helps the parties reach a mutually acceptable solution to their problem. Solutions arrived at in mediation tend to last over time because the people affected by the decisions are making them rather than having a decision imposed on them by someone else.

Use and knowledge of ADR has been increasing over the last two decades and will probably continue to grow. In fact, some states require ADR prior to litigating in certain types of disputes, and some state bar associations have requirements in their ethical codes that lawyers advise clients early on that they can resolve their disputes in ways other than litigation.

HINT:

Very few states have any licensing or educational requirements for mediators yet, and this may be a new career direction for paralegals. In fact, some paralegals already are doing mediation, either on a paid or pro bono basis.

utilizing ADR and resolving cases outside the court system. ADR seems to all work out well; last year we saved $9 million by using it.

I also work with a computer analyst on a task force to develop a new tracking system to help the field offices update their information. I will still be responsible for preparing the reports every quarter. The people I prepare the reports for like my pie charts and graphs, so I can be creative. The reports demonstrate the statistical information for pending and re-solved disputes.

More rarely, I have the opportunity to do legal research, such as legis-lative histories. I also work on larger projects as they are available. For example, DOJ and FDIC wanted to know if using the Federal Tort Claims Act was saving us money or if FDIC's other powers were more useful. A task force was developed.

My section is also involved with new legislation being developed by Congress. We are sometimes asked to review pending legislation before it becomes law. I would like to get more involved with these projects, but, unfortunately, they are usually projects with a very short turnaround, and the attorneys rarely use the paralegals for them.

I researched and drafted responses to congressional inquiries while working for another section at FDIC. Someone might write their represen-tative because they applied to work for the FDIC (for example, a law firm) and didn't receive any work. I investigated whether they had actually completed the application process and interviewed with a field office in their area, and whether their expertise could be utilized by FDIC.

KZ: It doesn't sound like you do much drafting.

LT: No. I do very little drafting, but that's because we rarely handle litiga-tion, since the lawsuits are rarely filed here in D.C. My attorneys don't have a caseload, and neither do I.

My attorneys monitor high-profile cases with issues important to the FDIC, and they work on appeals that are important to develop case law that is beneficial to the FDIC, and they write policy for the FDIC on special issues or procedures (for example, repudiation of contracts). The attorneys consider themselves to be a "think tank." Each one has a specialty and each one has a geographical region to handle and serve as a resource for, in addition to that specialty. They are expected to be experts for the FDIC, and the work is very interesting.

KZ: Have you always worked as a paralegal in banking?

LT: No. My first paralegal job was with the Legal Aid Society of Salt Lake. It was a great first job. I worked there for two years, which was a long time. Most of the people burned out or left after a year. I had two years to de-velop great interviewing skills. I drafted documents and worked out ser-vice of process problems (out-of-state, military, and service outside of the United States).

Prior to working at Legal Aid, I worked as a volunteer guardian ad litem for an attorney in Utah.

Pro bono and non-profit work are a real love of mine. Even now, I'm very actively involved with it. For example, I'm the Pro Bono Publico Committee chairperson for the National Capital Area Paralegal Association (NCAPA). Unfortunately, there are not a lot of employment opportunities in pro bono and non-profit work.

I received my paralegal certificate in 1984; most of my friends went to work for law firms and were making at least $2,000 a month in Utah. I was making $11,000 a year at Legal Aid.

While I was working full-time for Legal Aid, I worked part-time as a counselor at a shelter for battered women. Many of the women were also clients of Legal Aid. I was surprised that everything worked out so well. Many of the women attorneys I worked with at Legal Aid agreed to talk with the women at the shelter at my weekly support groups. They provided information concerning how to file protective orders, and they empowered the women by telling them about their legal rights and the resources available.

The real problem was the hours. I worked at Legal Aid from 8:00 A.M. to 5:00 P.M. and then worked at the shelter from 6:00 to 10:00 P.M. If there was an emergency (say a woman that needed to be checked into the shelter, fire alarms, or bomb scares), I often worked until midnight. After about a year and a half of this work schedule, I burned out. I left Legal Aid and continued to work part-time at the shelter. The evening hours gave me time to look for a full-time paralegal job during the day.

During this time, I got involved with FSLIC. A friend of mine asked me if I wanted to work on a three- to four-week project. The work was different from my work at Legal Aid and sounded very interesting. The project continued for nine months.

FSLIC was preparing for a major case against the previous directors and officers of a large savings and loan that they were liquidating. The case involved major document organization and production. I spent the majority of my days reading through the documents involved and preparing summaries. We had determined which names, projects, and so forth, were important to the case. Because of the volume of documents—over ten thousand—I trained temporary staff to Bates stamp and assist in reviewing them. FSLIC had developed an excellent database to store and retrieve the information. I learned how important documents were to a case. It would have been great to stay with this case until it went to trial, but I was working for RTC during 1990 when it finally did, almost four years after I first started working on it.

After FSLIC, I worked on several other freelance projects. I fell into freelance work by accident and worked on some very interesting projects for two years, in law firms and in corporate environments. The legal community saw me as a domestic law paralegal because of my employment with Legal Aid, and there were very few full-time jobs that required my skills. The only offers I received were from other non-profit organizations with limited salaries and promotion opportunities. Working freelance allowed me to enhance my skills in a variety of environments and make myself more marketable.

I developed my freelance resources by responding to letters notifying me that I had not been selected for a position I had interviewed for. I would thank them for notifying me of their decision and then express my interest in short-term projects. I worked on my own, without the assistance of an employment agency. At that time, paralegal employment agencies did not exist in Utah. I finally worked with SOS Legal Staff during their growth period.

Because of my previous experience with them FSLIC had been looking for me to work on another project. After two months, I was offered a full-time position as a paralegal. I supervised a small staff in the records retention department. My freelance experience worked out well, but I don't believe that I would have been brave enough to set out to be a freelance paralegal.

KZ: You've had a real range of paralegal work.
LT: Oh yes. I have enjoyed the different opportunities and the different work environments. Legal Aid specialized in domestic law. We also did immigration law and adoptions.

Utah went quickly from having one paralegal school to having five, and the market was flooded. That was one reason I accepted the job offer and the move to Los Angeles. I felt the job market would be better there and that I would have more opportunities.

KZ: Was it a good market?
LT: The most difficult thing about California was that it was important to have graduated from an ABA-approved paralegal school. In Utah, you needed to have an undergraduate degree and a paralegal certificate to work for the larger law firms. At the time that I graduated, my school was not an ABA-approved program, although I understand that it is now.

While working for RTC, I mailed out about fifty resumes and received two telephone calls. RTC was a very chaotic environment because of the attempt to mix people from FDIC and FSLIC and from outside both organizations. After a year of constant travel and that environment, I was ready for a different paralegal job. When I was offered a job in Washington, D.C., at the NBW field office, I accepted. I packed what I could in my car and moved most of my things into storage in Utah with my family. I had never been to D.C. and looked forward to the adventure of working there. I also had the opportunity to drive across the country and see some very interesting places.

KT: How is it being a paralegal in Washington D.C., since it's the seat of government for the country? Do you think it's a unique place to be?

LT: I really enjoy living and working in D.C. Most of the paralegals out here work for some government entity. However, most of the members of the professional paralegal association I belong to work for local law firms. The number of government paralegals who are members of NCAPA is very small when you consider the large number of paralegals the government employs.

Some of the paralegals in government are struggling to be seen as professionals. I do have an office—it's an interior office, but it's nice. There are other paralegals in the FDIC who are working in cubicles. As more attorneys are hired, paralegals working in cubicles will become more of the norm. To me, that's an indication of not being viewed as professional by the FDIC. We're not quite seen as secretaries, but we are viewed as support staff and given some clerical or secretarial tasks. Many paralegals here have worked their way up from a secretarial position. They will type and file, and not just their own typing and filing. I feel as if that damages the profession because the attorneys come to expect clerical work from their paralegals. I do my own typing because I think better while I'm typing into my computer. One secretary tried to teach me how to use a dictaphone, but it didn't work for me. I don't do other people's typing, and I think paralegals should have secretarial support if they need it.

KT: Why aren't the paralegals in government active in the professional paralegal associations?

LT: I'm not sure why they aren't, unless it's because most of the paralegals in government come up through the ranks and don't understand that being a paralegal is a profession and not just a job promotion. They don't seem to be aware that there's a professional paralegal association or what that association can do for them. I have tried to inform the FDIC paralegals about NCAPA. When I have extra copies of our monthly newsletter, I route them to the paralegals.

I also feel that paralegals working in government are generally underutilized. For example, at RTC they hired ten paralegals, and with the exception of a few of them they were hired at Grade-9. Yet we were assigned to review fee bills from outside counsel and write letters in regard to those bills concerning exceptions that would not be reimbursed by RTC. It was very, very boring work, and our paralegal skills weren't used, in my opinion. I would finish the required work very quickly and then request more. This worked out very well. I ended up with more challenging, interesting work and responsibilities that better utilized my skills. I developed my assertiveness skills.

As a paralegal, you can't just wait around and hope that an attorney will delegate challenging work. Two of the paralegals who were hired by

RTC when the office first opened ended the year with some very interesting responsibilities. I had an opportunity to work on dissolving subsidiaries and on some other very interesting projects. The other paralegal was assigned to monitor bankruptcy cases. We were determined to change the existing environment and ended up in much different positions from the other paralegals, who complained among themselves about the boring work.

There is a lot of work in D.C. for the paralegals, but it could be more substantive. Instead it's very administrative. Some paralegals are happy doing this type of work, and there are other sections within FDIC which utilize paralegals better. For example, in the appellate section and the trial litigation section, paralegals write briefs, and their attorneys have a caseload with more limited administrative responsibilities. Paralegals in these sections are assigned work similar to what paralegals working in a law firm do. But, of course, other than my freelance work, I've never worked in a law firm.

KZ: Do you like your job?

LT: Overall, I do. It would be great to have clerical staff assigned to me so that I could delegate appropriate work. I have learned American Sign Language because the legal technician assigned to me is deaf. He does a lot of filing, faxing, and copying. He would like more challenging work, but he is too busy with the clerical work for his attorneys. Each legal technician works for four to five attorneys, which doesn't leave much time for them to assist paralegals.

Everyone is trying to find more interesting work, but we're all too busy with our paperwork. It's a dilemma. The attorneys have blinders on; they don't think about how paralegals and legal technicians could be better utilized. We could do a lot to make their job easier, but we need to be assertive. The attorneys are not sitting around thinking, "How can I make Lori's life more interesting?"

I'm working on a development plan to enhance my skills to better assist my section. I'm also taking classes at George Washington University, in the government relations program, and I'm in the legislative certificate program. Because Congress is so close and involved, this should be a worthwhile area.

KZ: Do you have any hope that your immediate work situation will change?

LT: Everything takes time. I'm assigned to a team of about ten attorneys, but I can get work from anybody in the section. That leads to another frustration with the job—it feels as if everything I do is piecemeal. I never feel that I work on a project from start to finish. It's frustrating. And I worry that the paralegals here, who have never worked elsewhere and who aren't involved in a professional paralegal organization, will think that this is all that paralegals are capable of doing.

This is such an important time for paralegals. Licensure is becoming an important issue, and I worry about paralegals who don't understand the profession or even see their job as a profession. I also worry about paralegals who assume that, if the profession becomes licensed, they will automatically be grandfathered in. What if all paralegals must take an exam because they *aren't* necessarily grandfathered in? Many paralegals have no clue to what being a paralegal actually involves. What if they lose their jobs and have to search for new ones? I don't see how they're going to stand a chance of getting a traditional paralegal job. It concerns me.

KZ: Are you in favor of licensing or mandatory education requirements?
LT: I have mixed feelings, especially about testing, for a lot of reasons. For example, some paralegal schools require their paralegals to graduate with a specialty in only one area. How would those paralegals be tested or licensed? Before I moved from Utah, I was studying to take the National Association of Legal Assistants (NALA) test. It's a difficult test, with different sections, such as litigation and ethics. I thought that the ethics section was great. Paralegal education should focus on ethics and the unauthorized practice of law. The NALA test is a good starting point.

I am concerned about who can call themselves paralegals. When I left Legal Aid, they hired the word processor to replace me. He was a very smart person, and I'm sure he ended up doing a great job, but where are the standards for being a paralegal? Lawyers have standards they have to meet, and that's what I would like to see for paralegals. The title should mean something—not only that an employee who is a paralegal meets certain standards (for example, education and experience) but that the work given to paralegals meets certain standards. Paralegals would be assigned less non-paralegal (clerical) work. I'm a professional, and I want to be treated as a professional.

It's a tough call. I've been a paralegal for almost ten years, and I don't know what's going to happen with our profession in regard to licensing. Questions concerning regulation and licensing have come up in the past without much happening. Because of the involvement across the nation regarding these questions and the number of bar associations looking for guidance, the time has come to define the paralegal profession.

A lot of state bars are looking into licensing of paralegals. I'd like to see paralegals take control of that licensing rather than have someone else decide how we're going to be defined and licensed. I know the ABA held hearings all last year throughout the country on non-lawyers and related topics. It will be interesting to see their results.

The president of NCAPA asked me to give a talk about what paralegals are doing with pro bono work. Pro bono work is important. I just had a call on my answering machine from a law firm asking me to help set up a pro bono program for their paralegals.

It's interesting to see how far the profession has come.

KT: What do you see for yourself in the future?

LT: Since I was fourteen, I've always thought I wanted to be an attorney. That was my goal. I pursued the paralegal field as a way to explore the legal profession before making the three-year commitment. I'm thirty-four now, so I'm not sure if I will get to law school. There are a lot of law schools in and around D.C., and a lot of new attorneys are competing for limited jobs. But an attorney at RTC was in her fifties when she finished law school. I guess it's never too late. Going to law school might be something I will do in the future.

I don't see myself working as a lawyer in a big law firm. I would like to dedicate my skills to more cause-oriented, non-profit organizations, but from what I understand from friends just getting out of law school, there are huge financial obligations that make non-profit work impossible. I am also very interested in getting involved in the legislative process—the FDIC has an internal legislative division—or I might like to work for a member of Congress someday.

I would like to be an attorney for Green Peace. That would be an ideal position for me. I could combine my interest in law and my love of the ocean.

For the most part, I enjoy working with the section that I am with, and I feel I can get more involved with challenging projects. D.C. is a great place, but you definitely get what's called "Potomac Fever." People don't willingly do anything for you unless you can do something for them. It's very political. You have to be more careful of what you are doing, and you can get a little paranoid about moving in any aggressive direction for fear of stepping on someone's toes. People can be very sensitive if they view your actions as invading their area.

KT: Do you have any words of wisdom for someone who might be looking at government paralegal work?

LT: Be assertive. You need to look very carefully at what paralegals do where you apply for a job. You need to know if the work is administrative or if it's what I consider to be real paralegal work. It's great that there are opportunities, but it's frustrating to get involved with an agency and have the job turn out different than you perceived. The local paralegal associations can assist you. They might have a member who works where you are looking and can discuss the job responsibilities. You can also interview a government paralegal and see what he or she actually does.

There's interesting work out there in the government, but you need to be assertive to get the challenging work from the attorneys. The first attorney I worked for at RTC asked me to put together a binder, so I punched holes, indexed, and generally put a lot of effort into the project. Everyone around me was saying, "That's really dumb. Why are you doing that?" But I just did the best I could at this mundane task. My efforts helped the attorney to see that he could count on me to do a good job, no matter what the

HINT:

The Paralegal's Guide to U.S. Government Jobs, 6th edition, is a comprehensive resource for any paralegal trying to find a position in the federal government. The book gives an overall description of the federal hiring process, contains and discusses the employment form used by the federal government, and describes 70 law-related federal careers for which paralegals may be qualified. This $14 manual can be obtained by contacting Federal Reports, Inc. at (202) 393-3311.

job involved. That way we built up the mutual trust that allowed me to get more challenging work from him. He gave me some very interesting projects during my year with RTC. If I had refused his original binder project or done a sloppy job, he most likely would never have asked me to help him again.

You have to do a good job and not be timid. You have to ask a lot of questions. I worry about people who are timid in this profession. It's a good profession with a lot of opportunities.

CHAPTER 5

Non-Profit Organizations

Paralegals in non-profit organizations share many of the same motivations that other non-traditional paralegals have for pursuing a non-traditional career. The desire to be better utilized than a traditional paralegal is heard among this group.

The paralegals interviewed in this chapter were looking for more challenge and more self-determination on the job. "[I have] an appetite for challenge. In the private sector, it's almost like working for a factory. The more you produce, the more you get paid. . . . I'm not satisfied to do that." (David L. Hay)

These paralegals had an overall sense that they could accomplish more outside of the traditional paralegal world. ". . . I knew there had to be something else out there, and I wanted to see what it was and give it a try . . . Part of it was just a basic curiosity and thinking that, surely, all these skills can be utilized someplace else." (Donna Barr)

But paralegals in non-profit organizations are different from other non-traditional paralegals in some ways. For example, monetary gain is not one of their motives. ". . . if I were in the private sector, I could probably start at $10,000 a year more than I make now." (Hay) "It's not great money here, and it won't get any better than it is for me. I think I've pretty much hit the ceiling as far as salary goes, and that creates pressure on me." (Mary Kelly Finegan)

But, even if the job isn't financially rewarding, these paralegals seem more than satisfied with their job choices. "I took a cut in pay, and it was worth it!" (Barr) There are several reasons for this satisfaction. One is that they have enormous independence and thrive on the challenges. "The job I have now gives me a lot of freedom. I have a great deal of responsibility, and there aren't a lot of people looking over my shoulder." (Finegan)

Another reason for high job satisfaction is the altruism of non-profit organizations. ". . . finally I'm doing something that's worthwhile . . . Conservation work is more near and dear to my own heart . . ." (Whisman) ". . . it's so much more than a job. I think I'm addicted to helping people . . . I don't know what I would do if I had to go back to a profit corporation where the goals are so different." (Finegan)

The self-confidence and professional pride of this group of paralegals come through loud and clear. When asked what skills and qualities most help them in their positions, they answer: "The ambition and the drive—that's a needed quality . . . you have to put your foot forward, be ambitious, and have an internal drive." (Hay) ". . . my intellect. I've been told I'm very bright. . . . I don't have any real limits in understanding things and learning things." (Finegan)

Finally, the non-profit paralegals view themselves as flexible, always moving from problem to problem and from project to project. Because their jobs require them to jump around so much, they view themselves as jacks of all trades and masters of none. "Yes, I may be master of none, but I know how to deal with emergencies, and I have survival skills in many, many areas of law." (Finegan) "I don't have all the answers. I'm not a specialist; I'm a generalist. And something is always coming up that leads me to say, 'I never heard of that before. Let me look into that and I'll get back to you.' I like that a lot." (Hay)

INTERVIEW J

*I wanted something that would
move me along a career path,
either here or someplace else, so
that I could not only use my legal
skills, but also get more involved in
the business side of real estate. I
do a lot of contract negotiations
and things that I wouldn't normally
do in a law firm because they
would be done by the attorneys.*

Donna Barr

Company: Archdiocese of Denver
City: Denver, Colorado
Department: Secretariat of Administration, Finance, and Planning
Title: Real Estate Paralegal
Salary: $30,000
Benefits:
  Insurance: medical, dental, life, long-term disability, accidental
              death
  Financial: pension plan (optional tax-deferred annuity programs,
              term life insurance, group banking, credit union)
  Vacation: 12 days
  Sick time: 10 days
  Misc.:   personal time as needed

Previous Work Experience:
Two years as a property manager. Sixteen years as a paralegal for the
U.S. Small Business Administration and small, medium, and large law
firms.

JOB DESCRIPTION

General Summary

Assist with all aspects of real estate transactions by the Archdiocese, including sales and acquisitions of property, leasing of property owned by the Archdiocese, foreclosures, lease terminations, zoning issues, granting of easements, water rights matters, and tax issues.

Principle Duties

Closings

1. Gather facts; negotiate terms of contract.
2. Draft contract.
3. Coordinate with other parties, make changes to contract, and handle execution of contract.
4. Order and review title work; obtain special coverages and endorsements.
5. Review survey, work with surveyor to coordinate changes, corrections, etc.
6. Review loan payoff documents or new loan documents.
7. Review contract for critical dates and monitor calendar to ensure that deadlines are met.
8. Work with real estate agent, title company closer, loan officer/closer, and parish.
9. Prepare closing documents or review if prepared by another party to the transaction, including deed, bill of sale, settlement sheets, new loan documents, and any necessary agreements.
10. Coordinate escrow closing.
11. Follow up after closing: Obtain and review title policy, obtain recorded original document, prepare final communication to parish.

Lease Terminations

1. Obtain information on delinquencies, review tenants' leases, and prepare 3-day demands.
2. Draft summons, complaint, and affidavit of mailing.
3. File complaint, mail, and have served.
4. Review return of service and prepare file for return date.
5. After judgment is entered, have writ of restitution issued and delivered to sheriff.

Taxes

Handle applications for exemptions, filing of annual exempt property reports, and payment of property taxes.

Leases

Negotiate, draft, and obtain signatures on leases.

Zoning

Apply for rezoning, meet with neighborhood associations regarding zoning issues, handle determination of use.

Organizational

Create database of all properties, maintain and form files.

Foreclosures

Handle public trustee foreclosures.

KZ: Your job is with the Archdiocese of Denver. What is an archdiocese?
DB: The archdiocese is a geographic area. Colorado has three dioceses, and each has a supervising bishop. Some bishops become archbishops, and therefore their diocese becomes an archdiocese. The Archdiocese of Denver is the northern twenty-four counties in Colorado. If you drew a line through Denver east to west across the state, the geographic area of the diocese would be everything north of that line. It's fairly large and includes the metro-Denver area.

The arch-diocese is a non-profit corporation. In this case, it happens to be a corporation sole, which means that the archbishop is the only officer and the only director. In terms of organization, he signs everything.

KZ: Are you in a particular division of the archdiocese?
DB: Yes. The normal word in a corporation would be a department. In the archdiocese, the equivalent is a secretariat. Our department chairman's official title is Secretary of Finance, Administration, and Planning. Real estate falls within this department.

KZ: How big is the real estate section?
DB: There's an overlap with other people, such as the risk manager, but only three of us work strictly in real estate. John McGuire is the manager of real estate property. Although most of his background is in architecture and construction, he has a real estate broker's license, too. Then there's me and an administrative assistant.

KZ: But there are no attorneys on staff here?
DB: No. I report to John as my immediate supervisor, and both of us are responsible to the secretary of finance, administration, and planning. We don't have in-house counsel. I discussed that with John when I first came here and with our outside counsel, because I was concerned about mal-

Supervision of Paralegals by Attorneys

One basic rule of the legal field is that paralegals must be supervised by the attorneys for whom they work. Generally, attorneys can delegate to a paralegal any task usually performed by the attorney, so long as the attorney remains responsible for the work product. However, there are exceptions to this. As stated in Guideline 3 of the *American Bar Association Model Guidelines for Legal Assistant Services*;

A lawyer may not delegate

- Responsibility for establishing an attorney-client relationship.
- Responsibility for establishing the fee for legal services.
- Responsibility for a legal opinion rendered to a client.

A paralegal who performs any of the above functions can be accused of unauthorized practice of law, as can the attorney who allows the paralegal to perform them.

It is easy to see how these three exceptions apply to the traditional paralegal in a law firm. It is a little more difficult to apply them to a non-traditional paralegal, especially one who works for a company which employs no attorney. We can look at the exceptions one by one:

- *Responsibility for establishing an attorney-client relationship.* This exception is probably not a problem for the non-traditional paralegal because he or she is usually employed by the client and so would not be establishing an attorney-client relationship.
- *Responsibility for establishing the fee for legal services.* This exception also would not be problem for the non-traditional paralegal because he or she is employed by the client and would not be charging fees for legal services.
- *Responsibility for a legal opinion rendered to a client.* This exception is the problem for non-traditional paralegals. They are hired for their legal skills and ability to perform legal work, but this means that they are giving legal opinions and making legal judgments as they perform their work.

Whether this third exception is a serious problem is unclear. After all, many companies employ people who perform law-related work (title examiners in title companies, for example), but nobody worries about unauthorized practice of law. If that same person is titled "paralegal," or if that same person has a paralegal background, does he or she automatically face the danger of unauthorized practice of law? To answer yes to that question seems a little extreme. Perhaps the more practical answer is that the non-traditional paralegal is not giving legal opinions to clients from the public but only to his or her employer/client, and is therefore *not* performing the unauthorized practice of law.

Note: Unauthorized practice of law by non-traditional paralegals has not been fully resolved by case law or state statute. Therefore readers are strongly encouraged to discuss these issues with office supervisors. When in doubt, seek guidance.

practice issues. We do have general malpractice insurance that covers all the professional positions—the accountants, other managers, and so forth—so I'm covered under that professional liability policy. I talked with our outside counsel, and for purposes of supervision they agreed that they would be my supervising attorneys if there were ever any question. I'm not supervised on a daily basis by an attorney. This means that I choose when I contact our attorneys—if I have something I want them to look at or if I need advice. It is up to me whether or not I involve an attorney or paralegal from our outside counsel.

KZ: Do you think that's an unusual situation?

DB: There must be many other paralegals out there in the same position. I feel a little awkward about it when I teach my paralegal real estate class because I stress being under the supervision of an attorney, and here I am, not under that supervision. But it is a paralegal position, and I do work directly with attorneys; it's just that I have this little extra space.

When I first came here, we discussed what my title was going to be— possibly "Assistant Real Estate Manager" or "Real Estate Specialist." The secretary of the department preferred that my title be "Real Estate Paralegal" because he felt that would carry more clout and would impress people more.

KZ: That's a great statement for the paralegal profession.

DB: Yes. He said, "I want people to know that you have expertise and that you're a specialist in the legal field." So my title is "Real Estate Paralegal" because of its prestige.

KZ: Is there anything else you'd like to add about the structure of your department?

DB: I'm the first and only paralegal they've ever had here. The position was created when I came.

KT: Why was it created?

DB: Well, the true story is that our outside counsel, my boss, and the department secretary were discussing how much there was to do. Our outside counsel said, "What you guys need is a paralegal." When they asked if he knew anybody, he said, "Well, as a matter of fact I do." And here I am. The position wasn't created with me in mind, but it was one of those "who you know and being in the right place at the right time" kind of things.

KT: So that's how you got into this position.

DB: Yes, but I had been specifically looking for a non-law-firm job and had been networking, including contacting the attorney who recommended me to the archdiocese. I had started looking for jobs about four months before I interviewed here. I didn't send one resume to a law firm. I thought, "Working in a law firm is something I know I can do, I can probably always find a job there, but I really want to try something else." I interviewed at places like the federal public defenders office, Cellular One, and with a couple of real estate developers. I was just trying to move in some direction other than a traditional law firm.

KT: Why?

DB: Partly a basic curiosity and thinking that, surely, all these skills can be utilized someplace else. And I think that being in real estate is fortunate because it easily transfers to more business environments than, say, product liability. There are simply some areas of law that are not quite as versatile.

KT: That's probably true. For example, it's difficult to see how litigation skills would translate directly into the business world.

DB: Yes. As I said, part of it was just a curiosity about what else was out there. But another part of it was the frustration of having been in law firms for fifteen years. I wanted to work for people who realize that you have a life outside of work and that there are more important things than billable hours and the whole package that comes with that. I was really frustrated with the stress, even though I'm one of those people who do better under stress. It's probably because I've worked in law firms for all these years.

KT: But there's such a thing as too much stress?

DB: Yes, there is. For example, one attorney I used to work for was a single woman, about 30, never married, no children, was on the partnership track, and just couldn't understand if you had to take off work for a sick kid or if you had to leave by 5:00 to pick up your kids from day care. She had no concept what that was all about, as opposed to a place like this which is very family oriented. Family is important, and if you have to take some time off for a sick child, it's understood that that's a part of daily life.

I left the traditional paralegal world because I knew there had to be something else out there, and I wanted to see what it was and give it a try in a less stressful environment. But I was also thinking about my future and planning for that.

KT: Meaning that you were looking for a career path?
DB: I wanted something that would move me along a career path, either here or someplace else, so that I could not only use my legal skills, but also get more involved in the business side of real estate. I do a lot of contract negotiations and things that I wouldn't normally do in a law firm because they would be done by the attorneys.

KT: So do you feel that it's less hierarchical here than in a law firm?
DB: Probably, but we're such a small group of people that it's hard to say. Between John and me, there's less hierarchy than there would be between an attorney and a legal assistant, but, after all, it's only the two of us.

KT: Do you have a vision of where you might go from here?
DB: Well, there are a couple of possibilities. Here at the archdiocese, the direction I could go in is fairly limited. Specifically, John may retire in the next few years, and they may divide his job into the real estate side and the construction and maintenance side. One thing I aspire to is taking over responsibility for the real estate side. Beyond that, there would be no place for me to go here. Of course, maybe I could do that for twenty years and be happy with it.

KT: How long have you been here?
DB: Nine months. But if I try to project down the road, assuming that I don't want to stay here forever, I think that the experience that I'm getting here is going to be transferable to another corporate environment, not just to a paralegal position in a law firm.

KT: Can you give me an example?
DB: Right now, I'm negotiating a lease with a woman in California who represents a bank-holding company. We rent a building to a savings and loan which is part of that bank-holding company out in Lakewood. Her title is "Real Estate Negotiator." I know a man who used to do the same type of thing for Safeway. There are all kinds of corporations out there that employ people who have real estate knowledge and skills. By learning the business side and getting more involved with the financial aspects, the contracts, the environmental inspections—that part of it I didn't get deeply involved in when I was working for a law firm—I think that, if I want to move on, I will have a lot more possibilities in the private sector.

KT: Maybe this is a good time to ask you what you do on your job.
DB: Basically, all the things that I would do in a law firm—occasionally foreclosures and evictions, drafting contracts, leases, deeds, and agree-

ments. As far as the documents go, the level of complexity is probably not as high as when I was working for a law firm, but on a daily basis, there is a lot more variety. Leases, contracts, and deeds are the main documents that I prepare. I coordinate all the real estate closings. If we're buying a piece of property, I get the title work in, review it, and work with the title company if we want to make any changes and if they have any special requirements that we have to meet. I make sure that the closing documents are reviewed, signed, and delivered to the title company in time for closing, and then I get the policy and deed. In terms of the process from beginning to end, I'm the one everything goes through for the closing.

Exempt and non-exempt property taxes are a big part of my work, and that's one of the reasons the archdiocese hired me. That work was being done by a paralegal at our outside counsel, and we were paying many, many thousands of dollars for it. The logic was "If we had somebody in-house, we could get a large part of this person's salary back from not having to pay the law firm to do this; we could also get better control of it if it were in-house, and we'd have our own paralegal for the other ten months of the year when we're not dealing with the tax-exempt and non-exempt property."

KZ: Has having you on-board made any difference financially for the archdiocese?
DB: Yes, our legal fees, I've been told, have gone down since I started here, so I'm paying for my existence, and that makes me feel good.

KZ: What else do you do?
DB: Being a non-profit and religious organization, we've got between 350 and 400 tax-exempt property reports that have to be filed with the state every year by April 15, and we have a number of properties that are taxable because they're vacant land or not being used for religious purposes, so I have tax statements coming in for taxes that have to be paid. On a regular basis, I file all the applications for tax exemptions. For example, if the parish buys a piece of property that it's going to use for a playground or a school, I file the application for tax exemption. I've had to learn that part of the statutes. I recently testified before a state senate committee on a bill that would change some parts of the exempt property filings if it passes.

What else do I do? The variety is actually very interesting. A week ago, I went to a ditch company meeting on a Saturday morning because they were making amendments to their bylaws and we own stock in the company. The archdiocese owns many water rights and oil and gas leases. One evening last week, I went to a homeowner's association meeting to give them a description of what we were intending to do with a piece of property in their neighborhood, so that before we go into the county to apply for permits, we'll have the homeowner's association on our side.

Often, the archdiocese has to have property rezoned, and so I attend zoning hearings. We have farm property—I recently called a grain broker to sell wheat. We've got a cemetery up near Central City where somebody has blocked off one of our access roads, so we've got a potential prescriptive easement litigation coming up there which will be very interesting. We have a gravel pit in Jefferson County; when they mine the gravel, they sift through the finer particles because there's a lot of gold out there. One day I had to go downtown and pick up a little jar that had about $10,000 worth of gold flakes and gold dust in it. That's probably one of the oddest things I've done.

KZ: Is it different being the client rather than the law firm?
DB: It's a very different perspective. I don't bill time. There are a few items for which I do keep track of time spent, but that's for administrative and time management purposes. For the most part, I don't keep track of my time. I hated billing time for fifteen years and I love not having to do it now. But having billed my time for all those years, it's very different now, when I review a bill from the law firm, I think, "Nine hundred dollars! We only talked about this twice!" Of course, every time you make a phone call to the firm, the meter starts ticking. Because of that, I do things that won't run up the legal fees.

KZ: Give me an example.
DB: If I have a meeting with one of the firm's paralegals or attorneys, or with our water law attorney in Boulder, I go there to meet with them, knowing that that will keep travel time off of our bill. I've given instructions to use the regular mail instead of messengering things unless I tell them otherwise. I don't want that eight bucks in messenger fees on my bill. It's a different way of looking at it.

Of course, I'm in a unique position; Before I came here, I was a paralegal with the real estate attorney at the firm, so we're friends, and we work together well. But now I'm his client, and sometimes I can tell him what to do or can decide not to take his advice!

KZ: What do you dislike about your position, or about being a non-traditional paralegal, if anything?
DB: Sometimes I get frustrated, partly out of expectation and habit, with the lackadaisical approach here. If I don't put a letter in the out box by four, it doesn't go out that day. It just sits there in the basket until the next day. In a law firm, that would be unheard of. Or if I take something to the word processing unit at four-thirty and say that it needs to be done by the end of the day, she'll look at me as if I'm crazy, as if to say, "Why would you need it by the end of the day? Tomorrow is fine." For the most part, the "If we don't get it done today, we'll do it tomorrow" attitude is refreshing be-

cause you don't have that constant pressure of meeting unrealistic deadlines, but sometimes it frustrates me. Sometimes I put a stamp on a letter and walk it to the post office at the end of the day because I want it to get out, and then I put the twenty-nine cents on my expense account to get reimbursed.

KZ: Any other thoughts you'd like to share?
DB: I took a cut in pay to come here and it was worth it!

INTERVIEW K

To be involved in these deals you need to understand what's happening and pick up concepts and issues quickly. I have to manage about fifty to seventy-five files, so I have to be able to jump from one project to another. Since we provide a service to our field offices, all the work that we do here is based on what they need.

Janis Whisman

Company:	The Nature Conservancy, western regional office
City:	Boulder, Colorado
Department:	Legal Department
Title:	Protection Paralegal
Salary Range:	Not available
Benefits:	
Insurance:	medical, dental, life, disability, accidental death
Financial:	
Vacation:	10 days
Sick time:	8.5 days
Misc.:	overtime, compensatory time

Previous Work Experience:
Three and a half years with a small plaintiff's medical malpractice and product liability law firm. One and a half years with a sole practitioner in bankruptcy and personal injury. One year in the real estate department of a large law firm, working as a paralegal, including work as a legal secretary coordinator.

JOB DESCRIPTION

Summary of Position

Under the supervision of the regional attorneys, provide paralegal assistance to the regional attorneys and field-office staff in the western region on all real estate acquisition, transfer out, and exchange transactions. Coordinate these projects by obtaining project information, preparing documentation, handling closings, and resolving stewardship issues. The position requires extensive understanding of real estate law and significant use of independent judgment. It involves communication with government agency representatives, title insurance companies, attorneys, Conservancy staff, landowners, and brokers. The protection paralegal supervises no staff.

Duties

Under the supervision of the regional attorneys:

1. Draft, review, and revise legal documents related to land transactions for the western region, including option and purchase agreements, escrow instruction letters, deeds, conservation easements, deeds of trust, mortgages, promissory notes, and legal correspondence.
2. Oversee the acquisition, transfer out, and exchange of property by obtaining and reviewing appraisals, title work, environmental hazard assessments, project packages, and other transaction documentation.
3. Coordinate and independently handle the details of real estate transactions by working with government agency representatives, title insurance companies, attorneys, Conservancy staff, landowners, and brokers. Handle post-closing tasks such as obtaining, reviewing, and confirming the accuracy of closing documentation.
4. Serve as a resource for Conservancy staff on questions regarding real estate projects, legal procedures, and Conservancy policy.
5. Maintain effective organizational and tickler systems for protection projects.
6. Perform other paralegal duties as assigned.
7. Periodically assist other western region legal staff with duties as necessary.

Minimum Requirements

1. Bachelor's degree in paralegal studies or certificate of completion from an ABA-approved paralegal training program.
2. Four years of paralegal experience and a demonstrated knowledge of complex real estate transactions.
3. Excellent written and verbal communication skills, including an appropriate legal writing style.

4. Ability to take initiative, work independently, and maintain efficiency under stressful conditions.
5. Ability to work effectively with Conservancy staff and a wide variety of other professionals.
6. Demonstrated organizational skills, attention to detail, and ability to manage multiple projects.
7. Commitment to conservation and the goals of The Nature Conservancy.
8. Proficient computer skills.

KZ: How did you end up at The Nature Conservancy? Was it a deliberate choice to leave law firms?
JW: No. I got laid off from my previous job, was looking for a new job, and happened to notice an advertisement in the newspaper. I've always been interested in the environment and thought working in real estate at The Nature Conservancy would be a neat job. I applied for it and got hired. The attorney I used to work for was very involved in the Exxon-Valdez litigation, so that's what got me interested in doing more environmentally oriented law. I did have a little bit of real estate background, but it didn't apply much to what I'm doing now.

KZ: What are you doing?
JW: I coordinate real estate closings for six of the eleven states in The Nature Conservancy's western region. In a nutshell, the Conservancy's mission is to preserve endangered species by protecting their habitat. After the science division identifies where the endangered species reside, the protection division goes to work with the community to protect their habitat.

Local communities like the Conservancy's non-confrontational and cooperative approach. Protection of a species' habitat can be done in a variety of ways, but usually, the Conservancy negotiates with landowners to buy property where these endangered species live, and then either manages the property itself or transfers ownership to a government agency or to another conservation organization. Another method is to place a conservation easement over the property, which restricts certain activities that would further endanger the habitat.

Under an attorney's supervision, I draft documents; review appraisals, hazards reports, and title information; and do whatever else is necessary to accomplish a closing.

KZ: What states are in the western region?
JW: Arizona, Colorado, Idaho, Montana, New Mexico, Washington, Alaska, Oregon, Utah, Nevada, and Wyoming.

KZ: Does your job entail travel?
JW: The only traveling I've done so far has been to Washington, D.C., where our home office is, for skills training. They have different seminars

during one week of the year, and I've gone back there to participate in those. We are going to try to do some travel to individual field offices during the next fiscal year. Those trips will probably be in relation to a particular project. I do talk with people in other states about their projects, so I get the chance to widen my horizon that way, at least.

KT: If you're not traveling, what is a typical day like for you? Or is there a typical day?
JW: It usually involves a lot of time on the phone speaking with attorneys, title companies, government agency representatives, and our field office representatives. The field representatives are in direct contact with the property owners, and they put all the deals together and then talk with us about putting them in writing. I talk with them quite a bit. I also draft a myriad of real estate documents, and I do my own typing because I don't have a secretary.

KT: To summarize, you are in charge of making sure that everything goes smoothly so that you can close.
JW: Right.

KT: I would have thought that your real estate background from law firms would have been helpful.
JW: It wasn't, because the position I was in at the firm was much more administrative than paralegal. The only thing I was doing that's similar to what I'm doing now was keeping a list of all the projects that we were working on and the status of those projects. But most of my time there was spent seeing what came in the mail during the day and dividing that up among the secretaries. I did a lot of proofreading of the product they produced. I never got involved in the details of how the transactions were going to be structured. I do a lot of that here. I quit that job because I didn't think that my paralegal skills were being utilized very well.

KT: Do you feel they're being utilized now?
JW: I think so, although there is always room for improvement.

KT: How is your department organized? Are the attorneys on-site?
JW: Yes. We have two attorneys and two paralegals, and we have a couple of people who handle the database maintenance for the western region. The two attorneys are right here and they're accessible every day and at almost any time during the day.

KT: So you are directly supervised.
JW: Right.

KT: What primary skills are you utilizing?
JW: I would say the ability to organize and to work under pressure are the

primary skills I use. To be involved in these deals you need to understand what's happening and pick up concepts and issues quickly. I have to manage about fifty to seventy-five files, so I have to be able to jump from one project to another. Since we provide a service to our field offices, all the work that we do here is based on what they need. Basically, if they call us up and say, "This is what I'm doing, and I need an option contract drafted right away," you've got to be able to juggle that along with all the other things that are happening.

KT: Do you have an undergraduate degree that you feel you're using now?
JW: Yes. I do. My B.A. degree is in communications, from the University of Colorado. I chose that because I wanted something that didn't have so many requirements that I wouldn't be able to take some fun classes too, and something that was general enough to help me in any area I decided to work in.

KT: And you've found that it has helped?
JW: I think so.

KT: An underlying theme for non-traditional paralegals seems to be that they are able to do a lot more in their current jobs than they were able to do in law firms.
JW: I would agree, to a certain extent. The first job that I had was mainly administrative, and I was frustrated with that. I had more responsibility in my last two positions, but my tasks were still tied to whatever the attorney was doing right then. Here, I feel a lot more involved in the planning, and as a result, I'm able to do more substantive work.

The other thing that's been a big help to me is that, although the deadlines are there and they're important, there's not as much tension for me as there was in litigation. And I really appreciate knowing that I can work a set number of hours a day and usually count on meeting my personal commitments, unless something really unusual happens.

KT: How is this position better or worse than the traditional paralegal job?
JW: I think it's better because it's more predictable, as I've just described. It's better, too, because the people I work with here are more approachable and team oriented. And I feel that I'm finally doing something worthwhile. I felt that way before when I worked on personal injury cases, especially on the larger, more complex medical malpractice cases, but here it seems as if I have a little bit more influence globally. Conservation work is more near and dear to my own heart, too, and I like the work a great deal.

KT: It sounds like you get a lot of satisfaction out of it. Do you feel that there is a career path here?
JW: There isn't a career path for paralegals here, unless I decide to try

something other than paralegal work. Even then, the path is not well defined. I suppose that could be taken positively because it means there are all sorts of possibilities for me; instead, it's a drawback because not many people have a good understanding of the skills a paralegal has. In order to move from this job into another, I'd first have to educate those around me about what I can do. If I could accomplish that, I think similarities between jobs and required skills would surface and more avenues would be open to me.

KT: I'm surprised by that answer. I would have thought your career opportunities would be better at the Conservancy than in a law firm.
JW: I'm surprised, too, that there isn't an overall career advancement plan, but maybe it's due to rapid growth. I do know the Conservancy is working to standardize job titles and descriptions, so maybe career paths will develop out of that.

KT: To change the subject, I'm assuming that you don't bill hours or keep your time.
JW: No, we don't, although that may change. There are a couple of projects that the other paralegal is keeping track of her time on. That's on a testing basis right now, but if anyone were to become interested in how much time we're spending on various field offices' projects, I'm sure that's what they would do.

KT: That about covers it from my side. Any comments or words of wisdom?
JW: I think I mentioned that this is more exciting for me because it's something that I've always cared about. That's how everybody else in the office feels, too, so it's an encouraging place to work. We all get bogged down by things like not having a career path, but because, in a sense, we're all working on the same thing, there's a camaraderie that I never felt at the law firms where I've worked.

KT: You have a mutual purpose.
JW: Right. We're all doing a different part of the job, but the goal is the same for everybody. I like that.

INTERVIEW L

My title is program coordinator. My salary is in the mid-twenties, and the benefits are very good because the Philadelphia Bar Association sponsors the program. They do all the bookkeeping and a couple of other nice things for us. They provide all our benefits, so we have the same medical and dental benefits the bar association offers. We're fully covered in that area, which is nice.

Mary Kelly Finegan

Company: Philadelphia Volunteers for the Indigent (Philadelphia VIP)
City: Philadelphia, Pennsylvania
Department: Not applicable
Title: Program Coordinator
Salary Range: mid-$20s
Benefits:
   Insurance: medical, dental, life, disability
   Financial:
   Vacation: 20 days
   Sick time: 10 days
   Misc.:   5 days personal time

Previous Work Experience:
Technical publications coordinator with Electronic Data Systems (EDS) for approximately six months. Litigation paralegal for a large law firm (300+ attorneys) for one and a half years.

JOB DESCRIPTION

Duties

- Refer cases to attorneys by calling volunteers directly, or work with "contact" person within an organization on referrals.
- Input appropriate data to the computer regarding referral of cases.
- Monitor cases already referred by sending periodic status report forms and client questionnaires to be completed and returned.
- Check and monitor cases for all relevant deadlines.
- Communicate with clients to gather additional information, when necessary.
- Send the referral package to the volunteer attorney within the prescribed time frames.
- Coordinate litigation services for volunteer attorneys.
- Answer questions and inquiries from volunteer attorneys.
- Contact opposing counsel and/or the judge to obtain an extension or a continuance, when appropriate.
- Review intake forms for information and screen cases for eligibility.
- From time to time, perform general clerical tasks, such as photocopying and answering the phone.
- Perform all other duties, as assigned.

In addition to the above, the program coordinator may coordinate VIP training sessions by obtaining speakers, scheduling sessions, and preparing program notices and publicity, with appropriate follow-up to recruit volunteers.

General Job Qualifications and Requirements

- A high school graduate with considerable relevant job experience, or an individual with paralegal training or college experience. The individual must possess knowledge of the legal system and the general nature of litigation.
- Immediate supervisor: assistant director or staff attorney
  Reports to the executive director.

KT: You work for the Philadelphia Volunteers for the Indigent Program, or Philadelphia VIP.
MKF: Right.

KT: And the department you're in is the legal department?
MKF: No. We're a poverty law firm. It's a referral program. We have three attorneys and three paralegals who serve as a clearinghouse for people living below the poverty level who can't afford attorneys on their own. We get

cases from different agencies throughout Philadelphia. The agencies refer people who are financially eligible and need legal assistance. We're responsible for finding volunteer attorneys to represent them.

We review the files, screening for merit and eligibility, and then we try to find a suitable volunteer. We send the file out to the volunteer, and then we follow up with all kinds of support—court reporters, paralegals, title searches, and other things that might be needed during the course of a case. The program is a 501(c)(3) organization, so it's non-profit.

KT: The law firm itself is called Philadelphia Volunteers for the Indigent Program?
MKF: The non-profit organization is called that. As I said, it's a poverty law firm, although calling it that is a little misleading because we don't handle cases in-house. We can, but we don't very often. We try to get volunteers rather than handle the cases ourselves because it's more efficient.

KT: What is your title?
MKF: My title is program coordinator. My salary is in the mid-twenties, and the benefits are very good because the Philadelphia Bar Association sponsors the program. They do all the bookkeeping and a couple of other nice things for us. They provide all our benefits, so we have the same medical and dental benefits the bar association offers. We're fully covered in that area, which is nice.

KT: That is nice.
MKF: Especially for a pro bono program. That's one down side of working for a pro bono. I'm very, very lucky that I'm in a metropolitan area where a metropolitan bar association sponsors us. I'd say that most pro bono programs wouldn't have the benefit of that organizational structure.

KT: You get quite a few vacation days, too.
MKF: Right. Four weeks of vacation.

KT: Do you feel you need it?
MKF: Yes, desperately. I get to the end of the year sometimes and I somehow run out of time. It's a very difficult job in a lot of ways. It takes a lot out of you emotionally; it takes a lot out of you mentally; it takes a lot out of you physically. It really depletes you. I've found in the four years I've been working here that it's cyclic. You go through burnout stages, and then you get yourself going again, get excited about the job, and good things happen. Then you burn out again pretty quickly. So there are plenty of opportunities for using those four weeks of vacation. It sounds like a lot, but it really isn't.

KT: What about your previous work experience?
MKF: I worked as a litigation paralegal for one of the biggest law firms

here in Philadelphia—three hundred plus attorneys. I worked there for about a year and a half, and that's how I got the job I have now. I was volunteering for the program.

I also worked for Electronic Data Systems, EDS, in Washington, D.C. That's the company that Ross Perot founded twenty-five or thirty years ago. That job didn't last very long. There was a cookie-cutter, blue-suit, pinstripe, work ethic. It was great for some people, but it was a different work style than mine. The job I have now gives me a lot of freedom. I have a great deal of responsibility, and I there aren't a lot of people looking over my shoulder. Those are things that I appreciate about the situation I have now, as compared to the EDS environment.

KT: The law firm environment was probably more structured, too.
MKF: It was very structured. I was good at it because I like detail, which is something I've had to let go of since I've been here at VIP. This position is very stressful. I'm being pulled in hundreds, literally hundreds, of directions each day, so my attention to detail is an aspect I've had to let slide. But I did like that part of the law firm environment. And I liked learning. When I started at the law firm, law was new to me, so I was learning all about the legal process, and that was fascinating. I liked working with the large document cases—organizing things, tying up all the loose ends. All the things that I don't have now!

KT: Is that why you find your job so stressful?
MKF: Definitely. It's not easy to follow through on things, and that's hard to tolerate if you're detail oriented. We're very overworked; we have incredibly big caseloads, and we don't have a lot of office support, so we do a lot of things for ourselves. It's hard to manage all that.

KT: What is your average caseload?
MKF: It's supposed to be seventy, eighty, ninety cases—somewhere in there.

KT: That's a lot!
MKF: It's actually much higher than that. It usually averages over a hundred cases. I don't always count them because sometimes, when you know it's high, it's better not to know. But I do remember that, during my first year here, we had to close our intake because our caseloads were so high. At that time, I had 174 cases. In that kind of environment, it's just impossible to function because you're dealing mostly with cases that have deadlines. You have to get an answer filed by a certain date; there's a hearing or an appeal on a certain date. When cases keep coming in the door, it's like working for a shooting gallery. When things start to stack up, I picture the *I Love Lucy* episode where she's working on the assembly line. Remember that?

KT: Oh yes! The chocolates.

MKF: Exactly. That's what this job is like sometimes. It requires a lot of stamina. When things get backed up, it really does get rough.

KT: How do find your volunteer attorneys? Do you have a list of attorneys who have expressed an interest in volunteering?

MKF: We recruit through the bar association. We have a database in our office of all our volunteer attorneys. We have over a thousand right now. What we do with the law firms—for example, the one I used to work for—is establish a contact person at each firm. One individual, usually a partner, acts as a conduit for the cases going to that firm. I just call the contact person and say, "I really need someone for this litigation case. There's an answer due next Friday, it's an auto accident, etc." The contact attorney takes the facts down and does the legwork for me. We have that system with about fifty law firms of all different sizes throughout town. That works well for us.

KT: Can you describe a normal day for you?

MKF: Well, one of the things that I was glad I left behind when I left the law firm was time sheets. They were relatively easy because I only had what I thought was a big caseload—fifteen or so. But when I came here and realized how many different things I'd be called on to do in a day's time, and how many different skills were required, I was even more glad I didn't have to do time sheets because it would be hard to break down a day, especially when you're doing mostly telephone work. I can't tell you how many times I'll be on the phone and, because I don't have a secretary, I'll have to put the first person on hold, go to the second person, write their phone number down, go back to the first person, finish with that person, start to call the second person, the phone will ring again . . .

I don't know what I do with my time. Sometimes I get to the end of the day and I don't know if I've done anything. On the other hand, there are days when I have wonderful things that I bring home in my heart that I know I've done for people. Today, I got a lawyer for a man who was on the verge of becoming homeless. I'll go home tonight knowing that his situation is taken care of.

KT: Tell me about him.

MKF: He needs to get disability payments from Social Security, but he was denied at an early level. He's elderly and has a brain tumor, and he's about to be evicted from his home. He can't get new housing without the disability payment. I think he was denied unjustly, and I can't imagine why, knowing his disabilities. I've been working since July to try to find a lawyer for him.

KT: Why is it so hard to find someone? Is it because of the expertise needed?

MKF: It's a combination of things. In this case, he didn't have a hearing

Pro Bono / Volunteer Work

Pro bono work is the representation of clients, especially indigent clients, free of charge. Traditionally, attorneys have done pro bono, but many paralegals also perform this volunteer work. Some law firms encourage pro bono work, and firms even give paralegals time out of their work week to perform it. Professional paralegal associations also encourage, and are active in, pro bono work. Some have pro bono sections which organize opportunities for their members to provide pro bono services to the public. In fact, pro bono work was one of the things NFPA had in mind when writing its Affirmation of Professional Responsibility. The entire affirmation was written to "delineate the principles of purpose and conduct toward which paralegals should aspire." Guideline 5 promotes pro bono work:

... A paralegal shall serve the public interests by contributing to the availability and delivery of quality legal services.

Discussion: It is the responsibility of each paralegal to promote the development and implementation of programs that address the legal needs of the public. A paralegal shall strive to maintain a sensitivity to public needs and educate the public as to the services that paralegals may render.

HINT:

Doing pro bono work can be a way for a paralegal not only to gain new skills but also to network with attorneys and other paralegals. Many paralegals have found their first job, or a new job, through the connections they've made doing pro bono. If you have a chance to do pro bono and can spare the time, take the opportunity. You never know where it might lead, and it certainly will give you satisfaction!

date, and there were other cases that did have dates, so I had to refer those cases first. I've had his file for a long time, and I've been trying, but he was a second-level priority until very recently. Now, all of sudden, with a hearing date, he has become much more of a priority. This is how things work. Cases are on the back burner, and then they become emergencies.

KT: It's got to drive you crazy.
MKF: Oh, it does!

KT: How do you get a client like this man? Do they walk in off the street?
MKF: We don't do intake. That's one thing we absolutely don't have time for, and we don't have the resources or staff. The reason that my program was put together was to help community legal services. Fifteen or twenty years ago, the federal government created the Legal Services Corporation, which provides low-cost, or no-cost, legal assistance to people living below the poverty level. The federal government channels funds through this corporation, which are then dispersed into a number of regional offices. There's one in Philadelphia called Community Legal Services.

At the end of the Carter administration and the beginning of the Reagan administration, they had a large staff, over a hundred attorneys, because they had very good funding. But over the last twelve years, the funding has been cut, sometimes in pretty big chunks, and the staff has gone down to about fifty or sixty. It has created a lot of pressure, not just for the staff but also for the clients, because at the same time that the number of people living below the poverty level jumped, the number of attorneys available to help them decreased. My program was put in place to assist those attorneys.

The agencies do all the intake. They screen the cases, and certain kinds they take themselves. Other kinds they just don't have the expertise to handle, such as tax or real estate, and those are sent to us. There are other poverty law firms that help different groups of people, such as Women Against Abuse or the Support Center for Child Advocates, which works with abused and neglected children. There's another that works with elderly people and another that works with disabled people. There's a whole network in Philadelphia, and all these groups know that they can send their cases to VIP if they don't have an attorney available to help.

These clients, in effect, have already exhausted all of their resources, except for VIP. We're the last stop on the line. If we can't help them, there really isn't anywhere else we can send them.

KT: How often do you come across someone that you just cannot help?
MKF: It happens a couple of times a month for different reasons. We turn people down sometimes because they're over our income guidelines. We turn people down sometimes because of deadlines that are just too close. If a deadline is within ten working days, we can't even try. If you take in a case like that, you're extending to the client a hope that you can find someone in that short a time, and that's very dangerous. So in order to protect ourselves, and to protect the client, we don't even take those cases on.

From time to time, we have a case we just won't be able to find someone for. I have two cases on my desk right now—litigation cases—one of which I've had since June. Opposing counsel has been very cooperative, obviously, in waiting for this, but I just don't think I can wait any more. I think I'm just going to have to bite the bullet and turn the person down.

Those are some of the reasons we can't help a particular person. Sometimes clients will get a loan or borrow money from a family member to get their own lawyer; they'll let us know, and we'll close the file.

KZ: Do you usually find out what happens to the cases you refer?

MKF: Yes. We send status reports to our volunteers at two months and six months, and we ask them to let us know when they conclude the case, how it was resolved, and the number of hours they put in. We keep track of how many hours were contributed to the program for funding purposes. Most of our funding comes from foundations or charitable organizations. We factor out by the average billable rate in Philadelphia to determine how many hours, in dollars, are being donated.

Too, the attorneys know that we provide many support services, so they contact us when they have a question about their case. Sometimes their cases touch on poverty law areas that they're not familiar with. For example, about three weeks ago, we got a telephone call from one of the legal services offices about a woman in the hospital who was dying within a week. She had a young son, she was a widow, and she needed a will with a guardianship clause for taking care of her son. There wasn't anyone at legal services who had the kind of probate experience that was necessary, so we got someone from one of the top five law firms at the last minute, who was willing to work over the weekend to get the will executed.

Today I got a telephone call. The woman has passed away, and all sorts of complications have come up with her house. The guardian was going to hold her house in trust for her son, but the house has a welfare lien on it. Now, with all these complications, we have to get an expert on welfare law to help us out.

KZ: Is part of your function to advise the volunteer attorneys?

MKF: I don't give legal advice, since I'm not a lawyer. I try to get somebody who is an expert in the area to assist the volunteer attorney. One good thing about working in this program is that I deal with so many areas of law, and I come across people who are experts in their field. I have a lot of resources to fall back on. It's great experience for the volunteers here because they're in close contact with all these experts.

KZ: Good experience for you, too, and good connections that you're making which might help you if you ever decide to move on to something else.

MKF: I wonder about that sometimes. It's an emotional issue. A job like this involves so much of who you are because your emotions are tied into it. When I worked at the law firm, or at EDS—yes, I went home with my paycheck every other week; it was a job. But now it's so much more than a job. I think I'm addicted to helping people.

I don't know what I would do if I had to go back to a profit corporation, where the goals are so different. It's not great money here. I think I've pretty much hit the ceiling as far as salary goes, and that creates pressure on me. But, on the other hand, I would find it really difficult to leave.

As far as experience goes, I deal with so many different areas and so many experts, hear so many lectures, and act as the go-between in so many situations that I do learn so much about the law. It's fascinating. I think if I weren't so hooked on helping people, I might find a good way to use these experiences for my own material benefit.

KZ: Is your boss is an attorney?
MKF: Yes. We work under the supervision of attorneys. When I have questions regarding the law I take them to my attorney. She keeps an eye on my office in a general way, and she makes sure that I'm not blowing deadlines. She keeps an eye on me from afar. It's good to have someone to ask questions of, because I don't understand the issues in some cases.

This is essentially a sales job. The first rule of sales is that you have to know your product. I look at the job as trying to sell these cases to the private attorneys, and in order to do that I have to know the area of law that the case revolves around. The job is challenging in that way. It requires a lot of skills.

KZ: What skill, or skills, do you think you use the most?
MKF: That's a hard one. I think the talent that has helped me most in this job is my intellect. I've been told I'm very bright, and that's been an incredible help when dealing with so many areas of law. I don't have any real limits in understanding things and learning things.

Also, I'm very curious about what I'm doing. That helps me, too. When I'm trying to find volunteer attorneys, for example, I'll say, "Isn't this an interesting twist, isn't this great experience?" That attitude intrigues the volunteers.

I'm also very well organized. Even though my office looks like chaos, I can imagine what it would be like if I didn't have the organizational skills that I brought with me. Beyond that, there's stress management. I was a pretty relaxed person when I came here. But I was nowhere near as flexible as I am now. It's like life in the trenches—you have to be prepared for anything. I don't think you could survive in this job for any length of time without being very, very flexible.

You have to be able to deal with difficult situations, too. Sometimes clients call up furious. They insult me and the program, and then hang up on me. You have to be able to roll with it. Volunteer attorneys, never having been outside the ivory tower of the private firm, don't always understand how it is working here, that you might come to work in the morning and find a cockroach on your desk. They don't understand what it's like not having people to help you out by making copies. Sometimes we have to skim the surface of our cases, and that's difficult for the volunteer attorneys to understand.

KT: Isn't it discouraging sometimes?
MKF: Very.

KT: You must feel as if you're trying so hard to help, but that sometimes no one appreciates it.
MKF: Absolutely. In fact, on the case I was telling you about—the elderly man with the brain tumor—I had talked to an attorney who was interested in the case, so I sent it out to her. This was a week before the hearing. I'd told her that the hearing was coming up and to please let me know if she could get it prepared in time. She was talking about giving it to someone else in her firm if she couldn't do it, so I said, "Just let me know, because I know the hearing is real close, and I can get a continuance if needed. There shouldn't be any problem with that."

So I sent the file to her, and I said everything in the cover letter—I told her about his disabilities, that he was about to be evicted. She sent the file back with no warning on the next day. Of course, I didn't get the file until two days before the hearing. She'd attached a nasty note saying that it seemed unfortunate that the file was not referred out until a few days before the scheduled hearing, with the file materials incomplete, and none of the things that would need to be done having been done over the last seven months.

I thought, "Well, thank you!" I can understand her getting the file, seeing the date of the intake as July and knowing I called her in February—maybe it appeared to her that VIP was grossly negligent and just sitting on this file for the last seven months. But that's not what happened. I had told her that I'd tried for months to get a volunteer. I'd told her that we'd had two sessions to train people to handle this kind of case, but no one was willing to take the case. That was a very difficult day.

It can be very disappointing. It's a hard job because you have to care in order for it to work. But you can't care too much, or you'll drive yourself nuts, and you won't be able to function. But you have to care because you have to be sensitive to the clients, right? Well, basically, that means you end up caring. So when you care, you get hurt, and this situation was disappointing to me, and a couple of other similar things happened to me. The long and the short of it was that on Thursday afternoon I was saying "I'm getting a new job. I can't even stand this any more. I'm going into a new field. I'm going to be an interior decorator." I actually ended up in tears early in the afternoon. It was just too much. I lost my wristwatch, and life fell apart for me. It was almost three o'clock when I was supposed to do the interview with you, and I said "Oh no, I have to call Karen, I can't do an interview in this condition." I was a wreck.

So that happens, and then you bounce back, and good things happen, and you go on. But those are the sacrifices you have to make, being in a job like this. Working in a job like this requires emotional sacrifices. You have to be willing to endure the highs and lows emotionally as well as professionally.

KZ: Well, I'm in a non-profit job myself, and although my position isn't the same as yours, it's similar in that sometimes it seems very thankless.

MKF: Yes, it's hard. I have a million bosses. I answer to the clients, I answer to the volunteer attorneys, I answer to the agencies that send us the files, I answer to my boss, and I answer to the attorney who supervises us. I answer to everybody, and nobody answers to me. That's difficult.

KZ: I think there's a real challenge in having a job that has a lot of demands and a lot of variety. You get to wear many different hats, which is exciting, but you feel as if you never do any thing particularly well. On bad days, it can seem very depressing. On good days, it seems very challenging.

MKF: Exactly. It can be stimulating. But it's hard.

One of the things I've used to counsel myself is to explain the job to myself, and to others, in this way: My brother is a paramedic for the Philadelphia Fire Department. I find a lot of similarities between what he does and what I do. He knows the basics about a lot of different medical conditions. He can keep people patched together until he gets them into the hands of a professional.

I console myself regarding my "jack of all trades, master of none" experience by saying, "Yes, I may be master of none, but I know how to deal with emergencies, and I have survival skills in many, many areas of law." I know enough to say, "You need to get to an attorney right away" or "That's not really a problem" or "You really don't have a case." And that's a skill most attorneys don't have. Most attorneys don't have that broad of a base of experience. I don't know of any other paralegals who do, either.

INTERVIEW M

I've had some great opportunities. In one case, I went to a workshop in Washington, D.C., on the Drug Free Schools and Community Act. I came back and drafted a policy, and gave workshops at the various schools to explain the act. It's my responsibility to make sure, first, that they're aware of it and, second, that they're going to comply.

David L. Hay

Company: Dallas County Community College District
City: Dallas, Texas
Department: Legal Department
Title: Legal Assistant
Salary Range: $21,864–$32,796
Benefits:
    Insurance: medical, dental, life, disability, accidental death
                  (cafeteria plan)
    Financial:
    Vacation: 12 days
    Sick time: 12 days
    Misc.:   2 days personal time

Previous Work Experience:
Seven years as an administrative assistant. One year as a word processor. Secretary/paralegal trainee at a private firm for four months. Paralegal internship with the City of Dallas. Deposition summarizer in a private firm for three months.

JOB DESCRIPTION

General Summary

Perform complex and responsible legal assistant services requiring initiative and discretion based on knowledge of local, state, and federal law. Assist in preparation and review of legal documents; write resolutions, agenda items, and backup to Board meetings; organize and prioritize workload.

Principal Duties and Responsibilities

- Perform research; identify cases; analyze issues and summarize findings related to pending caseload. Assist in the preparation of legal documents.
- Investigate new and existing cases involving community colleges as directed by supervisor. Update legal counsel on pending status and available options.
- Investigate current and pending legislation related to higher education as directed by supervisor. Summarize findings and provide input to legal counsel to establish new guidelines as required.
- Draft policy and procedures as required by changes in legislation, public policy, and legal decisions related to higher education.
- Attend meetings with legal counsel, takes notes, and provide follow-up on items requiring action.
- Prepare resolutions, agenda items, and backup for board meetings as required.
- Organize and prioritize correspondence and legal documents.
- Organize and coordinate functions related to the election of DCCD board of trustees members.

Minimum Educational/Experience Requirements

Associate degree as a legal assistant plus two years of general office experience, or two years of college plus two years of experience in a similar law-office-based position. Ability to interpret and apply administrative policies, rules and regulations, and local, state, and federal legislation. Ability to perform detailed research and investigation and analyze findings. Demonstrated written communication skills.

KT: Your current position is in the non-profit sector, the Dallas County Community College District [DCCD] but you haven't always worked in that arena. Can you tell me about your previous work experience?
DH: My current position is the only one with a public entity. All my other jobs were in the private sector. I was a secretary/legal assistant trainee for a firm that dealt primarily in oil and gas, and my end of it was materialmen's liens. They had several clients on retainer of between $10,000 and $20,000 a

month, so when the oil industry fell through, so did the position. That was a part-time position which helped me through school. I drafted documents, did a little filing, assembled evidence packets, assisted with discovery—and I got a taste of research.

I worked as a deposition summarizer for about three months in another law firm. It was three to four hundred pages a day to read. That experience taught me what I *didn't* want to do.

KZ: It sounds miserable to me.

DH: Yes, but there were people who thrived on it and who loved it.

Without giving away the name of the firm, it was one that dealt mostly with tort claims, and it is considered by many to be one of the leading tort firms in the Dallas/Ft. Worth area. As a matter of fact, in the hallways, they had pictures of accidents—for example, a plane crash. That's how they decorated the hallways of the firm. The person who established the business is now heavily involved in handgun control throughout the state of Texas.

In the deposition summarizing, I started out with car accidents and slip-and-fall cases; then I graduated to more complex things. One was military aircraft—a failure of the aircraft wing—and that was very technical. It was a deposition from an engineer, and not having an engineering background, or any classes, training, or knowledge, I actually had to sit and draw pictures to figure things out.

Some people who did that type of deposition summarizing were automobile specialists. The firm wanted me to become specialized in aircraft. I didn't stay there primarily because I didn't want to do deposition summarizing full-time and I saw that my chances for upward mobility to legal assistant were nil.

I did an internship, pro bono work, with the City of Dallas, including some deposition summarizing, but it was a much more relaxed atmosphere—maybe fifty pages a day. I didn't spend all day doing it, either. I did filing of documents and some document preparation, and I assisted in the preparation of trial notebooks. One of the things I liked about that atmosphere is that a public entity has a limited budget and no one there is going to turn down free help, which is what I amounted to. Once word got around—and it took me two or three weeks to discover this—whenever I wanted something more challenging or wanted to go to a different department, all I had to do was ask.

I got a chance to do a lot of different things. We have a street here in Dallas that is famous for one of the oldest professions. I got an opportunity to see things and prepare for—well, I guess you would call it a trial. I prepared statements the officers had made to be used in prosecuting individuals involved in this profession. It was an education in itself. Then I came into my current position.

KT: And how did that happen?

DH: Dumb luck! Nothing beats it. I had been a part-time secretary to the secretary to the legislative liaison of the DCCD prior to graduating from school. So I stopped in to see how everyone was doing because it was around the Christmas holidays, plus I wanted to copy my résumé on their laser printer. While I was here, my future boss walked out and said, "I need help with the elections. How would you like to talk about it?" So, after the holidays, I got in touch with him and began the interview process. I started out as a research assistant in board of trustee elections.

At that time, we had elections in even-numbered years, and two seats were up for re-election. Every ten years they do a census and redraw the lines in the county. Then all the seats are up for re-election. The board members draw lots to determine what the terms are. They range from two to six years. Preparing for the election is something the legal department is responsible for. The process is long and can be tedious.

If nothing else, I thought, the job would provide me with good experience as a legal assistant and perhaps act as a springboard to bigger and better things. I was hired in January, and our elections were in May. I was hired with the understanding that I would work through the election, as a full-time, temporary research assistant, for the sole purpose of assisting in the elections. If anything else came along, it would be additional work, but there were no guarantees. That meant that from January to May, if something came across my boss' desk, there was time, and both of us were in agreement that I should get involved with it, I would do it.

KT: But obviously, your situation changed.

DH: Yes. In March, my boss told me that he might be able to hire me as a legal assistant. He didn't specify if it would be permanent or temporary part-time, but he said he had put in a good word about me to the chancellor. Never having had a legal assistant, he had some questions: What can I do, what am I qualified to do, what would I like to do?

As time went along, I was given more responsibility in addition to the elections. Just before the elections in May he asked, "How would you like to be permanent full-time? We have the approval of the Chancellor." After the elections, the position was created. They had to go through the process of opening it up to the general public by advertising it in the newspaper. I've now been here almost three years.

KT: Basically, the job was created for you?

DH: It worked out that way.

KT: What does your job consist of?

DH: A little bit of everything. When I went to school to be a legal assistant, we got a smorgasbord of the different areas of law, and what the legal assistant can expect to do in those different areas. In addition to knowing contracts, torts, and litigation, the legal assistant assists the attorney or boss in making a trial notebook, picking a jury, taking notes during a trial, keeping abreast of a case—all to help the attorney prepare for going to a hearing, trial, or some type of legal meeting.

For a public entity, it's the mirror opposite of that. Very few times do we go to court. I've never helped my boss pick a jury. I've been in depositions two or three times only. I don't have a caseload of thirty-five or forty cases, whereas a traditional legal assistant in the private sector would. It's legal work, but maybe more administrative.

For example, we have a satellite, called the Center for Educational Telecommunications, which produces and airs educational programs. We are the largest center in the Southwest. In order to establish that, and to continue and maintain it, we have to apply for a grant and licenses from the federal government. My job is, first, to make sure we're in compliance with the law, and, second, to make sure that all the parties involved comply and submit the appropriate information—the business end, which does the financing; the Center for Educational Telecommunications, which must submit records to the government, and our end, which has to report any litigation or pending litigation.

KT: So trying to comply with state and federal laws is a big part of your job.
DH: I do anything that comes from the federal government, such as the Drug-Free Schools and Communities Act. We're having a bi-annual review wherein the campuses, the vice-chancellors, and the provost have to submit a progress report. I'm working with them to make the report ready and available so that if an audit is done, we're in compliance. The Drug-Free Schools and Community Act monitors criminal activity on campus—illegal drugs, sale and possession, distribution. It also covers some other offenses that campus security departments have to keep a record of. The bi-annual review ensures that our program is keeping this under control and makes suggestions as to how we can improve and follow those guidelines.

The legal department also handles an AIDS policy and the Americans with Disabilities Act. We want to make the district locations accessible to all walks of life. For example, we have to make sure that the campus is providing services for a handicapped person, such as readers if the person is blind or interpreters if the person is deaf. Right now, I'm putting out feelers to see how the campuses are doing with that.

KT: Do you have a typical day?
DH: No. I'm given a list of things that need to be taken care of.

KT: By whom?
DH: My boss, legal counsel for the district. I make weekly progress reports

for him. As far as a typical day, well, sometimes things come in out of left field. Often a person will call, wanting to know what options they have if they've been discriminated against. I may be able to keep the incident from blowing out of proportion.

KZ: Well, that raises an interesting question. Where is the line between practicing law and not practicing law?

DH: I'm not telling them that they need to go down to EEOC. It depends on what it is. An administrator wanted me to approve a release form to get some information from an employee's physician. The form, which was generated internally, was less than perfect, but I couldn't tell her to use it or not because that would have been crossing that line you refer to. We have a law firm we've been doing business with, and because of the volume of business, I can pick up the phone and say, "This is the situation. I've got a release here. This is how it reads. I need something better than this. Is there a way you can help me out?" The law firm, of course, can recommend something.

KZ: Or your boss could, if your boss were in the office.

DH: Right. In his absence, I deal with the law firm, and for the most part, that works out.

Another thing I do is bankruptcies. I started working with them because I had shown an interest. They trickle in. Most of them are not students who have taken gross, unfair advantage of the system. An exception would be a student accepting funds through the Guaranteed Student Loan Program who then cheats on his taxes and files bankruptcy to avoid paying back any of the loan. Usually a bankruptcy is from someone who has come across hard times.

I do remember one corporate bankruptcy. A company we had written classroom materials for filed bankruptcy before they paid us. That was a $5,000 debt—the largest bankruptcy problem I've dealt with.

I have the type of boss who allows me a free hand. He doesn't say, "Step one is . . . , step two is . . . ." He just hands me a file, gives me an outline of what's going on, and says, "We have a deadline of X." So when a bankruptcy comes up, I have the option of asking my boss how to handle it or of calling on the law firm we do business with. But when someone wants to know about a bankruptcy, I don't want to have to say that I'll find out. I want to know the answer for myself, so I write to the Bankruptcy Court, and I'm finding that's the best way. They don't take phone calls or see people regarding a particular matter. They'll only respond if you send them something in writing, and their turnaround is usually within ten days. They've been very helpful. Therefore, I don't have to rely on an outside firm every time. And, remember, an outside firm is going to charge us—there is such a thing as billable hours.

KT: Which I assume you don't have.
DH: That's right.

KT: You seem to work very autonomously.
DH: When I first came here, and even now to a degree, my supervisor would say to me, "This is something that came across my desk. It involves this, that, and the other thing. Is that something you'd like to do?" I never turned him down. That doesn't happen so much now. But I don't turn him down for a lot of reasons—I want to learn as much as I can and get involved in different areas. If he needs something done, I want him to know he can trust me.

I've had some great opportunities. In one case, I went to a workshop in Washington, D.C., on the Drug Free Schools and Community Act. I came back and drafted a policy, and gave workshops at the various schools to explain the act. It's my responsibility to make sure, first, that they're aware of it and, second, that they're going to comply.

It used to be that anything the colleges needed to do they'd turn over to us. That isn't the case so much any more because we're trying to make them more independent. But I give them guidance, and if major problems develop, I'm here to help. Every once in a while something unusual will come up such as the time a towing firm caused some damage to an employee's car. I got an opportunity to perform as a paralegal in the private sector would. I went out to the scene, took pictures, and helped negotiate with the towing firm without going to court.

So it's difficult to say exactly what I do, except that whenever something comes up that a legal assistant could do, I do it. Most of the people in the district know now that this position exists, so they know to call me. I've been fortunate, and I don't know if that's through my personality, but I try to make sure that I'm able to help them out. I don't want to refer them to the attorney, because if I do that, they don't need me.

KT: It sounds as if you're very successful in your job. If you had to put your finger on the qualities that have made you successful in your position, what would they be?
DH: An appetite for challenge. In the private sector, it's like working for a factory. The more you produce, the more you get paid—the billable hours scenario. I'm not satisfied to do that. In addition to working here, I'm involved in the Dallas Association of Legal Assistants and the Ft. Worth Paralegal Association, and I do volunteer work. So I am not happy or content just to go with the flow.

The ambition and the drive—that's a needed quality. To make yourself available, to create situations. For example, we're just getting around to putting the service mark on all of our college names. I saw a memo regarding that on my boss's desk, and I said, "Could I see this?" and he said, "How would you like to handle it?" You have to put your foot forward, be ambitious, and have internal drive.

Computers

Although the law tends to be somewhat traditional, in recent years it has become more and more computerized. Most law firms currently use computers for one function or another. This is confirmed by a recent *Chicago-Kent School of Law Annual Legal Software Survey*, which reported that more than 90 percent of the top 500 law firms now use computers for litigation. Typically, computers are used in the following ways in the legal field:

1. Word processing of legal documents such as pleadings, contracts, wills, correspondence, and the like, using such programs as WordPerfect 5.1 or 6.0 or Microsoft Word.
2. Computerized research using programs such as WESTLAW or LEXIS. Computerized research allows the user to access and search for key words or topics within huge databases that contain the complete text of state and federal cases and statutes.
3. Calendaring and scheduling of deadlines, appointments, and any other dates, through docket control programs such as Legal Calendar and Docket.
4. Billing and timekeeping through programs such as Timeslips and Verdict. These programs enable the user not only to keep track of all time spent on a particular client or matter but also to bill that time to a particular client or cost center.
5. Litigation support using programs like Litigator and ZyINDEX. Through these programs, the information acquired during the course of litigation can be organized, stored, retrieved, and summarized in various ways, so that the case can be managed and controlled efficiently.
6. Database creation and management with programs such as dBASE IV and Q&A. With these programs, the user can store, search, sort, and produce reports, both for in-house use and for use in cases.
7. Financial statements and analysis, budgeting, and statistical or numerical reports with spreadsheet programs such as Lotus 1-2-3 and SuperCalc. These programs can be used to support the firm or company's business or to support a case.
8. Desktop publishing through programs such as Pagemaker to design documents on a computer rather than use a professional printer.
9. Support of specialty areas of law through programs designed to support a specific legal market, such as Lawyer's WillWriter and Divorce Settlement Assistant.

One of the newest computer products to hit the legal field is CD-ROM. This can be expected to alter the practice of law enormously. [See the box entitled "CD-ROM" in Chapter 4.]

HINT:

As the legal field becomes more and more computerized, it will be essential that paralegals be familiar with, and able to use, at least some of the programs mentioned above. Take full advantage of any computer classes or workshops that are offered by your school, professional paralegal organization, or employer.

Networking a little bit in the organization, making yourself more visible, is important. When I first came here, it didn't take long to find out that if you're in the district office, you're on your own. When business like this bankruptcy comes along, it gives me an opportunity to go out to the campuses, talk to the business officers, or the presidents themselves, and make myself known and visible.

Ongoing education is important, too. Because we're a public entity, we are allocated so many free hours a month on a WESTLAW satellite—a training center for computerized research. I can go through the training and if I need to look up an important issue in a hurry, those facilities are available. When I worked for the city, their budget was so tight that they had to discontinue WESTLAW for a while, which is incredible when you look at how much a lawsuits costs.

KT: What do you dislike about your position, if anything?
DH: I can't complain about variety!

What do I dislike? It depends on your point of view. I have probably a more secure job than in the private sector, but if I were in the private sector, I could probably start at $10,000 a year more than I make now. When I got out of college, I wanted to be in litigation. I still do. If the right opportunity were to come along, I would take it.

I've got deadlines and pressures, but that's going to be so in any industry.

KT: You've somewhat answered the question as to whether you have any future plans.
DH: I'll stay here for a while and make the most of what I've got—to learn, to read, to absorb. I say that as I'm looking at my reading stack right now! I've got a very helpful boss. In fact, one of the things he has offered, but

which I haven't followed up on, is the chance to work a couple of days a week in the law firm that we do business with, as a legal assistant. That way, I could get experience in the private sector. I may do this in the future. Ultimately, I'd like to be in litigation. And with a little more education and depending on how the market is, I might pursue being a paralegal manager.

I don't have all the answers. I'm not a specialist; I'm a generalist. And something is always coming up that leads me to say, "I never heard of that before. Let me look into that and I'll get back to you." I like that a lot.

CHAPTER 6

Entrepreneurs

The three paralegals interviewed for this chapter are quite different from each other—one is the owner of a company which handles permanent and temporary placement of paralegals; one is a freelance paralegal; and one is a partner in a company providing services to the secondary mortgage market. But they are similar because all three used the skills and knowledge they gained working as paralegals to go into business for themselves.

These paralegals started their business ventures because they *didn't* feel limited in the profession. "A lot of people think this is a dead-end career, that it's very limiting. If you think it's very limiting, then it will be." (Scott Collister) Rather than view it as limited, they view it as providing the individual paralegal with broad skills which can then be translated into a myriad of positions. To them, a paralegal is someone who can ". . . look at a problem, work it through, come up with several options, then pick an option for a reason and articulate it." (Collister)

Having transferred these skills into their own entrepreneurial ventures, these paralegals attribute their success at least partly to their being goal setters and planners. "You've got to have a plan. It may not always work, but you need to have one." (Jo Barrett) "I'm very much a goal setter. . . . You just put your head down and work at it, and when you look up, boom, you've hit a goal. So you put your head back down, look up, and boom, you've hit another one." (Collister)

On the other hand, success may have less to do with planning than with being in the right place at the right time, seeing a need, and taking the initiative to fill that need. "It wasn't as if I had planned all this in advance. . . . It evolved, and I just continued to market it. . . . I just responded to the needs of the marketplace." (Shelley Widoff)

But even if these paralegals are running their own businesses, without the title "paralegal," they still identify strongly with, and view themselves as a part of, the paralegal profession. High levels of participation in professional paralegal associations and continuing legal education demonstrate this view. "I believe that to stay on top of things you need CLE. There's always a change in the law that you need to know about." (Barrett)

They also show their close ties to the profession by their thoughtful predictions and concerns regarding future. ". . . I've always wanted to promote paralegal professionalism." (Widoff) "I think that more and more attorneys will utilize the services of freelance paralegals. I would guess that you'll see a real change in three to five years." (Barrett) "One of my pet peeves is the amount of divisiveness in the profession and the lack of unity. . . . We all agree that we need to get up and get going [on setting educational standards for paralegals] . . . but we can't agree on what size step we should take. Because of that, we're going to go nowhere. That's what has been holding this profession back. . . . (Collister) ". . . what I would like to see is a defined territory in which [paralegals] could work as professionals. . . . That may require certain credentials or certification, but that is where I would like to see paralegals go." (Widoff)

Not surprisingly, these paralegals enjoy the business side of their work. "Once I started freelancing, well, it's just been a real challenge. I've learned so much about running a business." (Barrett) In fact, in some cases, the business side may provide more satisfaction than the law components of their jobs. ". . . law as a business is where I've gained most of my satisfaction, as opposed to practicing law, which I never cared for. I've been very satisfied with the business side." (Widoff)

These paralegals thrive on their own, don't mind risks, and are extremely independent. "I did not have a single client when I left the law firm. . . . One of the partners at the firm said that I was gutsy." (Barrett) "I was totally comfortable with starting my own business. . . . I didn't see it as a risk. It was just a natural way for me to express myself . . . I perform the best when I'm working for myself . . ." (Widoff) "I'm a very independent person, and I don't want a security blanket. I want to be out on my own, to make it or break it—no guts, no glory." (Collister)

INTERVIEW N

I meet with attorneys, I meet with their clients (because, of course, the attorneys are my clients), I prepare the documents to open the estate, go to court to get the executor appointed, go to the auditor's office for tax releases, contact the banks and brokerage firms to verify date-of-death balances, transfer cars, arrange for property to be moved out of a house if it's necessary, arrange for an auction, arrange for items to be shipped to a beneficiary, open and close bank accounts. I'm out of the office a good deal, and I have a lot of correspondence.

Jo Barrett

Company: Freelance Paralegal, Sole Proprietor
City: Columbus, Ohio
Department: Not applicable
Title: Probate Paralegal
Salary Range: Not available
Benefits:
    Insurance: Not available
    Financial: Not available
    Vacation: Not available
    Sick time: Not available
    Misc.:   Not available

Previous Work Experience:
Ten years of secretarial experience for various corporations. Five years as a legal secretary for a large law firm and eighteen years as a paralegal for the same law firm.

JOB DESCRIPTION

General Summary

Assist attorneys in the administration of estates, guardianships, and trusts, as well as estate tax preparation and miscellaneous probate matters such as adoptions and name changes.

Principal Duties

- Interview client with attorney at initial conference.
- Prepare documents to admit will, appoint executor, inventory and appraisal, accounts, estate tax returns, income tax returns, release from administration, appointment of guardian and related documents, stock transfer papers, tax release, etc.
- Identify and value assets (jewelry, automobiles, bank accounts, securities, IRA's, real property, notes).
- Handle estate checking accounts, including paying bills, making deposits, and assisting with investments.
- Prepare transfer documents for real property, check deed records and legal descriptions, record deeds and certificates, etc.
- Distribute to beneficiaries.
- Remind attorneys of due dates.

JB: I went to paralegal school in the Fall of 1972—at that time a ten-month course at the Capital University Law Center Legal Assistant Program. Capital is the only paralegal program out of nearly 700 programs nationwide that is co-sponsored by a law school and a local bar association. In 1972, it had just begun, and I was in the very first class. I got there because I had been a legal secretary at Bricker and Eckler for five years.

KT: These are all places in Columbus?
JB: Yes. An attorney representing one of the firm's clients in a bankruptcy proceeding hired me as a legal secretary in 1968. I worked as a legal secretary there for five years when the program was started at Capital. The acting dean wanted twenty-five warm bodies for the class, so he made the rounds of all the large law firms where he had friends to get them to send their legal secretaries.

The first class was a probate specialty. It was three months of legal systems and legal research, and six months of probate, wills and trusts, guardianships—everything relating to probate court. Since I'd been at the firm for five years, was really interested in the law, and had a small son to support, they chose me. They paid my tuition. I worked full-time, went to school two nights a week, and spent twenty to twenty-five hours per week on homework.

I was a paralegal for eighteen years in the Probate Department and loved it. My mentor, David C. Cummins, and I were a real team. We worked together very well. He had a stroke and heart attack in December 1989 and died about a month later. That's when I started thinking about freelancing for the second time.

The reason I say for the second time is that I first started thinking about it in 1982 or 1983. One of my friends from Legal Assistants of Central Ohio (LACO), our local paralegal association, was a corporate paralegal and the first paralegal in Columbus to start her own business. I thought that was very exciting. I started making my notes and getting organized. When I thought I was ready, I talked to my boss about it. At that time I still had a son in school, and my boss said, "You don't want to give up the security of the law firm." He didn't think it was the right time. I thought, "Well, you know, he's right, but he's probably a little selfish also, because he'd have to train someone else." In any case, I decided to put it on the back burner.

Following his death in January of 1990, I didn't really think about it, but my father died of cancer in a short three and a half months. During that time, when I was out of the office a lot dealing with his illness and death, I thought, "You know, my boss died, and my dad died. Life is too short. Why don't you try this freelance thing? You're not getting any younger."

It all came together. I dragged out my old notes from 1982, started making lists of what I needed to do, and gave the firm my notice. That was October of 1990, so I've been freelancing for three years now.

Starting a Freelance Career

HINT:

Paralegals considering a freelance career may want to read two new books:

1. Hussey, Katherine and Benzel, Rick, *Legal Services on Your Home-Based PC*, TAB McGraw-Hill, Philadelphia, 1994.
2. Warner, Ralph, *The Independent Paralegal's Handbook: How to Provide Legal Services Without Becoming a Lawyer*, Nolo Press, Berkeley, California, 1993.

   Hussey focuses on freelancing, whereas Warner deals primarily with the independent paralegal (one chapter deals specifically with the freelance paralegal), but both discuss a wide range of topics important to freelance paralegals, such as setting up shop, finding clients, and avoiding the unauthorized practice of law.

KT: How's it going?

JB: It's going fine. I did not have a single client when I left the law firm. I didn't have time to do any marketing, and I didn't think it was ethical to do it on the firm's time. I just figured that the Lord would take care of me, that there are many sole practitioners out there who must need help. I thought it would work out.

KT: That's kind of gutsy, though.

JB: One of the partners at the firm said I was gutsy. I did put a small announcement in the *Daily Reporter,* which is the legal newspaper here, just saying I was going to open an office and would be assisting attorneys in the administration of estates, guardianships and trusts, and tax work. Lo and behold, one came, and he told somebody else, and another one came . . .

I now work for over forty clients—sole practitioners, small firms, and one large firm. The large firm lost their paralegal at the same time I left Bricker, and was just too busy to interview and hire. They wanted to hire me, but I had this freelance dream. So they made an offer to me to work just two or three months and we'd see how it went.

KT: Two or three months on a freelance basis?

JB: Right. I've been working for them since the very beginning. They love it. They don't have to pay any benefits or overhead. They call me when they need me. I'm working on about ten matters with them at present. Some months it's a little slow, but for the most part, it's very busy.

They pay me monthly, and it covers pretty much all of my expenses. On the other hand, the sole practitioners can't afford to pay me monthly—they pay me when they get paid. It's good, because I could practically live on what I make from the large firm, so when the sole practitioners pay me, it's almost like getting a bonus. I have a really good relationship with them.

I've been very fortunate, and I think a lot of it is because I was in the law firm for eighteen years. I was very active in the Columbus Bar Association. I am a member of the probate court committee, the elder law committee, and have been a member of the lawyer/legal assistants committee. I am also a charter member, a founder, of the local legal assistants group, Legal Assistants of Central Ohio. Six of the first paralegals from Capital University Law Center Legal Assistant Program started the association in October 1973. Because of that, everybody knew me.

KT: You'd built up your reputation.

JB: Yes. While working for Bricker for eighteen years, I met a lot of other attorneys, people from banks, and appraisers. Because I had so much experience and exposure, that really helped. The only advertising I have done is in the annual Columbus bar directory.

KZ: Your clients have found you by word of mouth.

JB: Yes. Even the referees over at the probate court have recommended me to attorneys. My business has been continual. I did have one slack period, around August of 1991, but I found out that many attorneys go on vacation in August. Business picked up again in October, and it's never stopped since. Sometimes I wish it would slow down a little.

KZ: It sounds as if you almost have more than you can handle.

JB: Yes . . . in fact, I have two paralegals who help out from time to time as I need them. One of them works as a freelance paralegal for a firm in the mornings, so she's free in the afternoon. The other one can work evenings and weekends. A bookkeeper does all my billing.

KZ: Whom you contract out to?

JB: Yes. She enters all my time sheet information in the computer program and prints work sheets, which I review carefully. She wants my bills to go out by the fourth of every month, although it depends on when the end of the month falls.

KZ: Are you in an office-sharing situation?

JB: I'm in an office building right across from the courthouse, where Probate Court is, which makes it convenient. It's a building that two attorneys own. There are probably thirty offices, rented on a no-lease, thirty-day basis. It's just great. Almost everyone in the building is an attorney. I didn't move in here thinking I would work for them; I moved in because there was no lease and the location was excellent. The building supplies a receptionist, coffee, conference rooms—all the things you might need.

The first year I didn't work for anyone in the building. I don't think they knew what I did. But after the first year, attorneys started approaching me. Now I work for about a half a dozen attorneys in the building. I prefer to work for people outside the building, because they call or I call them when we need to meet. With some of them I have a scheduled, standing appointment, and it works out well that way. The attorneys in the building tend to "pop" in, which sometimes is inconvenient.

KZ: Do you do all your own computer work?

JB: Pretty much. I use WordPerfect, and I have programs to do federal and state tax, accounts, inventories, and to value securities. Most of the documents can be done on the computer. Some forms still have to be filled out on the typewriter, but my secretarial background helps there, and I'm quite efficient.

I have had secretarial help during this three-year period. One secretary, Cathy, stayed with me for about a year and a half. She came for three hours in the morning, so I could shut off my phone and get a lot done.

When she left, I decided not to get anybody else. I'm about ready to start looking, though. Having somebody like Cathy who only comes in three hours a day is perfect. I try to do as much as I can by myself because that helps with costs.

KT: What do you typically do during a day or a week?
JB: Oh, gosh. I do it all!

I meet with attorneys, I meet with their clients (because, of course, the attorneys are my clients), I prepare the documents to open the estate, go to court to get the executor appointed, go to the auditor's office for tax releases, contact the banks and brokerage firms to verify date-of-death balances, transfer cars, arrange for property to be moved out of a house if it's necessary, arrange for an auction, arrange for items to be shipped to a beneficiary, open and close bank accounts. I'm out of the office a good deal, and I have a lot of correspondence. I have about eighty estates and guardianships right now that are all active.

I'm starting an office at home. I come down here on Saturdays and sometime Sundays, so I want a home office to save some traveling time.

KT: But you'll keep the other?
JB: Yes, I'll have both.

I'm fifty-four. Long-range, I'd like to slow down and work part-time, maybe when I'm sixty. When it's time for me to slow down, I'll work out of my home two or three days a week for the sole practitioners that I want to work for.

Working in probate, I deal with death all the time. So often you pick up that death certificate and see that someone retired and then died right after. I have seen this for twenty some years. I don't want to retire and die; I want to ease into retirement. Not that that's going make me live any longer, but that's my game plan. You've got to have a plan. It may not always work, but you need to have one.

KT: Something to aim for, at least.
JB: There are a lot of freelance paralegals in Columbus now. By a lot, I mean fifteen or twenty. Some start without any experience, and, quite frankly, I don't know how they make it. Many sole practitioners are general-practice attorneys, without expertise in certain areas. The reason they hire you is that you do have the expertise. They want you to know how to do something because they don't have time to train someone.

KT: Do you like being a freelance paralegal?
JB: I do. But I liked being at Bricker and Eckler, too; I liked being a legal secretary. I wouldn't stay in a job that I didn't like. It just seems that whenever I've started getting a little bored, something else has come along.

Freelancing has been a real challenge. I've learned so much about running a business. I went to courses that the Small Business Administration offered on running a business. There is so much that I have to do administratively, but I really enjoy my work.

I also enjoy meeting people. I have some long-time friends whom I've met through my work. One friend, a widow whose husband died in 1976, was a client of the firm. As a paralegal, I could give clients more time than my boss could; he wanted them to call me. I did a lot of hand-holding and made some good friends in the process. I think I was warm and sympathetic at a time when they needed that.

There are a lot of stressful days, difficult days when someone young dies and leaves small children. Some deaths make you wonder, "Why did this happen?" It's emotionally draining at times. For example, I have to empty out an apartment if someone dies with no family. I have to go through their drawers and closets and get rid of all of their possessions.

KT: It's sad.

JB: It is. It's an invasion of this person's privacy, but somebody has to do it.

I don't have an undergraduate degree. In my era, girls were nurses, teachers, secretaries, or clerical workers. My parents were poor, so my older brother went to college. After high school, I worked as a secretary. So I feel especially blessed that I am where I am.

KT: It's been a good career for you.

JB: I think so. When I'm sitting at a paralegal meeting with eight or ten people who are talking about their college days, I feel that I missed that. But I'm not done yet! I have plans to go back to school, soon, I hope. With my close friend's death, I have more time now, and it's something that's always been in the back of my mind. I plan on getting my undergraduate degree.

Probate work is very rewarding. You see a person come in so upset with his or her spouse's or parent's death, not knowing what the next move is. Then, six months to a year later, you see that the person has figured out what they're doing and has learned so much.

KT: Anything else you'd like to mention?

JB: I do a lot of CLE. The Columbus Bar Association offers many seminars, and I attend as many as I can afford. Our legal assistants association sponsors seminars, and as an associate member of the Ohio State Bar, I attend some bar association seminars. I believe that to stay on top of things, you need CLE. There's always a change in the law that you need to know about.

KT: What do you see as the future of paralegals? Any thoughts on that?

JB: In Ohio, at least, the large law firms are cutting back. They're not hiring full-time as they used to. I think that more and more attorneys will utilize the services of freelance paralegals, especially in probate. I would guess that you'll see a real change in three to five years.

KZ: So fast?

JB: Yes, I think so. I get a lot of calls from attorneys asking, for example, "Do you know anyone who freelances in bankruptcy?" The large firm I work for told me that they wish they could have freelance paralegals in all areas because it's more economical for them.

KZ: Do you think there are any bad sides to freelancing?

JB: Some attorneys think that I'm taking business away from them. And, of course, some paralegals are pushing to serve the public directly. I don't need to serve the public directly. I do get calls from people who want to hire me because they've heard that paralegals are cheaper, but, of course, I can't practice law.

As a freelance paralegal, I cover myself all the time with memos. It takes extra time to write them, but I'm concerned for my liability. That's another reason that I meet regularly with my attorneys. Someone might say, "She does everything herself, and the attorney comes in once a month and signs papers." Well, that is not true; that is not the type of relationship that I have with the attorneys I work with. Plus, I am on the Unauthorized Practice of Law Committee for the Columbus Bar Association. When I was asked to serve on the committee I jumped at the opportunity even though I don't have the time. I can assist the committee in handling complaints against paralegals.

I'm ethical and honest. I do things the right way. When the National Federation of Paralegal Associations came out with professional liability insurance, my accountant didn't think I needed it, but I signed up for it anyway. I thought it was money well spent. It looks good on my resume. I hope that I never need it, and I think that I would be covered under the policies of the attorneys I work for. But it doesn't hurt.

Malpractice Insurance for Paralegals

Generally, paralegals are covered under the malpractice insurance of the sole practitioner of firm for which they work. "Respondeat superior" is the guiding theory: An employer is deemed to be responsible for any wrongs that an employee commits while the employee is within the scope of his or her employment.

However, just because a paralegal is employed by an attorney, he or she is not off the hook. A paralegal can be sued individually by a client, although normally a client would sue the attorney or firm instead, because the attorney or firm has the "deep pockets" (money or assets) that a paralegal may not have. Still, paralegals have been sued individually, and they can face penalties or admonishments by the local bar association in their state if they conduct themselves improperly. An example is a 1982 case, *Florida Bar v. Julio A. Pascual*, 424 So.2d 757, in which a paralegal was enjoined by the Supreme Court of Florida from the unauthorized practice of law. The paralegal had represented his employer's client, given legal advice, and corresponded with another lawyer, all without disclosing his non-attorney status and without the supervision of his employer.

As malpractice claims have skyrocketed in recent years, malpractice insurance for paralegals has come on the market. Very few insurance companies currently offer this type of insurance, but the National Federation of Paralegal Associations (NFPA) provides professional liability insurance to its members. Traditional and non-traditional paralegals can purchase this insurance and be covered as paralegals, notaries, or as board directors or committee members of professional paralegal associations. Purchasers are also covered for any libel and slander claims and are provided with legal defense. Rates for this insurance vary, depending on whether the purchaser is a traditional paralegal, say within a law firm, or a freelancer. For a traditional paralegal, the cost is $150 to $165 per year, with coverage ranging from $100,000 per claim/$300,000 aggregate to $250,000 per claim/$500,000 aggregate. The cost for a freelance paralegal ranges from $450 to $788 per year, with coverage ranging from $100,000 per claim/$300,000 aggregate to $1,000,000 per claim/$1,000,000 aggregate (see Figure 6-1). Obviously, the cost is higher for a freelance paralegal because the risk is greater.

If the day comes when paralegals can obtain licenses to practice limited areas of law on their own, without attorney supervision, malpractice insurance will be a necessary and mandatory component of that paralegal's practice.

HINT:

Not all policies held by attorneys cover their staff. Be forewarned about this, and discuss it with a prospective employer prior to taking a new position.

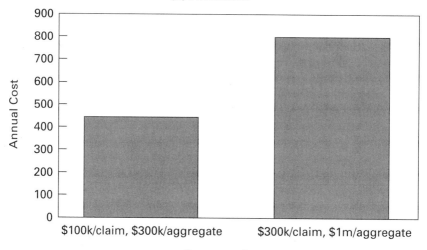

(a) Freelance

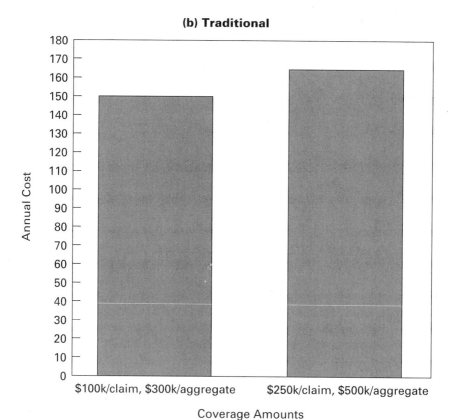

(b) Traditional

Figure 6-1   Costs of Malpractice Insurance for Freelance (a) and Traditional (b) Paralegals (*Courtesy National Federation of Paralegal Associations*)

INTERVIEW O

Salaries were horrible at that time because neither our job nor its value was defined. I felt that if I had lawyers as clients, I could set my own rate, and that's what I did. I started out by getting a part-time position on an estate matter with an attorney, who then allowed me to use his office address and telephone number to develop my clientele.

Shelley Widoff

Company: Paralegal Resource Center, Inc.
City: Boston
Department:
Title: President
Salary Range: $100,000+
Benefits:
  Insurance: HMO
  Financial: 401(k)
  Vacation: long weekends whenever possible
  Sick time: who can afford to be sick?
  Misc.:   being your own boss!!

Previous Work Experience:
Paralegal in a general-practice law firm for four years. One year as a legal-assistant manager in a large law firm. Teaching in, designing, and directing paralegal education programs.

JOB DESCRIPTION

Principal Duties

- Manage a paralegal service and placement business.
- Direct the legal assistant programs at Boston University.
- Write a column entitled "On the Docket" for *Legal Assistant Today* magazine.

SW: I feel that I'm even a little more non-traditional than some of the paralegals you've been speaking to. Although I began as a traditional paralegal, very early on I took a non-traditional route. Where I am now took me fifteen years to get to. It's been an evolution. Maybe it would be best for me to tell you how I started.

KT: I'm already intrigued by what you've said.

SW: I started as a paralegal in 1972, so I go back a way. At that time, no one really knew what a paralegal could do, would do, and should do. After taking the training, even I didn't know what I could do when I interviewed for employment. I was not particularly self-assured, not having been put to the test, but I did know two things. I knew that I did not have the credentials to be a lawyer, and I knew that I did not wish to be a legal secretary and that there was a position in the middle that I was seeking. I never gave up searching for that position. My first job was as a traditional paralegal for about four years in a general-practice firm.

That period is when I did all of my learning and developing. It was a wonderful experience—almost like going through law school. Lawyers mentored me, and I learned corporate, real estate, and probate work. I did not do much litigation. After I found my strengths and had been a paralegal for four years—one of the few experienced paralegals around—I became a non-traditional, freelance paralegal. I knew what paralegals did and how they did it, and I could better relate to the effective utilization of paralegals. I had a wealth of knowledge that few other people had at that time.

I guess that makes me a pioneer of sorts. Salaries were horrible at that time because neither our job nor its value was defined. I felt that if I had lawyers as clients, I could set my own rate, and that's what I did. I started out by getting a part-time position on an estate matter with an attorney, who then allowed me to use his office address and telephone number to develop my clientele.

KT: Was this in Boston?

SW: Right. Looking pretty official, with a downtown office and address, was my head start. Then I prepared a professional, inexpensive brochure that explained how I, as a trained, experienced paralegal, could service members of the bar. I obtained lawyer clients, primarily sole practitioners,

and I did many out-of-office operations which lawyers had perhaps neglected or hadn't enough time to do. There seemed to be a need for my
services.

KZ: Did you obtain your clients mostly through word of mouth?
SW: Yes. I also knocked on a lot of doors. Many attorneys were trying to
figure out what paralegals could do, but they didn't have enough work for
a forty-hour week for a paralegal. So by my freelancing by the hour, their
needs were satisfied, as well as mine.

At the same time, I was very interested in teaching paralegals. I felt
that paralegals weren't learning what they should be learning in the classroom because the attorneys who were teaching them had never even utilized a paralegal.

Since I was on a different track, I was asked to speak at paralegal programs, and because I was freelancing, the students were interested. All of a
sudden, I was presenting them with an option they'd never considered
before. I sat through some paralegal classes for a half-hour before speaking, and I wasn't all that impressed with how and what the paralegals
were being taught. They were being given a lot of legal theory but not
much of what they would do as a practicing paralegal—not unlike the
education I had. Since I had the time and energy and could use the income,
I thought that it would be great to share my knowledge and the nuts and
bolts of paralegal practice with students, and I sought to be hired as a paralegal instructor.

That wasn't to be because the school that I had spoken at was ABA-
approved and they feared that they would lose their ABA approval if they
hired me because I was "only" a paralegal. Supposedly, I didn't have the
credentials to teach for them. That really disturbed me, and it's something
I've never forgotten.

There were a lot of complaints to the director of this school from the
students about an estate administration course. The students were interviewing for jobs upon completion of the course, but they hadn't been prepared to do practical matters such as filling out petitions to file in court,
which is what employers were trying to hire them for. This gave me my
first teaching opportunity. The director called me in to trouble-shoot for
the course. I devised a practical curriculum to go over the basics over four
or five sessions. All the students who had paid for the previous course
were able to come to my course for free. It was a great public relations
move for the school. The course evaluations all said, "Why didn't Ms.
Widoff teach this course from the beginning?" "She taught us what we
should know." So I got the reassurance I needed that I was on the mark
and perhaps the ABA was not.

That's when I decided to start my own paralegal program. I had the
time to do it, since I was working for myself. I approached Northeastern
University with my idea for a paralegal program whose unique feature

would be team teaching by a paralegal and a lawyer. I knew that I needed the credibility of a lawyer, but I felt that the two of us together would be what the students needed. That was 1979, I believe. I taught the entire thing, with a colleague. We put together a workbook for the course.

I became popular enough that I was soon approached by a major firm in town to consult as a legal-assistant manager. By this time, law firms were hiring paralegals in numbers, and paralegals at this firm were complaining about being underpaid and overworked, about whether they were part of the professional staff, whether they should be paid overtime, and similar management issues. The firm wanted me to resolve these problems, and I worked there for a year.

During that time, I started Boston University's legal assistant programs. BU had made a commitment to a more complete and comprehensive curriculum, which I designed in compliance with the ABA guidelines. It included a continuing-education component for practicing paralegals and used paralegal/lawyer teaching teams. Interestingly enough, almost ten years later, the paralegal/lawyer team teaching approach gained acceptance by the ABA. Now the ABA encourages paralegals to teach in the classroom. I had gone to the paralegal educators' conferences and made such a big stink about it that they finally accepted it. Now it's a given—there's really no controversy about it.

I also started a paralegal listing in the Yellow Pages in Boston around this time. Mine was the only name under it. More and more paralegals were being educated, and I started receiving resumes. Also, lawyers were calling who needed paralegals; some were even asking me to screen paralegals before they hired them. Out of that, I started a permanent and temporary placement company.

I didn't receive a hundred calls in 1976, but by 1979 I did. When lawyers called me for a freelance service in an area in which I had no expertise, such as litigation, I might have a resume on hand of someone who did have that expertise, so I matched them up. It wasn't as if I had planned all this in advance and put out a shingle thinking, "There's a need for temps." It evolved, and I just continued to market it.

Now, a good 15 years later, I am President of the Paralegal Resource Center, Inc. I have a staff of paralegals who do document retrieval and the like. We get calls from attorneys who need documents or legislative research or anything involving a public record. We obtain whatever they want, on an hourly basis. Right now, I manage those activities. I also have a placement director, who deals with permanent placement requests. We interview and screen candidates for openings in the market.

I am also the director of Boston University's legal assistant programs. I developed not only their certificate program but most recently a bachelor of science program in paralegal studies. We offer both a postgraduate and an undergraduate curriculum. Those are my major commitments.

KZ: That's a lot. You must work an enormous amount of hours.

SW: I have, but I'm trying to quiet down now because I had a baby two and a half years ago. I'm thinking of starting a second career because I feel my first career has almost reached a pinnacle in a certain sense. Where I am now is very comfortable, and professionally I feel very satisfied and successful, but *personally* I never felt as successful or fulfilled as I have since I had my daughter.

KZ: In regard to the Paralegal Resource Center, you said you have a staff of paralegals who go out on assignments. Is this a permanent staff?

SW: Some are permanent and on my payroll. We also use independent contractors. It depends on the assignment. For instance, a real estate assignment involves going to the Registry of Deeds, which requires specialized training, so we contract with title examiners to do that work and they bill the company. If someone needs something at the federal courthouse or the secretary of state's office, I have people on staff to do that.

KZ: How many of those do you have?

SW: I've had up to three full-time persons doing this work. It varies between one and three.

The business climate here for law firms and paralegals is reflective of the general economy. In 1989, 1990, and 1991, things were booming and the demand was there. Now it's following the economy, and we've downsized a bit. But it's consistent, and there certainly is business.

KZ: But you've been able to keep it going for ten years or more.

SW: Yes. What's nice about the company is its three divisions—permanent placement, temporary placement, and services—which keep it stable in the marketplace. When there's a great need for permanent and temporary placement, the services might quiet down because the firms are fully staffed. Now, with downsizing, firms are a bit understaffed and overworked, so we get more calls for paralegal temps and paralegal services. They're delegating to temps or sending the work to us to be done. Sometimes each division of my company goes up and down, but when you add all three areas together, it's a very substantial, consistent business.

KZ: That's very smart of you.

SW: I just responded to the needs of the marketplace. I should mention that we do paralegal work exclusively.

KZ: No legal secretarial?

SW: No, because that was always a concern of mine. In order to professionalize the paralegal position early on, I had to separate the two because everyone was trying to merge them. "I need a legal secretary/paralegal," employers would say. I felt that if I tried to do both, the paralegal profession would lose credibility. I've always stuck to my guns about that.

KƦ: I admire that. What do you think has led to your success?

SW: Several things: not taking no for an answer when I strongly believe in what I'm doing; I have always considered myself to be a professional, and I've always wanted to promote paralegal professionalism. I majored in business administration and psychology for my undergrad degree, and I always felt that I had a business sense. When I entered the paralegal field and saw what it was all about, I realized that law was a business. Certainly, one of the things you learn in the legal field is the business aspect of billing your time. I learned the economies of scale and how paralegals could make a law firm efficient and even be a profit center. Once I learned all of that and looked at it from a business perspective, when I went freelance, it was comfortable to me.

I was totally comfortable with starting my own business. People always say, "What a risk you took," but I didn't see it as a risk. It was just a natural way for me to express myself and perform the best. I perform the best when I'm working for myself and I'm competitive with myself in doing better and better and more and more.

KƦ: What do you see for your future—for yourself and for the profession?

SW: For me, I would like to see early retirement!

KƦ: That sounds great. Although why do I have the feeling that you would get bored if you stayed home and did nothing?

SW: I only mean temporarily, in order to make a transition to my second career, whatever that may be. I think more and more people these days are starting second careers at age forty. Maybe I'll go into some related field, but not exactly what I'm doing now. Perhaps I'll deal more with academia or do writing or consulting. Or I may totally leave the field and find something that interests me. I can't put my finger on what that would be right now, but I would like the time to think and redirect myself.

For the paralegal profession, I see a need for a defined territory in which paralegals could work as professionals. Right now we can only work for lawyers. It would be nice to work side by side and still be independent. That may require certain credentials or certification, but that is where I would like to see paralegals go—more responsibility and independence in delivering legal services to the people who need them desperately, and not allowing the lawyers to have a monopoly.

KƦ: You're talking about limited licensing.

SW: Yes. I think that may be the future. Running a paralegal service, I've learned what a paralegal can do. On top of that, I get more and more calls from the general public asking for paralegals to help with this and that.

Non-Lawyer Practice of Law (or Limited Licensure)

Perhaps the major controversy in the paralegal profession today is whether the role of paralegals should be expanded to enable them to practice law without the supervision of attorneys. Currently, paralegals are not allowed to provide legal services directly to the public (with a few exceptions, such as paralegals who work for administrative agencies). In other words, paralegals can only offer legal services through the attorneys who employ them.

For various reasons, many people think that this situation should be changed. They believe that paralegals should be able to practice law independently, within a particular and very limited area of law, after proving that they have the expertise to do so. Having proven their expertise, paralegals would be granted a limited license to practice law in that area.

Probably no two paralegals have exactly the same opinion on this topic. However, the positions of four major organizations which are highly influential in the paralegal profession sum up the various opinions, as follows:

The American Association for Paralegal Educators (AAfPE) takes perhaps the simplest stance. In its Statement to the ABA Commission on Nonlawyer Practice, the AAfPE said it ". . . takes no position as to whether non-lawyers should be allowed to provide legal representation directly to clients. If it should be determined that some practice should be allowed in limited areas, AAfPE institutions are capable of providing educational programs that would be responsive to the special needs of such a group."

The American Bar Association (ABA) is a powerful national organization of attorneys which has enormous influence over the paralegal profession, primarily because most paralegals are still employed by attorneys. The ABA was so concerned about this issue that it appointed a commission on nonlawyer practice, which held nationwide hearings throughout 1993. The commission's findings are expected in the spring of 1994.

Simply put, the ABA has two opposing concerns: (1) that the public needs to be protected from people who are not fully trained in the law, and (2) that a large percentage of the American public cannot afford legal help. The question then becomes whether any group of people other than attorneys should be allowed to offer legal services to the public. The group that most quickly comes to mind is paralegals. But if they are allowed to practice, how will they be regulated, and what types of legal services will they be allowed to offer?

Of course, some attorneys feel that paralegals can never be trained well enough to offer legal services directly to the public, and if they *were* trained well enough, they'd be attorneys. Some paralegals accuse these attorneys of feeling threatened by paralegals and of being motivated only by the desire to keep their monopoly on the legal field. On the other hand, many attorneys who are concerned about the consequences of bad legal advice are motivated by a genuine concern for public welfare.

Partly because paralegals do not attend law schools and are not *fully* trained in the law, they could charge less for their services than attorneys. Allowing paralegals to offer legal services directly to the public might solve the problem that many Americans face of not being able to afford legal help.

NALA's position is that paralegals should work only under the direct supervision of attorneys. This organization is the author and administrator of the voluntary Certified Legal Assistant (CLA) exam. NALA believes that this exam sets a national standard of paralegal competence and that there is no need for paralegals to progress further into limited licensing.

Critics argue that NALA opposes paralegals offering legal services directly to the public because if that happens, the CLA exam will no longer serve any function and NALA will lose any profits it gains from administering the exam. In other words, if paralegals are allowed to practice law in limited areas on their own, they will have to take an exam in that area of law, which will probably be administered by a company or government agency within their state. Therefore, the CLA exam might become meaningless.

NFPA adopted a resolution in September 1992 which, for the first time, directly supported the idea of limited licensing. In its Resolution 92-M1, NFPA promotes the idea of licensing, and thereby regulating, *all* paralegals, state by state. It also endorses limited licensing (called specialty licensing by NFPA) so that they can offer legal services directly to the public. NFPA ". . . endorses a two-tier regulatory scheme consisting of licensing and specialty licensing programs as its preferred form of regulation. The licensing programs must contain minimum standards and provide for an expanded role of practice for qualifying paralegals, contain provisions for a method of consumer redress, and contain a CLE provision requiring a minimum of 3 hours per year continuing education in a legal or specialty field . . ."

Unfortunately, we have to explain that paralegals work for lawyers only. Once again, it's the monopoly that only lawyers can hire paralegals. Of course, these things are being discussed in committees right now; the non-lawyer practice of law is a big ABA issue, and I hope that if the committees say no, we won't let it die but will keep pushing for it.

I was very active in professional paralegal associations, and I think that opened my eyes to the opportunities for those who enter the field. Regrettably, there is perhaps a little more apathy among paralegals in terms of political activism or concern over their future than there was in the past. I hope that readers of your book who are interested in entering the profession know what professional support groups are available. I would also like paralegals to be globally oriented. That might lead to some support for paralegals here and increase job opportunities.

I want paralegals to be more aware locally, nationally, and internationally as to the opportunities available to them. One way of doing that is to belong to professional paralegal associations and to read literature relative to the profession.

I have to say, though, that relating to law as a business is where I've gained most of my satisfaction, as opposed to practicing law, which I never cared for. I've been very satisfied with the business side.

INTERVIEW P

It was interesting to work up a particular strategy and then get on the phone and tell your lawyers to do it, after asking them if it was a good idea. Six weeks later they'd come back and say, "Well, it worked; we got a judgment." It was also nice to have lawyers call up and say, "These are the three things that we perceive we can do. You tell us which way you want to go." The shoe was on the other foot.

Scott Collister

Company: DataTrace Mortgage Investment Services, Inc.
City: Houston
Department:
Title: Vice President
Salary Range: Too early to tell
Benefits:
   Insurance:
   Financial:
   Vacation:
   Sick time:
   Misc.:   being your own boss!

Previous Work Experience:
Seven years as a paralegal, litigation paralegal, and claims and tort litigation manager with the Air Force. Two years as a litigation paralegal with a private law firm. Four years as a litigation manager and assistant vice president with a bank.

JOB DESCRIPTION:

General Summary

Provide services to the secondary mortgage market.

Principal Duties

Primarily operations oriented—software development and statutory and regulatory compliance.

Males and Minorities in the Paralegal Field

Traditionally, paralegals have been white women, probably because law was long dominated by white males who hired white, female legal secretaries, who then worked their way up to the first paralegal positions. This has not changed enormously, but recent surveys show that the profession is becoming more diverse as males and ethnic minorities enter the field. Most surveys show that women make up between 90 and 95 percent of all paralegals. It is unknown how many of those women are minorities.

Many local professional paralegal organizations are doing their best to make ethnic minorities and males feel welcome in the profession. Some organizations have specialty sections, made up entirely of males or ethnic minorities, which address the needs and promote the professional interests of their members. For example, the Dallas Association of Legal Assistants formed a minority section in 1991, which has the following goals:

1. To increase minority employment in the legal community in the Dallas metroplex area.
2. To encourage networking among minority paralegals.
3. To educate the community on minority involvement and promote the paralegal profession in the community.

It had been thought that as males entered the profession, salaries might increase for *all* paralegals. But the Rocky Mountain Legal Assistant Association was surprised to find in its 1992 Salary and Employment Survey that salaries had increased 6.8 percent between 1990 and 1992 for female paralegals, but had increased 18.1 percent for males during the same period (see Figure 6-2). The greatest disparity occurred among paralegals employed by corporations, where males averaged $8,000 more per year than females!

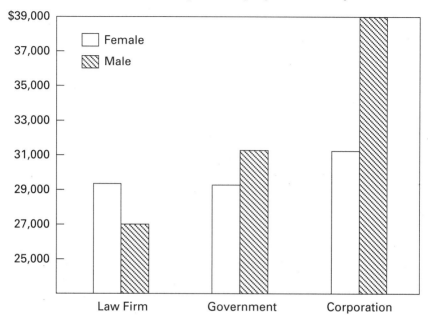

(from 1992 $ Salary and Employment Survey)

Figure 6-2   Average Salaries by Gender and Type of Employer
              (*Courtesy Rocky Mountain Legal Assistant Association*)

SC: I've been a paralegal for about thirteen years. I joined the Air Force in 1980 and went to their legal training school. I had some good jobs and some not so good jobs there, but overall it was an extraordinarily formative experience. I worked initially for a legal office doing general legal assistance for the folks on the base. After two years—I was stationed in England—I went to the headquarters for England, where we processed all the courts martial for the command. It was fascinating; the people there were very good to me and taught me a lot.

After my four-year tour was up, the chief enlisted legal officer for all of Europe asked me to work for him in Germany. I was not going to reenlist for another four years—although it was fun, it wasn't *that* much fun—so they got me an extension for two years, and I went to Germany and worked at the headquarters level in the claims office.

They were having a lot of problems processing their claims, and they needed somebody to streamline everything and whack it back down to size. The kind of work they did there was, say, a household goods claim that a serviceman filed because the Air Force moved him from one base to another and his car got dented. But it could also be medical malpractice claims or "a wrongful death suit" if a jet fighter went down on a training mission.

KT: Anywhere in Europe?

SC: Right. That was a very good job. When I got out of the service, I went to work for a law firm for two years.

KT: Was it a hard transition from the military to a private law firm?

SC: I really wanted to get out of the Air Force because I have a low tolerance for the extraneous things that go on in the service, like adherence to regulation. Surprisingly, though, the transition from military life to civilian life was very hard. I was used to having a security blanket in the military. But I'm a very independent person, and I don't want a security blanket. I want to be out on my own, make it or break it, no guts no glory, that kind of thing. I guess subconsciously we all want a level of security, and you certainly get that in the service.

That transition was hard, but the transition from the legal work we did in the military to the legal work we did at the law firm was not a problem at all. And that's primarily how I viewed that experience—as a transition for me. I came back to Texas, went to work for the law firm, and learned that one motion is called this in the military and called something else in Texas, that the discovery rules are this in the military and that in Texas.

After about two years, as wonderful as the people at the law firm were to me and for me, I came to the conclusion that had I started my paralegal career at a private law firm, I probably would have ended it after two years. I didn't really enjoy it.

KT: Any reasons for that?

SC: They used you on an as-needed basis, and I prefer to work one-on-one with a particular attorney on cases that I know about and can see to some sort of conclusion. I also recognized some of the things that are inherently limiting about our profession, and I saw that there were ways to get around them. However, for me, at least, those ways did not exist at a law firm.

So I got a wonderful job at First Heights Bank, which is a "SouthWest Plan" institution. The "SouthWest Plan" had a provision whereby if you bought a failed savings and loan and agreed to manage the outstanding litigation against it, the FDIC would pay you back. So we essentially managed the litigation for the FDIC.

In-house we didn't do much legal work, but we managed law firms that were doing, say, 200 cases for us. That was fun because we had to submit a litigation plan to the FDIC, laying out what the facts of the suit were, what the allegations were, what our strategy was, and how much it would cost to resolve it.

KT: Sounds fun.

SC: Oh yes! I was given responsibility for certain cases. I got to write up my plans and conduct the lawsuits the way I thought that they ought to be conducted.

KT: You got to follow things through from beginning to end, unlike at the law firm.

SC: Right. It was interesting to work up a particular strategy and then get on the phone and tell your lawyers to do it, after asking them if it was a good idea. Six weeks later they'd come back and say, "Well, it worked; we got a judgment." It was also nice to have lawyers call up and say, "These are the three things that we perceive we can do. You tell us which way you want to go." The shoe was on the other foot.

After three years in the legal department, watching the department grow, I was promoted to the bank training program. They recognize individuals in the bank whom they wanted to pull from "non-banking" areas, such as accounting, or legal, or marketing, and put into the true bank side. I graduated from that program on Wednesday, October first, and I gave my notice on the third.

KT: And that's when I called you.

SC: Yes. I quit to start my own company.

KT: Tell me how that came about.

SC: A friend of mine and his wife run a successful company that does title searches for law firms with foreclosure clients. Since they do research at the courthouse, they also do filings and document retrieval there, and they do all of that on a nationwide basis. They've been very successful for the past five years and they're growing by leaps and bounds.

The new company my wife and I have formed with them will service the secondary mortgage market. Secondary mortgage is a department in a bank that pools the bank's mortgages and sells them to an investor. Sometimes the bank needs documents from the courthouse to perfect the chain of title. For example, a deed of trust may have been filed but is not in the loan file at the bank. We'll get that for them. There's a lot of buying and selling of mortgages, especially with the refinancing craze, so it's become big business. We're hoping to carve a niche for ourselves in doing the job right the first time and getting it right all the time. That entails—and this is what a lot of people say but very few do—providing a level of service that people haven't seen before.

We can do that because of the way we've structured the company and structured the database that we use. We shopped some of our competition today, and one told me, "Here's what we'll do: boom, boom, boom." And then he said. "After I send everything out for recording, you get two reports." Well, we have a client that doesn't want two reports. They want a report every week in a particular format, and that's what they'll get from us. Another client might want something else, and we'll set it up that way. Some of our larger competitors have big computers that nobody on-site knows how to program. It would cost them a lot of money to program the computer to give you a report in the format that you want.

KT: I assume that you write your own programs, then.

SC: Right. I was very fortunate when I went to First Heights. There was one lawyer and one secretary in the department, and the lawyer was try-ing to manage the litigation through a database. He shopped for some soft-ware and picked a consultant who knew everything about computers but nothing about litigation. The lawyer told the consultant what the program should do. The consultant went away and wrote a program, came back, and left. Well, it didn't do exactly everything the lawyer wanted it to. In the meantime, the FDIC's rules for how to manage litigation changed. And then changed again and again.

When I walked in, there was a shell of a database sitting there that was very dusty and musty and old. They'd pretty much abandoned it. I didn't know much about computers, and certainly nothing about data-bases, but I got their permission to play in it and read the books, and I actually found it quite enjoyable—to the point that I was playing with the database when I should have been doing other work. Eventually, we got it to do what we needed it to do, and over the next three years, I was the in-house programming guy.

The upshot is that I'm the programmer for the new company. As one of the owners of the company, I don't have to tell the computer person what to do. You always lose something in the translation when you have to tell a consultant what you need.

KT: How's the company going? Although it's maybe too early to tell, I suppose.

SC: We think it's doing very well. The dynamic of the group—in terms of the experience involved and the way it meshes together—is a large part of what we're about and why it works as well as it does.

My friend and his wife have a lot of title and courthouse experience. His wife also spent some time in the legal field, and she knows several soft-ware programs and does our accounting. My wife worked for a law firm that did high-volume foreclosure work for banks. She was the head of that department. It turns out that the only way they could manage that kind of volume is through a database which just happens to be the same software that we're running. So she is familiar with the software and with supervis-ing a high-volume, deadline-intensive process, which is what our new busi-ness is. About a year and a half ago, she was promoted to Director of client relations for the law firm. So she is now our marketing director.

KT: You have a great combination of people.

SC: Yes.

KT: What was your motivation to go out on your own? I know you were approached by your friend, but do you think you would have gone out on your own someday anyway?

SC: Yes, definitely. The very first class that I took in college was small business management, and that was not an accident. I've been priming myself for self-employment for the past twelve years. My original idea was for a retail business. I did about six months of very hard research and condensed it into a business plan. I took my friend, who is now my partner, to lunch one day to get his opinion as a small-business person. He thought it was a great idea and he had toyed with that idea himself. A week later, I was watching a football game at his house. He started asking me questions, and I started asking him questions. That is when he pitched *his* idea to me, and here we are.

KT: That's wonderful. The skills that you gained in the legal field are so valuable in what you're doing now. I think paralegal skills translate well into other things.

SC: That's a great way of putting it.

I was the president of the Houston Legal Assistant Association in 1992–93. During my term, that was one of my big messages to paralegals. A lot of people think this is a dead-end career, that it's very limiting. If you think it's very limiting, then it will be. Sure, if you work for a law firm for thirty-five years as a paralegal, you're never going to make partner. But there are so many things that you *can* do.

The job I had at First Heights Bank right before I quit was a newly created position. The bank had acquired a commercial bank, and some problems had arisen from that transaction that had not been resolved after six or eight months. They gave me the job of getting rid of those problems because of my ability to look at a problem, work it through, come up with several options, then pick an option for a reason and then articulate it. That, to me, is what being a paralegal is all about.

KT: I can't think of too many other professions that give you the same type of training in writing, analyzing, and organization.

SC: It's very valuable training. You are an obvious example of taking paralegal skills and applying them to something that, although different, is very closely related to paralegal work.

KT: We've talked about skills a little bit, but what personal qualities have helped you be successful?

SC: I'm not sure what the difference is between a skill and a quality, but I'm very organized. I was organized before I became a paralegal, and I was organized before I went into the military. Obviously, that helped me in both cases. Also, I'm very much a goal setter. I went into the military to put myself through college, and I set many goals for myself. I'd never done that before. I purposely asked to be shipped overseas so I could be independent. I had a couple of big goals and worked back down to a couple of intermediate goals. It was rewarding the first time I ever hit a goal, or hit a goal a little early, or hit a goal a little better than I had planned. Then I could look back and see how really easy it was to set a big plan and say, "At age twenty-five I'm going to be here." You just put your head down and work at it and when you look up, boom, you've hit a goal. So you put your head back down, look up, and boom, you've hit another one. Sometimes you look up and you're not going to hit that goal. But you just stop, regroup, set another goal, and press on. I think that's a big part of who I am.

KZ: Do you have any thoughts for the future?
SC: One of my pet peeves is the amount of divisiveness in the profession and the lack of unity.

KZ: NALA and NFPA?
SC: Yes. Last year, our local association commissioned a report on the future of paralegal regulation in this state so we could prepare ourselves for what's coming. Several forms of regulation are being proposed, and at the core of every proposal is higher educational standards for paralegals. The report said that if we increased the minimum education standards for admission to our membership, new members would then be in a position to meet whatever standards are imposed on them by regulations down the road. This made a great deal of sense.

Our association is very close to acting on this recommendation. We got little, if any, objections to higher educational standards, but we argued to the teeth about what those standards should be. We argued to the point that the whole proposal came frighteningly close to being destroyed. That represents what is wrong with this profession. We all agree that we need to get going, but we can't agree on what *size* step we should take. Because of that, we're going to go nowhere. I see that as what has been holding this profession back—we know we need to go forward, but we quibble about how far or how fast we should go. I think we'll get our act together eventually, but had we planned, had we done a little goal setting a couple of years ago, we'd be a lot further along now.

APPENDIX A

Résumés of Interviewees

CARLA Y. BARLOW

CAREER OBJECTIVE: To obtain a position as a paralegal in a corporate office utilizing specialized training and experience.

EMPLOYMENT:

GAYLORD ENTERTAINMENT COMPANY
• **May, 1992 – Present**

Responsibilities include the preparation of contracts for corporate sponsors, concessionaires performers (singers, dancers, etc.), releases and indemnities, corporate documents including but not limited to written consent actions, resolutions, secretary's certificates, meeting notices, etc., corporate filings (i.e. annual reports, foreign qualification, dissolutions, assumed name filings); maintain current list of officers and directors for each corporate entity as well as current mailing addresses; accept service for garnishments and wage assignments, forward to appropriate payroll entity, answer to appropriate court and field any problem related to same; prepare and maintain records for collection of cable and satellite royalties; maintain approximately 250 trademark/service marks. Fill all requests for information as regards to date of first use, provide specimens of use, etc.; assist with preparation of various SEC filings (i.e. proxy statement, S-8's, 10-K, Forms 3, 4 & 5); review and revise as necessary talent contracts.

FIRST AMERICAN NATIONAL BANK
• **October, 1984 – May, 1992**

Experience in the area of corporate law, real estate, litigation, bankruptcy, corporate insurance risk management and office management. Responsibilities include managing corporate legal department with a staff of 20 (including 6 attorneys), supervising 4 secretaries, maintaining law library, systems administrator for Novell network consisting of 14 workstations; acting as assistant risk manager for corporate insurance program, monitoring claims, collecting claims not covered by insurance, preparing renewal applications, etc.; paralegal duties, including but not limited to preparing regulatory reports (SEC filings, Federal Reserve filings and Comptroller of the Currency filings), preparing applications for branch openings and closings as well as corporate reorganizations, acquisitions and mergers. Responsible for preparing annual budget and maintaining monthly accounting of budget variances. (Copy of description of duties attached for more detailed information.)

• **October, 1981 – October, 1984**

Legal Secretary for 2 lawyers, Legal Department, performing legal secretarial duties as well as collecting over 500 judgments. Also performed office management duties including the annual budget and preparing regulatory filings.

• **July, 1976 – October, 1981**

Secretary to Director of Systems and Programming performing general secretarial duties.

CARLA Y. BARLOW *(Continued)*

THIRD NATIONAL BANK – September, 1971 – May, 1976

Secretary for manager of Collateral Department performing general secretarial duties and monitoring collateral pledged to secure loans. Monitoring including reviewing notes on a daily basis and evaluating pledged collateral (i.e. stock prices, life insurance cash values, etc.)

METHODIST PUBLISHING HOUSE – April, 1969 – March, 1970

Bookkeeping machine operator responsible for posting payments to accounts payable and balancing accounts at month-end prior to issuing checks.

EDUCATION:

1984 – Southeastern Paralegal Institute
1963–1967 – Livingston Academy High School

Continuing education includes various night classes and professional seminars in various areas of law.

PROFESSIONAL ACTIVITIES:

Primary Representative to national affiliate association (NFPA) – 1992/93
President – 1990 and 1991
Chairman, Continuing Education Committee – 1989
Served on Continuing Education Committee – 1988
Member Middle Tennessee Paralegal Association 1986 to present

DONNA MARIE BARR

HIGHLIGHTS OF QUALIFICATIONS

*Nearly 15 years experience in real estate/property management
*Work well under pressure and thrive on challenging projects
*Excellent organization, communication and writing skills
*Able to establish priorities and adapt quickly to changing needs
*Proven record of dependability with increasing responsibility

RELEVANT EXPERIENCE

Real Estate
*Drafted all documents in connection with commercial, agricultural and residential real estate transactions
*Handled all aspects of real estate closings
*Reviewed and evaluated title work, surveys, and appraisals in connection with real estate transactions
*Researched legal and factual issues for real property and water rights
*Conducted negotiations with title companies, opposing counsel and principals

Property Management
*Supervised leasing/maintenance staff for 200–400 apartment/commercial units
*Coordinated construction and leasing for new and remodeled units
*Purchased maintenance supplies and office equipment

Administration and Management
*Supervised daily operations of 150 person law firm, including operation of copy center and mailroom, purchasing, messengers and conference scheduling
*Recruited high caliber personnel: faculty members, leasing and maintenance staff, legal assistants and non-professional support staff
*Developed and implemented orientation program for new employees
*Effectively allocated staff resources
*Hired, evaluated, and terminated staff
*Conducted seminars and training programs on numerous topics

Litigation
*Successfully handled over 25 pending real estate litigation cases simultaneously
*Drafted pleadings for judicial foreclosures and actions to quiet title
*Assisted at client meetings and trials
*Organized trial exhibits

Corporate
*Prepared articles of incorporation, by-laws, corporate minutes and resolutions, and UCC forms
*Conducted UCC and corporate searches
*Developed and maintained control system for corporate clients

DONNA MARIE BARR *(Continued)*

WORK HISTORY

6/92–Present	Real Estate Paralegal Archdiocese of Denver, Denver, Colorado
9/89–6/92	Real Estate Paralegal/Office Services Supervisor/Paralegal Supervisor Kirkland & Ellis, Denver, Colorado
9/86–present	Part-time Instructor (Real Estate Law, Legal Writing, Law Office Administration and Introduction to Paralegal) Community College of Aurora, Aurora
4/85–9/89	Real Estate Paralegal/Paralegal Coordinator Kutak Rock & Campbell, Denver, Colorado
4/83–4/85	Real Estate Paralegal Kirkland & Ellis, Denver, Colorado
7/82–4/83	Real Estate Litigation Paralegal Carlsmith, Carlsmith, Wichman & Case, Hilo, Hawaii
7/80–7/82	Corporate and Real Estate Paralegal/Office Manager Dixon & Okura, Hilo, Hawaii
3/79–6/79 1/80–4/80	Administrative Clerk, Legal Department U.S. Small Business Administration, Honolulu, Hawaii (Temporary Positions)
10/76–12/78	Property Manager Creative Restoration, Millhouse Redevelopments and Simoni & Heck, Houston, Texas

EDUCATION

University of Houston, M.A. in Public Administration, 1976
University of Houston, B.A. in English, 1973, Magna Cum Laude

CURRENT COMMUNITY LEADERSHIP AND PROFESSIONAL AFFILIATIONS

*Vice Chair/Board of Adjustment and Appeals for City of Longmont
*Volunteer Mediator with the Longmont Community Relations Office
*Officer/Director of Rocky Mountain Legal Assistants Association
*Pro Bono Committee/National Federation of Paralegal Associations

References available upon request

JO BARRETT

PROBATE PARALEGAL

SUMMARY OF QUALIFICATIONS:

Certified probate paralegal with over 20 years of experience in the probate area.

Offering in-depth experience in the administration of estates and estate tax including:

-PREPARATION OF FIDUCIARY ACCOUNTS
-ESTATE AND INCOME TAX PREPARATION
-VALUATION OF SECURITIES
-ADMINISTRATION OF ESTATES
-FILE MANAGEMENT
-COURT FILINGS

Utilizing computer software for fiduciary accounts and estate tax returns.

PROFESSIONAL EXPERIENCE:

Free-lance paralegal - October 1, 1990 to present
-working with sole practitioners and small firms not requiring a full-time probate paralegal on staff
-working with medium and large firms not requiring a full-time probate paralegal on staff, and doing overflow work and filling-in during vacations and illness of employees

BRICKER & ECKLER - Probate Paralegal (1973–1990)
Responsible for administration of estates including: meeting with clients and attorney at initial interview to obtain asset and debt information; preparation of all probate court and estate tax documents; obtain estate tax releases; transfer and/or sell securities; prepare income tax projections; arrange for private sale or auction of personal property; meet with appraisers and realtors regarding valuation and/or sale of real property; handle estate's bank accounts including investments during administration

EDUCATION:

Graduate - Capital University Law School,
Certified Legal Assistant Program - Probate Specialty (1973)

ACTIVITIES:

Legal Assistants of Central Ohio - (a founder, past president, secretary, served on numerous committees - 1990 Outstanding Member), Advisory Board - 1992

Capital University Law Center, Certified Legal Assistant Association - Member of Board of Advisors (1984–1991)

Capital University Law Center, Certified Legal Assistant Alumni Association - Board Member and Co-Chairman, Scholarship Committee
Columbus Bar Association - Associate Member
Probate Law Committee
Lawyer/Legal Assistant Committee
UPL Committee

Ohio State Bar Association - Associate Member

SCOTT J. COLLISTER

Experience

Oct 93– Present	**Principal** DataTrace Mortgage Investment Services, Inc. Houston, Texas Provide nationwide services to investors in the secondary mortgage market.

Sept 89– Litigation Manager/Assistant Vice President

Sept 93   First Heights Bank fsb   Houston, Texas
Managed the conduct of a caseload of over 100 lawsuits filed for and against this Southwest Plan institution. Responsibilities include development and implementation of case strategy and administration, control of legal fees and supervision of fee counsel. Responsible for the completion of all litigation reporting to Senior Management, the Board of Directors and banking regulators. Developed computer databases for litigation and bankruptcy case tracking and reporting, docketing/calendar, and payment and reporting of legal fees. Selected by Senior Management for promotion into the Executive Training Program.

Aug 1987– **Litigation Paralegal**   Houston, Texas
Aug 1989   Richie & Greenberg, P.C.
Prepared pleadings, discovery documents and trial materials, including case summaries, trial notebooks and exhibits. Assisted at client interviews, meetings, trials and depositions. Performed factual and legal research, including public records searches. Document organization and deposition summaries. Performed skip tracing of defendants and asset searches. Other paralegal assistance as required.

Sept 1984– **Claims & Tort Litigation Manager**
July 1987   Headquarters, United States Air Force in Europe   Ramstein, Germany
Supervised the adjudication of claims filed for and against the United States under various statutes, regulations, NATO Status of Forces Agreement and other agreements with foreign governments. Directed $7 million annual budget for the payment of claims, including distribution, budgeting, forecasting and trend analysis. Supervised department staff. Developed policies and procedures for the prompt and efficient adjudication and processing of claims. Supervised the operations of 32 subordinate claims offices and provided policy and training for their personnel. Promoted ahead of contemporaries.

Aug 1982   **Litigation Paralegal**
Aug 1984   Headquarters, Third Air Force   Mildenhall, England
Examined the completed records of trial and nonjudicial punishment actions from 9 subordinate jurisdictions for legal sufficiency and technical detail and prepared records of trial for appellate review. Maintained trial docket for all trials in the jurisdiction. Supervised operations of 8 subordinate jurisdictions and provided policy and training for their personnel. Performed as law librarian for the international law library. Promoted ahead of contemporaries.

SCOTT J. COLLISTER *(Continued)*

Dec 1980 July 1982	**Paralegal**

Headquarters, 513th Tactical Airlift Wing   Mildenhall, England

Maintained legal calendar and trial docket. Implemented the course of preparation for trials, investigations and hearings. Processed and adjudicated claims for and against the Government. Monitored the trial of US military personnel in foreign courts for compliance with the NATO Status of Forces Agreement and related statutes. Assisted attorneys in the rendering of legal assistance, researched points of law and performed as law librarian. Performed as court reporter at legal proceedings. Promoted ahead of contemporaries.

Education   **College of the Air Force** – Degree in Paralegal Studies awarded August 1984.

Professional   **Immediate Past President, Houston Legal Assistants Association.**
Affiliations   **State Bar of Texas, Legal Assistants Division**, member since 1991.
Advisory Board Member & Adjunct Instructor, University of Houston-Downtown.

Mary Kelly Finegan

EDUCATION

Chestnut Hill College
Philadelphia, Pennsylvania
Program: English Literature/History School
Bachelor of Art awarded *cum laude*, May 1986

Cambridge University
Cambridgeshire, England
Program: University of New Hampshire Summer Study in English Literature
Scholarship and course credits awarded, August 1985

SPECIAL ACHIEVEMENTS

Appointed to the position of National Pro Bono Co-Coordinator, National Federation of Paralegal Associations, May 1993.

Elected to the Board of Directors, Philadelphia Association of Paralegals, November 1989, November 1990, November 1991 (Executive Committee), November 1992 (Executive Committee).

Subject of interview, *"Pro Bono Publico:* A Career of Service," *Legal Assistant Today,* September/October 1992.

Subject of interview, "Paralegals Use Their Heads and Hearts in *Pro Bono* Programs," *National Paralegal Reporter,* Vol. 15, No. 2, Fall 1990.

Subject of interview, "The Use of Paralegals," *New York Law Journal,* August 20, 1990.

Subject of interview, "VIP Provides Outlet for Frustration," *The Legal Intelligencer,* March 20, 1990.

Article published, "An Overview of the Volunteers for the Indigent Program," *The Legal Intelligencer,* March 14, 1990.

Subject of interview, *"Pro Bono* Opportunities for Paralegals," *The Legal Intelligencer,* March 7, 1990.

Subject of interview, "Spotlight on Mary Kelly Finegan, a VIP Paralegal, "*The Paralegal Forum,* November/December 1989.

EMPLOYMENT

Philadelphia Volunteers for the Indigent Program (VIP)
Philadelphia, Pennsylvania
Paralegal/Program Coordinator – April 1989 to Present

* Assesses client files in litigation, bankruptcy, real estate, tax, corporate law, intellectual property, immigration and other major areas of civil law for issues and possible legal remedies
* Negotiates with opposing counsel for extensions of time or dismissals of suit
* Recruits volunteer attorneys and paralegals from all major Philadelphia law firms

Mary Kelly Finegan *(Continued)*

* Prepares and files responsive pleadings
* Arranges support services for volunteer attorneys
* Utilizes computer database and word processing programs to track volunteers and cases to their conclusion
* Plans and coordinates Continuing Legal Education courses at the Philadelphia Bar Association in substantive law and legal practice in the areas noted above
* Performs in an administrative capacity as required

Schnader. Harrison, Segal & Lewis
Philadelphia, Pennsylvania
Litigation Paralegal - January 1988 to April 1989

* Assisted the firm's trial lawyers in all stages of commercial litigation, including legal research and the creation and management of document banks in large document cases
* Supported the firm's Domestic Relations Department through research, discovery and trial preparation
* Performed administrative duties including billing, accounting and training
* Served as special assistant to the firm's Associates' Committee

Electronic Data Systems (EDS)
Bethesda, Maryland
Technical Publications Coordinator – 1987

* Coordinated graphics elements of EDS' contract proposals to the federal government and the armed services to design and implement comprehensive software systems
* Designed, proofed and edited graphics and text, set printing dates and established schedule for completion

Complete references and writing samples will be made available upon request.

David L. Hay

SUMMARY

Professional, detailed individual with over ten years experience in legal and administrative positions. Strong research and investigative capabilities. Works independently with little direction. Follows-through with persistence to get the job done. Proven ability in handling difficult situations with utmost professionalism. Provide excellent interpersonal skills in communicating effectively with clients/customers at all levels.

EDUCATION

Associates in Applied Science (Legal Assistant Program), 1989, El Centro College, Dallas, TX

EXPERIENCE

1/90 to Present   *Dallas County Community College*
                   District Office   Dallas, TX

Legal Assistant

Assist in-house attorney with legal matters. Research, investigate, analyze, summarize and manage case files. Oversee and coordinate DCCCD Board of Trustee elections. Independently organize, draft and revise legal documents. Follow-up on cases representing attorney in his absence.

9/86 to 12/89   *El Centro College*   Dallas, TX

Student

Enrolled in Legal Assistant Program. Area of study: Civil Litigation, Wills, Trust & Probate, Torts, Research and Family Law.

During this period worked Pro Bono for Legal Services of North Texas as Legal Assistant and City Attorney's Office as Legal Intern. Responsibilities included interviewing low income residents, preparing pleading forms, summarizing depositions, and maintaining case files.

12/86 to 3/87   *Erhard, Ruebel & Jennings*   Dallas, TX

Legal Secretary

Analyzed, controlled and prepared legal documents. Researched and investigated location of missing persons. Maintained court calendar for attorneys.

David L. Hay *(Continued)*

9/85 to 11/86   *Life Insurance Company of the Southwest*   Dallas, TX

Word Processor

Directed department personnel in proper techniques and style of correspondence and summaries. Assisted subordinates in resolving nonstandard problems and situations. Edited and proofread source documents, correspondence, company records and statistical tables to ensure accuracy and compliance to format specifications. Acted as liaison interacting with customers to clarify instructions and determine document specifications.

3/77 to 1/84   *Wisconsin Novelty Company*   Milwaukee, WI

Administrative Assistant

Analyzed department problems and recommended changes in procedures to save company time, labor costs, and improve operating efficiency. Evaluated job performance of department personnel and recommended appropriate personnel action to management. Reviewed and researched client requests; provided customer service; coordinated and supervised field service personnel. Handled business correspondence and bookkeeping activity.

COMPUTER EXPERIENCE

PC and mainframe
WordPerfect 5.1
WANG word processor

ORGANIZATIONS

Dallas Association for Legal Assistants – board member

JANIS LEWIS JONES

PROFESSIONAL EXPERIENCE

NOV 1987 – PRESENT   *Senior Legal Administrator*
Toyota Motor Sales, U.S.A., Inc., Torrance

Evaluate factual and legal merits of new warranty/Lemon Law litigation; determine appropriate strategy and coordinate defense of cases with outside counsel; negotiate settlements; respond to subpoenas for corporate records; assist by providing company information and documents on dealer business litigation; provide training to Regional personnel on consumer/Lemon Law litigation; legal and factual research.

JUL 1986 – NOV 1987   *Entertainment Litigation Paralegal*
Lavely & Singer, Century City

Drafted pleadings and discovery documents including complaints, subpoenas, notices and responses to requests for production. Also interviewed clients and witnesses coordinated depositions and documents productions, and assisted with trial preparation.

MAR 1983 – JUL 1986   *Litigation & Entertainment Paralegal*
Gang, Tyre & Brown, Hollywood

As music publishing administrator, registered copyrights, negotiated and drafted co-publishing agreements, foreign sub publishing agreements, and mechanical and synchronization licenses. Also incorporated and maintained clients corporations; communicated with clients and their agents. Assisted in entertainment-related litigation matters; supervised document productions, computerized evidence, and performed legal research.

AUG 1980 – MAR 1983   *Litigation Paralegal*
Paul, Hastings, Janofsky & Walker, Los Angeles

Assisted in multiple major litigation cases; organized and computerized documentary evidence, analyzed factual data, prepared for and assisted at trial, summarized depositions and performed legal research.

AUG 1979 – JUN 1980   *Legal Services Coordinator*
Public Counsel, Los Angeles

Interviewed clients, legal aid attorneys and volunteer attorneys to coordinate legal representation for indigent clients.

EDUCATION

JUN 1980   **University of Southern California**
Bachelor of Arts Degree – Communications Arts and Sciences

JUN 1980   **University of Southern California**
Paralegal Certificate

Related courses, electives and continuing education: Legal Interviewing and Counseling, Advanced Legal Research, Ethics, Franchising Law, Advanced California Civil Litigation, California Partnerships and Corporations, Debate, Persuasion, Public Speaking, and Negotiating.

AFFILIATIONS:

Faculty and Advisory Board Member – Southern California College of Business and Law, Brea, CA – 1992 to present.

Los Angeles Paralegal Association – Member since 1980; Coordinator, Pro Bono Committee Annual Food and Clothing Drive, 4 years.

KATHLEEN M. KLIMA

HIGHLIGHTS OF QUALIFICATIONS:

* Ability to absorb and apply newly acquired knowledge quickly
* Experience with Word Perfect 5.1 and Multi Mate
* Well organized, punctual, and diligent
* Adaptable to new experiences

EXPERIENCE:

Loan Secretary:
* Order and review flood certificates
* Prepare package for small business loans to be submitted to the SBA
* Type closing documents
* Assist loan processor and loan officers as necessary to expedite loan closing

Paralegal:
* Researched Colorado Revised Statutes to evaluate accuracy of quotations in office procedural manual
* Calculated debt due for arrears in child support cases
* Generated general correspondence to clients and administrative offices
* Reviewed client files in response to information requests
* Experienced with client interviews

General:
* Skilled in customer relations and service
* Trained cashiers in cash and credit transactions
* Performed light office duties including typing, filing, copying, and creating tickler files

EMPLOYMENT HISTORY:

THE MONEY STORE INVESTMENT CORPORATION, Aurora, CO	Loan Secretary	Present
DISTRICT ATTORNEYS OFFICE FAMILY SUPPORT DIVISION, Englewood, CO	Paralegal Intern	1993 Spring
GLASSROCK HOME HEALTH CARE, Aurora, CO	Temporary	1990 Fall
BEST PRODUCTS, Houston, TX	Customer service	1986–1987

EDUCATION AND TRAINING:

COMMUNITY COLLEGE OF AURORA, Aurora, CO
   Associates of General Studies, (GPA 3.8)   1993
   Paralegal Certificate, ABA approved, (GPA 4.0)   1993

* Family Law	* Real Estate
* Business Organization	* Litigation
* Legal Writing	* Torts
* Law Office Administration	* Legal Research

WESTLAW Training Center, Denver, CO
   WESTLAW Certificate
Continuing Education for Associates of Arts

REFERENCES UPON REQUEST

MARIAN J. MILLER

EMPLOYMENT HISTORY:

September 1988-
Present

Legal Administrator, City & Borough Law Department
City & Borough of Juneau, Juneau, AK 99801

Personal assistant to City & Borough Attorney and supervisor of two legal secretaries. Assist attorneys with litigation, legislative drafting, legal document preparation,
and administrative appeals. Administer law department,
including yearly evaluation of support staff and budget
preparation and administration. Maintain records system
of CBJ legislation. Respond to citizen and staff inquiries for
information.

Major accomplishments include conversion of CBJ
Code to electronic media, creating a mining resource
notebook, organizing discovery documentation for major lawsuit, and creating CBJ committees table.

September 1985-
September 1988

Legal Secretary II, City & Borough Law Department
City & Borough of Juneau, Juneau, AK 99801

Administered law department, including accounts payable and annual budget preparation. Assisted attorneys
with legal document preparation, litigation, administrative appeals, and alcohol commitments. Prepared collection documents. Compiled, subpoenaed witnesses,
and tracked traffic court trials. Maintained CBJ Law Department records system. Responded and researched
citizen and staff inquiries for information.

Major accomplishments include creation and establish-
ment of records retention policy and compiling a CBJ
fees notebook.

April 1983-
1984

Legal Secretary I, City & Borough Law Department
City & Borough of Juneau, Juneau, AK 99801

Assisted CBJ prosecutor with criminal prosecution files
including compiling files, keeping calendar of court ap-
pearances, confirming court docket, gathering police
reports, sending subpoenas, contacting witnesses, preparing jury trial notebooks, and maintaining criminal file
records.

Major accomplishments include setting up procedure
for court trials, creating system for retaining prosecution
records.

MARIAN J. MILLER *(Continued)*

OTHER ACTIVITIES:

1993	Co-chair, City & Borough of Juneau Employee Council (elected representative)
1991	Nominee for Alaska Municipal League Excellence in Local Government Award
1990	Alaska Municipal Clerk's Association Conference Seminar Speaker regarding Codification
1989	Association of Records Managers and Administrators Continuing Education Program

MEMBERSHIPS:

1984-1993	Juneau Legal Assistants Association (held various officer positions)

EDUCATION:

1991	Associate Degree-Paralegal Studies University of Alaska Southeast Juneau, AK 99801
1976–77 &1982–83	Undergraduate Studies—Prelaw Michigan State University East Lansing, MI
1982–83	Undergraduate Studies—Business Administration Lansing Community College Lansing, MI

REFERENCES: Available upon request

ROSIE J. ODUM

CAREER OBJECTIVE:

To utilize legal skills in communications, research and organizational ability for work as a paralegal.

BUSINESS EXPERIENCE:

Sept '92–present   **FEDERAL EXPRESS CORPORATION**
Memphis, TN 38132

Dept: **Legal/Customer Support Group**
2005 Corporate Ave
Associate Paralegal

Research, prepare trademark applications, keep track of trademark tracking system, keep track of all corporate international data systems, prepare certificates for bank guarantees, prepare resolutions, research trademarks, work with marketing on ad system, research infringement matters.

Nov '87 – Sept '92   **FEDERAL EXPRESS CORPORATION**
Memphis, TN 38132

Dept: **Legal/Business Transactions Group**
2005 Corporate Avenue
Secretary V

Compiling data and generating special reports; coordinating closing documents for aircraft sale/leaseback financing; minimal drafting of amendments/contracts under manager's supervision; research; organize files; minimal support to lawyers and paralegals on respective LOD/POD calls; excellent communications skills with outside vendors, customers and or counsel; administering company policies and procedures relative to performance reviews, salary administration, personnel issues and timely flow of paperwork; composing correspondence.

Dept: **Corporate/EDP Audit**
2099 Directors Row, Memphis, TN
Temporary Secretary/FEC Clerical Pool

Performed secretarial and all other related clerical duties for the Audit Dept.

Dept: **Crew Resource Scheduling**
Temporary Secretary/FEC Clerical Pool

ROSIE J. ODUM *(Continued)*

Answer and screen telephone calls; arrange reservations, transportation and catering for crew members; operate CRT to retrieve information on flights for crew members; check deadhead airline tickets for accuracy of outgoing flights; maintain 90 Day File (total flight time); compile and calculate daily list of Open Time indicating positions to be filled for specific flights; assist in flight revisions, copy/distribute revisions to all appropriate departments; update current revisions on bulletin board in Crew Lounge; sort and distribute mail to crew members; knowledge of GMT (Greenwich Mean Time) required to determine local departure and arrival time for national flights.

April '87 – Oct '87   **INTERCHECKS**, Memphis, TN
Data Entry Clerk

Entered data on computer, proofread check for accuracy prior to shipping, and boxed checks.

Dec '86 – March '87   **MIDWEST FEDERAL SAVING BANK,** Minot, ND
Clerk

Sorted and counted checks, folded, sorted, weighed, stamped and mailed statements.

May '84 – Sept '86   **BIG RAY'S STORE**, Fairbanks, AK
Secretary

Handled business correspondence, typed letters, prepared reports, entered data on computer, verified and handled bad checks, prepared bulk mail-catalogs, opened and sorted the mail, took postage meter to have refilled, made copies, prepared the payroll, opened and closed the store, sold and displayed merchandise, prepared inventory, bookkeeping, daily business deposits, including counting the money and depositing it, send messages back and forth on telex, traveled to Anchorage to help with preparation of their computer, assisted the managers in managing the personnel, bought store and office supplies, filing, and prepared invoices.

EDUCATIONAL ACHIEVEMENTS:

Certificate of Paralegal-Legal Assistant, National Association for Paralegal Studies, Christian Brothers University, Sept. 1990–June, 1991.

Completed **CPS Course Review I and II**, State Technical Institute, October 24, 1989.

Certificate of Clerical Training, Northwest Mississippi Junior College, Senatobia, MS 38668, May, 1983.

High School Diploma, Horn Lake High School, Horn Lake, MS 38637, May, 1981.

REFERENCES: Will be furnished upon request.

ROSIE J. ODUM *(Continued)*

SIGNIFICANT ACCOMPLISHMENTS

Listed below are major projects on which I have assisted attorneys in the Legal Department. I have also listed other activities in the Department and awards that I have received in recognition of my contributions.

PROJECTS:

Aircraft Financing

- Compiled and organized closing documents for the sale/leaseback of eight (8) 747-100 aircraft with Polaris Holding Company resulting in proceeds of $200 million to the Company and favorable short term leases.

- Compiled and organized closing documents in sale/leasebacks of over $800 million of DC-10, B727 and B747 aircraft and eight (8) Valsan-modified B727-2S2Fs.

- Responsible for gathering and compiling information related to the Company's aircraft financing (Report for Leased Aircraft). This document allows easy access to the following information:

    -the owner of all lease airframes and engines;
    -owner participant;
    -debt participants;
    -file number; and
    -date of the agreement.

    This document will also allow easier access to generate closing documents for impending aircraft financing.

Other Transactions

- Assisted Sandra Mabry, paralegal with the organization of the booklet identifying annual aircraft opinion due dates.

- Assisted the International Group with the preparation of consents and research.

- Organized a Newhire Procedures Notebook for the Legal Department to assist in the preparation of all Newhire paperwork.

- Responsible for organizing the 1st Secretarial Meeting for FY'93 with 90% participation from the secretaries in the Legal Department.

    Participated in a one-day seminar for LEXIS training.

QATs

- Aircraft Documents; Filing Procedures
- Rewrite of the Profit Manual
- Organization of the Contract Files
- Committee for BTG's retreats, birthdays and anniversaries
- Wang Systems

ROSIE J. ODUM *(Continued)*

Committees

- Member of the Quality Deployment Team
- Member of the Legal Department's Newsletter Committee
- Member of the Suggestion Award Committee
- Member of the Thanksgiving Committee
- Member of the Christmas Party Committee, past two years

AWARDS:

Superior Rating (8) - March, 1992

Bravo Zulus

- Recognized by Harry Dalton and James Whitworth for assistance on contract matters and by Ed Wiley for work on aircraft matters
- MD-11 Leveraged Leases, July, 1991
- 727-2S2F Aircraft Financing, August, 1990
- 747-200F Sale/Leaseback, October, 1989
- Flying Tiger Line, Inc., June, 1989

VOLUNTEER WORK:

Participated in the Adopt-a-School program for the 1991 school year at Booker T. Washington High School.

Participated in the 7th Annual Junior Achievement Bowl-a-Thon sponsored by Federal Express Corporation.

Member of the Civic Affairs Corporate Neighbor Team of Federal Express Corporation, assisting the martin Luther King Center and the National Civil Rights Museum.

LYNDI S. REED

EXPERIENCE

11/92 to Present **Administrator, Corporate Real Estate**
Diebold, Incorporated, Canton, OH

Responsible for management of all corporate real estate activity including relocation, expansion/downsizing, site selection when necessary, lease negotiation and lease administration in approximately 430 cities in the United States and Europe including 101 branch facilities, 300 storage facilities and 56,000 square feet of office space. Financial responsibility exceeds $8,000,000 annually. Member of three Quality Improvement Teams - Energy, Security & Branch Relocation & Closing. Saved over $30,000 in storage fees during 1993.

8/88 – 11/92 **Freelance Paralegal/Insurance Agent**
Self-Employed, Canton, OH
Independent Insurance Agent

Responsible for entire agency operations, generation of leads, follow up, presentation, sale and service for insurance needs relative to group and individual health, life, disability and annuities.

Freelance Paralegal
Major responsibilities include collections for Attorney General's Office for delinquent taxes and Workers' Compensation premiums. Preparation of personal injury cases up to trial/settlement. Real Estate closings, Incorporations, Mergers and Acquisitions, Probate and Office Management.

8/89 – 4/90 **Information Clerk - Emergency Temporary**
City of Canton - Police Department, Canton, OH

Major responsibilities include interview and preparation of statements/reports for theft, criminal damage, missing persons, assault, juvenile, motor vehicle theft and vehicle impound. Clerical responsibilities for shift supervisors and patrol officers. Screening and handling all incoming telephone calls and complainants on station. Distribution of radios and guns to patrol officers.

5/87 – 1/88 **Vice President**
Career Studies Institute, North Canton, OH

Major responsibilities include development and restructuring of new and existing education programs; placement of graduates, recruitment of students; retaining instructors; development of public relations with governmental agencies and area businesses.

LYNDI S. REED *(Continued)*

3/81 – 5/87   **Paralegal**
                     GenCorp, Inc./General Tire, Fairlawn, OH

Major responsibilities included preparation of cases in antici-
pation of trial; development of evidence and answers to discovery requests; interviewing witnesses; formation, training,
and supervision of discovery teams for company wide document searches and deposition abstracting; liaison between
excess insurance carriers and law department; research, design and implementation of manual systems for adaptation to
computer systems; interfaced with in-house counsel, outside
counsel, company personnel, and governmental agencies; legal research - manual and LEXIS/NEXIS. Responsible for contract review and signature approvals for 84 GT Service stores
including any litigation these facilities were involved in. Responsibilities encompassed the areas of product liability, personal injury, workers' compensation, property damage, toxic
tort, antitrust, real estate and EEOC.

12/78 – 3/81   **Paralegal**
                     Wead & Murphy, Bucyrus, OH

Major responsibilities included handling cases from initial client interview to settlement or trial. Responsibilities encompassed the areas of criminal law, personal injury, real estate,
medical malpractice, probate, domestic relations, and workers' compensation.

EDUCATION   Quality Management Training - 1993 - Diebold

                     Producing Results With Others - 1993 - Diebold

                     ADA Compliance Seminar - 1993 - NACORE

                     Management Orientation Training - 1993 - Diebold

                     Word Perfect Advanced Training - 1993 - Diebold

                     Q & A Training - 1993 - Diebold

                     NACORE Atlantic Conference - 1993

                     Principles & Practice of Real Estate
                     Stark Technical College - 1993

                     Interpersonal Managing Skills - 1993 - Diebold

                     Process Improvement - 1993 - Diebold

                     Self Esteem & Peak Performance
                     Career Track Seminar - 1993

                     AD Bankers & Co. Insurance School, Akron, OH
                     Life, Health, Accident & Annuities - 1991

LYNDI S. REED *(Continued)*

Ohio Paralegal Institute, Canton, OH
Specialty - Civil Litigation _ 1978

Philadelphia Institute for Paralegal Training
Courses - Discovery & Trial Preparation, Computer Literacy,
and Antitrust - 1980 – 1984

GenCorp, Inc./The General Tire & Rubber Co.
Courses - Put It In Writing, Understanding Data Processing,
Human Issues in Management, WANG, Displayrite3, Word
Perfect, Mead Data Central LEXIS/NEXIS & CompuServe

MEMBERSHIPS AND VOLUNTEER ACTIVITY

1992 – Present	International Association of Corporate Real Estate Executives (NACORE) - Member
1993 – Present	National Association of Legal Assistants - Member
1987 – Present	First Class Food Co-Op - Member 1989 – 1990 - Board Trustee 1989 – 1991 - Produce Coordinator 1988 – 1990 - Coordinator 1988 – 1991 - Newsletter Editor
1987 – 1990	Walnut Woods School, Greensburg, OH - Co-Founder 1990–1991 - Board Secretary
1987 – 1988	Akron Bar Association, Akron, OH - Member Committee Affiliation - Computer Research & Law Office Management
1987	Academy of Court Reporting - Instructor Introduction to Paralegalism - 12 Weeks
1987– 1988	Women's Network - Member
1986 – 1989	Northeastern Ohio Paralegal Association Co-Founder & Member 1986 – 1988 - President 1993 – Present - Member
1978 – 1985	Cleveland Association of Paralegals - Member 1984 – 1985 - Board of Trustees 1984 – 1985 - Chairperson - Professional Development Committee
1979 – 1981	Big Brother Association - Bucyrus, OH - Member 1980 – 1981 - Vice President 1979 – 1980 - Trustee
1979 – 1981	Friends of Crawford County, Bucyrus, OH Guardian Ad Litem for Juvenile & Probate Court

KATHY GEDEON SCOTT

PROFESSIONAL   **THE PHILADELPHIA INSTITUTE**
EXPERIENCE: Philadelphia, PA 1991 – Present
Director, Career Development Center

Responsible for management of department and staff. Create and conduct career instruction seminars to all students on trimester basis. Perform one-on-one career counseling to all students. Promotion and marketing of Institute through public relations activities, including attendance at various Legal Association and Civic Organization functions. Speaking engagements. Publication of articles and press releases. Coordination of special projects with Executive Director and Dean. Comprehensive individual employment counseling assistance to entire student body. Editor of Institute Newsletter.

ENTERPRISE RESOURCES, INC.
Philadelphia, PA 1990 – 1991
Manager - Philadelphia Region

Responsible for all administration, marketing, recruiting and temporary and permanent personnel assignments for paralegals, legal assistants, legal secretaries, and general office services positions. Served the needs of existing law firm and corporate clients and solicited and retained new client organizations. Responsible for all aspects of office management. Speaking engagements and articles on various management and professional topics.

THE PHILADELPHIA ASSOCIATION OF PARALEGALS
Philadelphia, PA 1989 – 1990
Executive Director

Coordinated all activities for this 1,000 member organization. Handled all telephone contact and directed membership efforts. Maintained member database for entire Association. Participated in all monthly committee and Board meetings. Personal guidance and direction to volunteer Board of Director and Committee Chairmen. Speaker at numerous programs for law firms, corporations, civic organizations, and area schools. Coordinated and lectured at National Conference of Paralegals. Produced numerous published articles on motivation and management.

KATHY GEDEON SCOTT *(Continued)*

BLANK, ROME, COMISKY & MC CAULEY
Philadelphia, PA 1984 – 1989
Tax and Corporate Paralegal
Paralegal Firm Representative

Responsible for development and maintenance of various tax department summaries as well as Federal and State tax files; drafted IRS Petitions and Protests; corporate, individual and partnership returns; tax straddles, incorporations, liquidations, mergers, and "S" corporation. Co-Editor of firm International Trade publication; responsible for drafting articles and overseeing production. Firm representative for paralegals. Created paralegal directory and conducted firm meetings.

EDUCATION: Adelphi Business College
Garden City, New York
Legal Course

PROFESSIONAL   CLE Courses relating to labor and management issues, tax
DEVELOPMENT   and corporation law.
Management seminars and conferences.

AFFILIATIONS: Member, The Philadelphia Bar Association
Membership/Bar Admission and Placement Committee

Member, The Legal Assistant Management Association

Member, The Philadelphia Association of Paralegals

LORI THOMPSON

**LEGAL
EXPERIENCE:**

July 1989   FEDERAL DEPOSIT INSURANCE CORPORATION
to Present   California and District of Columbia

FEDERAL DEPOSIT INSURANCE CORPORATION
Corporate Headquarters, Washington, D.C.
Paralegal Specialist - Closed Bank Litigation & Policy Section

FEDERAL DEPOSIT INSURANCE CORPORATION
National Bank of Washington Field Office, Washington, D.C.
Paralegal Specialist - Special Projects & Litigation

RESOLUTION TRUST CORPORATION
Coastal Consolidated Field Office, Costa Mesa, California
Paralegal Specialist - Litigation/Bankruptcy & Transactions

FDIC DIVISION OF FSLIC OPERATIONS
Western Region Office, Los Angeles, California
Document Control Coordinator/Paralegal

* Retrieve new cases and prepare case summaries for all cases affecting FDIC or RTC for distribution to all region and field offices (monthly).
* DOJ Task Force Project in re Federal Tort Claim Act cases.
* Monitor case referrals to the Department of Justice.
* Perform factual and legal research and prepared written memoranda concerning the determination for all administrative claims (over 1500).
* Review documents for exclusion of privileged documents.
* Prepared documentation for financial institution reorganizations and closings.
* Organized and prepared discovery requests.
* Coordinated document organization for subpoena and FOIA requests.
* Prepared corporate subsidiary dissolution manual for office and Western Region.
* Responsible for document control and organization for Western Region office.
* Supervised closing and consolidation of NBW field office into FDIC Consolidated Office.
* Supervised closing and consolidation of Los Angeles office.
* Alternative Dispute Resolution Coordinator for Washington Office.

LORI THOMPSON *(Continued)*

May 1988
to June 1989

FEDERAL SAVINGS AND LOAN INSURANCE CORPORATION (FSLIC) AS RECEIVER, Salt Lake City, Utah.
Paralegal Supervisor

* Supervised litigation and records retention department.
* Prepared responses to subpoenas, complaints, interrogatories, & discovery requests.
* Established policies for litigation and record retention.
* Supervised closing and consolidation of office into FSLIC Western Region Office.

Sept. 1986
to April 1988

SOS LEGAL STAFF, Salt Lake City, Utah.
LEBOEUF, LAMB, LEIBY AND MACRAE, Salt Lake City, Utah.
WATKISS AND CAMPBELL, Salt Lake City, Utah.
Fee Lance Paralegal

* Trained and supervised temporary personnel.
* Indexed documents for major litigations.
* Summarized and prepared written digests for dBase computer system.
* Organized documents for witness files and litigation.

Aug. 1984
to Aug. 1986

LEGAL AID SOCIETY OF SALT LAKE, Salt Lake City, Utah.
Paralegal Supervisor

* Supervised work flow in high volume law office specializing in domestic law.
* Arranged all service of process, drafted pleadings and interviewed clients.
* Established form and procedure manuals for office.
* Researched factual and legal matters.
* Promoted Legal Aid to community through presentations to local agencies.
* Interviewed, screened, trained and supervised paralegals and paralegal interns.
* Coordinated and developed internship program.

Jan. 1984
to Aug. 1984

ROE, FOWLER AND MOXLEY, Salt Lake City, Utah.
Paralegal Intern

* Established and implemented computerized Micro law Retrieval system.
* Generated written digest and summary for documents.

March 1982
to Aug. 1984

LITTLEFIELD AND PETERSON, 426 South 500 East, Salt Lake City, Utah.
Researcher - Guardian Ad Litem

* Assisted attorney in Juvenile Court with alleged child abuse and neglect cases.
* Ascertained client needs and prepared written recommendations.
* Compiled information and investigated allegations.

LORI THOMPSON *(Continued)*

EDUCATION:

George Washington University   Washington, D.C.
Legislative Specialist Certificate Program   **Estimated Completion:** Winter 1994

Westminister College of Salt Lake   Salt Lake City, Utah
Legal Assistant Training Program   **Graduated:** June 1984

University of Utah   Salt Lake City, Utah
Bachelor of Arts Degrees   **Graduated:** December 1981

Major: Political Science   Certificate: Political Administration
Second Major: Sociology   Certificate: Criminology

FDIC/RTC In House Training

* Criminal Restitution, Crime Control Act of 1990, FIRREA, *D'Oench Duhme* Application, Professional Liability Litigation, Government Privilege, FOIA, Right to Financial Privacy Act and Privacy Act, Environmental Issues, Corporate Subsidiary Dissolution, Real Estate Foreclosures. Specialized training in Alternative Dispute Resolution (ADR).

**PARALEGAL
ASSOCIATION
ACTIVITIES:**

National Capital Area Paralegal Association (NFPA Affiliate). First Vice President (1994 – Present); Chair, *Pro Bono Publico* Committee (1993–Present); Director (1992–Present); Chair, Government Network (1993).

DC Bar: Active paralegal volunteer in Pro Se Plus Uncontested Divorce Clinics.

Montgomery Bar Foundation: Active volunteer paralegal in monthly Walk-In Legal Clinics.

Legal Assistants Association of Utah. Served on Membership Committee (NALA Affiliate). Assisted with organizing Annual Meetings. Assisted with the organization of annual Seminar for Professional Paralegal Association.

Los Angeles Paralegal Association (NFPA Affiliate). Active member of Corporate Section. Attended monthly and annual seminars.

Orange County Paralegal Association (NFPA Affiliate). Attended monthly seminars as offered.

SKILLS:

WordPerfect 5.1, dBase III+, Lotus 1–2–3, R & R Report Writer, FDIC Case Management System (CMS), WESTLAW and LEXIS.

KATHLEEN ANN WEIR

RESUME

PROFESSIONAL EXPERIENCE:

MARKET ANALYST:
Pioneer Hi-Bred International, Inc.
International Seed Company.

- Research and analyze potential markets for food corn sales in the Western States and British Columbia.
- Develop reports and presentations identifying both the food corn suppliers and manufacturers currently using food corn in products manufactured and sold in this region.
- Present ongoing analyses of the potential for this company to successfully enter and compete in this regional marketplace from both marketing and cost perspectives.
- Make presentations to current consumers, manufacturers and producers of foods, to effectively evaluate the potential and projected market share for Pioneer products.

FIELD REPRESENTATIVE - REBOUND:
Seattle Building & Construction Trades Council

A non-profit labor organization established to investigate alleged violations of prevailing wage laws, and to collect unpaid wages for workers as allowed under the Washington State Public Works Act and the Freedom of Information Act.

- Developed and resolved wage claim cases for workers through personal interviews, job-site observations, and audits of certified payroll records and actual paystubs.
- Drafted and submitted proposed legislation to increase the enforcement effort of the Public Works Act by the State Department of Labor and Industries.
- Drafted proposed language for changes and revisions to the proposed Prevailing Wage rules (WAC), Apprenticeship Act, and Employment Standards wage claim procedures.
- Interfaced with leaders of Organized Labor both statewide and locally, as part of an ongoing communication effort.
- Worked with local Business Representatives toward the adoption of State Affirmative Action Goal for Apprentices.
- Wrote articles for TRADE-WINS, monthly Labor newsletter.
- Interfaced with U.S. Department of Labor to establish policies and procedures in conformance with federal laws.
- Conducted in-house staff training on working with State Government both politically and legislatively.

KATHLEEN ANN WEIR *(Continued)*

ADMINISTRATIVE ASSISTANT to the Assistant Director:
State of Washington Department of Labor and Industries Employment Standards, Apprenticeship and Crime Victims Compensation Division.

- Part of senior management team that produced the division's goals and objectives, policies and procedures and proposed legislation and rules.
- Coordinated and reviewed bill analyses and fiscal notes.
- Created and implemented division-wide automated tracking systems for legislation, suggested replies and program work flow for all four sections of the division.
- Developed and implemented workload indicators for senior management in the absence of a Programs Administrator. - Researched the feasibility of implementation of more stringent child labor laws for the department.
- Served on a multi-agency task force created to draft suggestions for the participating agencies to use as guidelines to combat increasing abuse of child labor laws.
- Interfaced with State Legislators and Department heads, serving as liaison for Assistant Director in this capacity.

STAFF WRITER:
Owens Project, McGeorge School of Law
Sacramento, California.

- Updated annual publication called *Owens Treatise on California Rules and Forms of Civil Procedure.*
- Drafted text on legislative impact of rules and served on team developing and writing new chapter on class actions.

LEGAL ASSISTANT/PARALEGAL:
Cruz Saavedra Law Offices
Long Beach, California.

- Principal assistant and paralegal in law firm specializing in tax laws, bankruptcy and immigration law.
- Interviewed clients, researched cases, drafted memoranda and correspondence, and verified case file cities.
- Coordinated forms and procedures for Federal District Court, State Superior Court and Court of Appeals filings.

EDUCATION;

University of the Pacific, McGeorge School of Law,
Sacramento, California, 1986

Bachelor of Arts - English/Education, Buena Vista College,
Storm Lake, Iowa, 1982

References Furnished Upon Request

JANIS L. WHISMAN

OBJECTIVE   To obtain a challenging position which will utilize my education and paralegal experience and which will provide me with opportunities to enhance my abilities.

MAJOR SKILLS

Communication
- Thorough collection of information using oral interviews and review of written records
- Effective interaction with clients and experts
- Competent preparation and analysis of documents

Computer Utilization
- Capable support of PC and Macintosh local area networks
- Proficient use of numerous word processing, database and graphics applications
- Practical organization of disk space

Leadership and Project Planning
- Diligent management of group projects
- Creative resolution of issues
- Practiced individual/small group trainer

Organization
- Efficient task prioritization and use of time
- Skillful coordination of details
- Adept administration of paperwork

EXPERIENCE

12/91 – Present   **Paralegal** for Western region of the Nature Conservancy. Coordinated all real estate transactions and assisted in documenting property management issues for 5.5 states in an 11-state region. Work involved extensive verbal and written communication with coworkers, attorneys, title companies and government agencies. Position required regular exercise of independent judgment within guidelines for paralegal conduct.

5/88 – 10/91   **Lead paralegal** for environmental plaintiffs in Exxon Valdez litigation. Developed complex trail litigation, including product liability, medical malpractice and other negligence cases. Prepared legal documents, maintained databases, and conducted interviews of new clients, including class representative plaintiffs in Globeville v. ASARCO litigation.

9/86 – 4/88   **Paralegal** responsible for development of all personal injury cases and personal bankruptcy filings. Drafted legal documents and maintained extensive contact with clients, attorneys, paralegals and court personnel.

10/85–9/86   **Paralegal** for four-attorney team at Kutak, Rock & Campbell. Coordinated document production, supervised three secretaries and managed statistics for a large volume of sale-leaseback transactions.

EDUCATION

6/93 – 7/93   **University of Colorado, Continuing Education** (Boulder, Colorado)
Passed Registered Appraiser and Standards & Ethics courses.

5/85 – 9/85   **Denver Paralegal Institute** (Denver, Colorado)
Certificate of Completion - September, 1985. Overall GPA: 96%.

9/81 – 9/85   **University of Colorado** (Boulder, Colorado)
Bachelor of Arts degree in Communication - May, 1985. Overall GPA: 3.57.

JANIS L. WHISMAN *(Continued)*

MAJOR ACCOMPLISHMENTS AND INTERESTS

Exchange student to Switzerland at age 16. High school valedictorian (1/246; 4.0 GPA). Boettcher Foundation full college scholarship recipient. Phi Beta Kappa scholar. Dean's List honoree. Consistent community volunteer. Active pursuit of softball, backpacking, bicycling, reading, sewing, singing and traveling.

REFERENCES   Available upon request.

SHELLEY G. WIDOFF

EDUCATION:

MSA, 1992, BOSTON UNIVERSITY
CERTIFICATE, 1972, THE PARALEGAL INSTITUTE, NYC
B.A., 1972, SKIDMORE COLLEGE, Saratoga Springs, NY
Major: Business Administration and Psychology

PROFESSIONAL AND CONSULTING EXPERIENCE:

PARALEGAL RESOURCE CENTER, INC.
President – Established full service paralegal firm in 1976, specializing in permanent and "Paralegal Temp"—temporary paralegal placement. The firm also provides consulting services to law firms and educational institutions as well as general paralegal services to members of the bar and legal service companies.   (1976 to present)

BOSTON UNIVERSITY, LEGAL ASSISTANT PROGRAMS
Founder/Director/Lecturer – Conceived and implemented in 1981, a Certificate Program which included new concepts in paralegal training to provide for a generalist core curriculum, a specialist continuing professional education component for practicing paralegals and a legal internship. Responsible for all aspects of program from recruiting paralegal/lawyer faculty, budgeting, marketing, research and development. In 1991, designed and implemented Bachelor of Science degree program in Paralegal Studies.   (1981 to present)

MINTZ, LEVIN, COHN, FERRIS, GLOVSKY & POPEO, P.C.
Paralegal Management Consultant – Developed in-house training programs geared toward effective utilization of paralegals. Steps included uncovering existing problems in lawyer/paralegal working relationship, assessing expectations, evaluating the paralegal staff, implementing a salary and reward package and systematizing the law practice in areas where paralegals were to function cost effectively.   (1981 to 1982)

NORTHEASTERN UNIVERSITY, THE PARALEGAL PROFESSION PROGRAM
Founder/Director/Educator – Responsible for the design and implementation of the paralegal/lawyer team teaching approach using an innovation generalist curriculum and workshops which emphasized the paralegal's role and function in the law office.   (1980 to 1981)

SINGER, STONEMAM & KURLAND
Legal Assistant – Pioneered paralegal position in small general practice law firm. Assisted lawyers in the delivery of legal services in the areas of corporate maintenance, real estate transactions and estate administration.   (1972 to 1976)

PUBICATIONS:

"On the Docket," column, *Legal Assistant Today*, Journal for the Paralegal Profession, 1984 to present).

"Trends in Paralegal Practice, Education and Placement," *Lawyers Weekly of Massachusetts*, (Spring, 1993).

Lincoln & Darrow Workbook for Paralegal Training, Co-author, (Paralegal Resource Center, 1981).

SHELLEY G. WIDOFF *(Continued)*

Lincoln & Darrow Teachers Manual for Paralegal Training, Co-author, (Paralegal Resource Center, 1982).

"Making the transition from legal secretary to legal assistant," *Lawyers Weekly of Massachusetts*, (Spring 1981).

PROFESSIONAL MEMBERSHIPS:

American Association for Paralegal Education (AAFPE)
    Director, former Secretary

Massachusetts Paralegal Association (MPA)
    Secondary Representative to NFPA,
    former Primary Representative, Vice President and Newsletter editor

Massachusetts Bar Association (MBA)
    Chairperson, Committee on Paralegals

National Federation of Paralegal Associations (NFPA)

National Public Records Research Association (NPRRA)

APPENDIX B

Job Titles

There are a great number of positions for which a paralegal may be qualified. An idea of what these positions are titled can help a prospective paralegal in his or her job search.

I. Paralegals often have job titles which focus on the type of law to be practiced. This type of job title is most typical in a law firm, but may be used by other employers. Representative titles are

Administrative law paralegal
Admiralty law paralegal
Antitrust paralegal
Banking paralegal
Bankruptcy paralegal
Civil rights paralegal
Collections paralegal
Communications paralegal
Consumer law paralegal
Contract law paralegal
Copyright law paralegal
Corporate paralegal
Corporate securities paralegal
Criminal law paralegal
Domestic relations law paralegal
Education law paralegal
Employee benefits paralegal
Employment law paralegal
Entertainment law paralegal
Environmental legal assistant
Estate planning paralegal
Family law paralegal
Hazardous waste litigation paralegal
Health care law paralegal
Immigration law paralegal
Insurance law paralegal
Intellectual property paralegal
International law paralegal
Labor law paralegal

Landlord–tenant law paralegal
Litigation paralegal
Military law paralegal
Municipal finance paralegal
Oil and gas law paralegal
Patent law paralegal
Personal injury paralegal
Probate paralegal
Protection paralegal
Real estate law paralegal
Tax law paralegal
Tort law paralegal
Trademark law paralegal
Tribal law paralegal
Trusts paralegal
Water law paralegal
Welfare law paralegal
Worker's compensation law paralegal

II.   The federal government employs hundreds of thousands of people in over seventy law-related positions. The titles for these positions are listed below. A paralegal interested in working for the federal government may want to consider these positions, especially because many of them require a paralegal background.

Alcohol, tobacco, and firearms inspector
Border patrol agent
Civil rights analyst
Civil service retirement claims examiner
Clerk of courts
Compliance inspector
Contract administrator–negotiator/specialist
Contract price/cost analyst
Contract representative
Contract termination specialist
Contractor/industrial relations specialist
Copyright examiner
Criminal investigator
Customs inspector
Customs patrol officer
Dependents and estates claims examiner
Employee relations specialist
Environmental protection specialist
Estate tax examiner
Equal employment manager

Equal opportunity assistant
Equal opportunity compliance specialist
Equal opportunity specialist
Foreign affairs analyst/officer
Foreign affairs service diplomatic security officer
Foreign law specialist
Game law enforcement officer
General claims examiner
Hearings and appeals officer
Immigration inspector
Import specialist
Industrial property clearance specialist
Industrial security specialist
Insurance examiner
Intelligence analyst
Internal revenue officer
International relations officer
Investigator
Labor management relations examiner
Labor relations specialist
Land law examiner
Legal clerk/technician
Legal instruments examiner
Legislative analyst
Loss and damage claims examiner
Mediation specialist
Mediator
Military personnel management specialist
Paralegal specialist
Passport and visa examiner
Patent advisor
Patent examiner
Personnel management specialist
Procurement analyst
Public utilities specialist
Railroad retirement claims examiner
Realty specialist
Reemployment rights compliance specialist
Securities compliance examiner
Security specialist/officer
Social insurance administrator
Social insurance claims examiner
Social service representative
Tax law specialist
Technical information specialist

Trade specialist
Transportation industry analyst
Unemployment compensation claims examiner
Unemployment insurance administrator
Veterans claims examiner
Wage and hour compliance specialist
Workers compensation claims examiner

III. Sometimes paralegals have jobs which require either paralegal skills or a paralegal background. These positions may or may not include the word "paralegal," and may or may not sound like they entail law-related work. Examples of these positions are

Administrative hearing representative
Administrative assistant
Administrator, corporate real estate
Associate paralegal
Case management coordinator
Case manager
Corporate secretary
Computer litigation support
Court analyst
Director of client relations
Director, career development center
Executive assistant
Financial data collection trainee
Foreclosure processor
Freelance paralegal
Human resources staff analyst/paralegal
Insurance adjustor
Law office administrator
Legal research aide
Legal research specialist
Legal services administrator
Legislative assistant
Lemon law specialist
Litigation manager
Loan facilitator
Loan secretary
Mediator
Minerals title clerk
Nurse paralegal
Paralegal coordinator or manager
Paralegal editor, author

Paralegal instructor
Paralegal placement counselor
Parole/probation supervisor
Pro bono coordinator
Project coordinator
Project manager
Real estate negotiator, manager
Recruitment coordinator
Regulatory specialist
Risk management specialist
Resource coordinator
Senior benefits coordinator
Senior legal administrator
Senior paralegal
Social services or welfare examiner
Title clerk

APPENDIX C

Professional Paralegal Organizations

The following is a list of professional paralegal associations by state. Organizations followed by a 1 are affiliated with the National Association of Legal Assistants, Inc. (NALA); those followed by a 2 are affiliated with the National Federation of Paralegal Associations, Inc. (NFPA).

Membership in NALA and NFPA continually grows, so there may be new organizations which are not listed. Also, some local organizations choose to remain independent and are not represented in the list below. The addresses and phone numbers of these organizations tend to change as their officers change, so addresses and phone numbers have not been included. If you desire to reach any of these organizations, call the main office of NALA or NFPA and ask for the organization's current phone number.

1. National Association of Legal Assistants, Inc.
   1601 S. Main Street, Suite 300
   Tulsa, Oklahoma 74119
   (918) 587-6828
2. National Federation of Paralegal Associations, Inc.
   P.O. Box 33108
   Kansas City, Missouri 64114
   (816) 941-4000

ALABAMA

Birmingham

Alabama Association of Legal Assistants (1)
Legal Assistant Society of Southern Institute (1)
Samford Paralegal Association (1)

Mobile

Mobile Association of Legal Assistants (2)

ALASKA

Anchorage

Alaska Association of Legal Assistants (2)

Fairbanks

Fairbanks Association of Legal Assistants (1)

ARIZONA

Flagstaff

Northern Arizona Paralegal Association (2)

Phoenix

Arizona Association of Professional Paralegals (2)
Arizona Paralegal Association (1)
Legal Assistants of Metropolitan Phoenix (1)

Tucson

Tucson Association of Legal Assistants (1)

ARKANSAS

Little Rock

Arkansas Association of Legal Assistants (1)

CALIFORNIA

Los Angeles

Los Angeles Paralegal Association (2)

Sacramento

Sacramento Association of Legal Assistants (2)

Santa Barbara

Legal Assistants Association of Santa Barbara (1)

San Diego

San Diego Association of Legal Assistants (2)

San Francisco

San Francisco Association of Legal Assistants (2)

San Jose

Paralegal Association of Santa Clara County (1)

Ventura

Ventura County Association of Legal Assistants (1)

COLORADO

Colorado Springs

Association of Legal Assistants of Colorado (1)

Denver

Rocky Mountain Legal Assistants Association (2)

CONNECTICUT

Bridgeport

Connecticut Association of Paralegals, Inc.
(Fairfield County) (2)

Hartford

Central Connecticut Association of Legal Assistants (2)

New Haven

Connecticut Association of Paralegals (New Haven) (2)

DELAWARE

Wilmington

Delaware Paralegal Association (2)

DISTRICT OF COLUMBIA

Washington, D.C.

National Capital Area Paralegal Association (2)

FLORIDA

Gainesville

Gainesville Association of Legal Assistants (1)

Jacksonville

Jacksonville Legal Assistants (1)

Miami

Dade Association of Legal Assistants (1)

Orlando

Orlando Legal Assistants (1)

Ormond Beach

Volusia Association of Legal Assistants (1)

Palm Beach

Plaintiff Paralegal Association (Palm Beach) (2)

Pensacola

Pensacola Legal Assistants (1)

St. Petersburg

Florida Legal Assistants, Inc. (1)

Tampa

Bay Area Legal Academy Student Association (1)

GEORGIA

Alma

Georgia Legal Assistants (1)

Atlanta

Georgia Association of Legal Assistants (2)
Professional Paralegals of Georgia (1)

Lake Park

South Georgia Association of Legal Assistants (1)

Savannah

Southeastern Association of Legal Assistants of Georgia (1)

HAWAII

Honolulu

Hawaii Association of Legal Assistants (2)

IDAHO

Ketchum

Gem State Association of Legal Assistants (1)

ILLINOIS

Bartlett

Illinois Paralegal Association (2)

Bloomington

Central Illinois Paralegal Association (1)

Peoria

Heart of Illinois Paralegal Association (1)

INDIANA

Indianapolis

Indiana Paralegal Association (2)

South Bend

Michiana Paralegal Association (2)

Terre Haute

Indiana Legal Assistants (1)

KANSAS

Topeka

Kansas Legal Assistants Society (2)

Wichita

Kansas Association of Legal Assistants (1)

KENTUCKY

Lexington

Lexington Paralegal Association, Inc. (2)

Louisville

Louisville Association of Paralegals (2)

Paducah

Western Kentucky Paralegals (1)

LOUSIANA

Alexandria

Louisiana State Paralegal Association (1)

New Orleans

New Orleans Paralegal Association (2)

Shreveport

Northwest Louisiana Paralegal Association (1)

MAINE

Portland

Maine State Association of Legal Assistants (1)

MANITOBA

Winnipeg

Manitoba Association of Legal Assistants, Inc. (2)

MARYLAND

Baltimore

Baltimore Association of Legal Assistants (2)

MASSACHUSETTS

Boston

Massachusetts Paralegal Association (2)

Springfield

Western Massachusetts Paralegal Association (2)

Worcester

Central Massachusetts Paralegal Association (2)

MICHIGAN

Kalamazoo

Legal Assistants Association of Michigan (1)

MINNESOTA

Minneapolis

Minnesota Association of Legal Assistants (2)

Rochester

Minnesota Paralegal Association (1)

MISSISSIPPI

Hattiesburg

Society for Paralegal Studies (1)

Jackson

Mississippi College Society of Legal Assistants (1)

Madison

Mississippi Association of Legal Assistants (1)

MISSOURI

Kansas City

Kansas City Association of Legal Assistants (2)

St. Joseph

Northwest Missouri Paralegal Association (2)

St. Louis

Gateway Paralegal Association (2)
St. Louis Association of Legal Assistants (1)

MONTANA

Missoula

Montana Association of Legal Assistants (1)

NEBRASKA

Lincoln

Nebraska Association of Legal Assistants (1)

NEVADA

Las Vegas

Clark County Organization of Legal Assistants, Inc. (1)

Reno

Sierra Nevada Association of Paralegals (1)

NEW HAMPSHIRE

Manchester

Paralegal Association of New Hampshire (1)

NEW JERSEY

Clark

The Legal Assistants Association of New Jersey, Inc. (1)

Edison

The Greater Jersey Paralegal Association, Inc. (2)

Haddonfield

South Jersey Paralegal Association (2)

NEW MEXICO

Albuquerque

Legal Assistants of New Mexico (2)

NEW YORK

Binghamton

Southern Tier Association of Paralegals (2)

Buffalo

Western New York Paralegal Association, Inc. (2)

Jerisho

Long Island Paralegal Association (2)

New York

Manhattan Paralegal Association, Inc. (2)

Rochester

Paralegal Association of Rochester, Inc. (2)

White Plains

West/Rock Paralegal Association (2)

NORTH CAROLINA

Jacksonville

Coastal Carolina Paralegal Club (1)

Pineville

North Carolina Paralegal Association, Inc. (1)

NORTH DAKOTA

Minot
Western Dakota Association of Legal Assistants (1)

Moorehead
Red River Valley Legal Assistants (1)

OHIO

Akron
Northeastern Ohio Paralegal Association (2)

Cincinnati
Cincinnati Paralegal Association (2)

Cleveland
Cleveland Association of Paralegals (2)

Columbus
Legal Assistants of Central Ohio (2)

Dayton
Greater Dayton Paralegal Association (2)

Maumee
Toledo Association of Legal Assistants (1)

OKLAHOMA

Claremore
Student Association of Legal Assistants,
Rogers State College (1)

Midwest City
Rose State Paralegal Association (1)

Ponca City

Oklahoma Paralegal Association (1)

Tulsa

TJC Student Association of Legal Assistants (1)
Tulsa Association of Legal Assistants (1)

OREGON

Bend

Pacific Northwest Legal Assistants (1)

Portland

Oregon Legal Assistants Association (2)

PENNSYLVANIA

Erie

Erie County Paralegal Association (2)

Harrisburg

Central Pennsylvania Paralegal Association (2)
Keystone Legal Assistant Association (1)

Philadelphia

Philadelphia Association of Paralegals (2)

Pittsburgh

Pittsburgh Paralegal Association (2)

RHODE ISLAND

Providence

Rhode Island Paralegal Association (2)

SOUTH CAROLINA

Charleston

Tri-County Paralegal Association (1)

Columbia

Columbia Paralegal Association (2)

Greenville

Greenville Association of Legal Assistants (1)

Sumter

Central Carolina Technical College Paralegal Association (1)

SOUTH DAKOTA

Sioux Falls

South Dakota Legal Assistants Association, Inc. (1)

TENNESSEE

Chattanooga

Tennessee Paralegal Association (1)

Memphis

Greater Memphis Legal Assistants, Inc. (1)
Memphis Paralegal Association (2)

TEXAS

Abilene

West Central Texas Association of Legal Assistants (2)

Amarillo

Texas Panhandle Association of Legal Assistants (1)

Austin

Capital Area Paralegal Association (1)

Beaumont

Southeast Texas Association of Legal Assistants (1)

Corpus Christi

Nueces County Association of Legal Assistants (1)

Dallas

Dallas Association of Legal Assistants (2)

El Paso

El Paso Association of Legal Assistants (1)

Longview

Northeast Texas Association of Legal Assistants (1)

Lubbock

West Texas Association of Legal Assistants (1)

Midland

Legal Assistants Association/Permian Basin (1)

Texarkana

Texarkana Association of Legal Assistants (1)

Tyler

Tyler Area Association of Legal Assistants (1)

Wichita Falls

Wichita County Student Association (1)

UTAH

Salt Lake City

Legal Assistants Association of Utah (1)

VIRGINIA

Newport News

Peninsula Legal Assistants, Inc. (1)

Richmond

Richmond Association of Legal Assistants (1)

Roanoke

Roanoke Valley Paralegal Association (2)

Poquoson

Tidewater Association of Legal Assistants (1)

VIRGIN ISLANDS

St. Thomas

Virgin Islands Paralegals (1)

WASHINGTON

Ardenvoir

Washington State Paralegal Association (2)

Kennewick

Columbia Basin College Paralegal Association (1)

Spokane

Association of Paralegals and Legal Assistants of Washington State (1)

WEST VIRGINIA

Charleston

Legal Assistants of West Virginia, Inc. (1)

WISCONSIN

Madison

Madison Area Legal Assistants Association (1)

Milwaukee

Paralegal Association of Wisconsin, Inc. (2)

WYOMING

Casper

Legal Assistants of Wyoming (1)

GLOSSARY

AAS degree Abbreviation for Associates of Applied Science degree. Typically conferred by junior colleges and community colleges.

ABA-approved school A paralegal program which has met certain standards established by the American Bar Association.

administrative agency A board, commission, bureau, office, or department of the executive branch of government which implements a law originating with the legislative branch.

affidavits Any voluntary statement reduced to writing and sworn to or affirmed before a person legally authorized to administer an oath or affirmation.

affirmative action A term applied to the obligation to remedy discrimination based on sex, race, color, creed, or age with respect to, for example, employment, union membership, or college admission.

American Arbitration Association (AAA) A nonprofit organization that provides arbitrators for the arbitration of disputes.

American Association for Paralegal Educators (AAfPE) A national organization of paralegal teachers and educational institutions, which provides technical assistance and supports research in the paralegal field, promotes standards for paralegal instruction, and cooperates with the American Bar Association and other organizations in developing an approval process for paralegal education.

American Bar Association (ABA) The country's largest voluntary professional association of attorneys, commonly referred to as the ABA. Its purposes include enhancing professionalism and advancing the administration of justice.

Americans with Disabilities Act (ADA) A federal statute that prohibits discrimination against disabled persons in employment, public services, and places of public accommodation.

annual report A report issued yearly by a corporation informing stockholders, the government, and the public, in some detail, of the corporation's operations, particularly its fiscal operations, during the year. The contents of an annual report, as well as the report itself, are required by law.

Antitrust   Refers to statutes that prohibit monopolies in the production or sale of goods or services which interfere with trade or fair competition.

arbitration   A method of settling disputes by submitting a disagreement to a person (an arbitrator) for decision instead of going to court.

articles of incorporation   The charter or basic rules that create a corporation and by which it functions. Among other things, it states the purposes for which the corporation is being organized, the amount of authorized capital stock, and the names and addresses of its director and incorporators.

autonomous   Independent or self-contained.

bankruptcy   The system under which a debtor may come into court or be brought into court by his or her creditors, either seeking to have his or her assets administered and sold for the benefit of the creditors and to be discharged from those debts, or to have the debts reorganized.

bar association   A voluntary organization of members of the bar of a state or county, or the bar of every state, whose primary function is promoting professionalism and enhancing the administration of justice.

Bates stamping   Also known as Bates numbering. A system for placing a number on a document by using a manually operated machine.

billing   The system by which law firms track the amount of time spent working on each client's matters, and any expenses paid out for the client, so that the client may then be billed for that time and those expenses.

breach of warranty   The violation of an express warranty or implied warranty.

BS/BA degree   Abbreviation for *Bachelor's degree*. The lowest degree conferred by a college or university.

by-laws   Rules and regulations created by corporations, associations, clubs, and societies for their governance.

CEO   Abbreviation for *chief executive officer*. The officer of a corporation or other organization who has the most responsibility for managing its affairs.

certificate of good standing   Also known as a certificate of existence. A certificate issued by the Secretary of State, in most states, which proves the incorporation and good standing of a specific corporation in that state.

civil litigation   The process of resolving private disputes through the court system.

civil procedure   The area of law that regulates the method of resolving civil disputes in the courts.

CLE   Abbreviation for *continuing legal education.*

complaint   The initial pleading in a civil action, in which the plaintiff alleges a cause of action and asks that the wrong done him or her be remedied.

computer database   A collection of related items of data kept on and accessed through a computer.

computerized litigation support   Computer software which can organize, store, retrieve, and summarize information acquired during the course of litigation.

Conclave   An assembly of six national paralegal and law-related organizations: the American Association for Paralegal Educators (AAfPE), the American Bar Association (ABA), the Association of Legal Administrators (ALA), the Legal Assistant Management Association (LAMA), the National Association of Legal Assistants (NALA), and the National Federation of Paralegal Associations (NFPA).

continuing education   See **CLE.**

copyright   The right of an author, granted by federal statute, to exclusively control the reproduction, distribution, and sale of his or her literary, artistic, or intellectual productions for the period of the copyright's existence.

corporate attorney   An attorney, employed by a corporation or business, who represents only the corporation or business.

corporate minute books   Books in which the proceedings of meetings of a corporation's stockholders or directors are recorded.

deed   A document by which real property, or an interest in real property, is conveyed from one person to another.

deed of trust   A deed that creates a trust in real estate, executed by a disinterested third party as trustee, and that is given as security for a debt.

deposition   The transcript of a witness's testimony given under oath outside of the courtroom, usually in advance of the trial or hearing, upon oral examination or in response to written interrogatories.

desktop publishing   A type of computer application that automatically produces page layout and design. Used to produce advertising, magazines, etc.

discovery   A means of providing each party, prior to trial, with access to facts that are within the knowledge of the other side, to enable the party to better try his or her case.

drafting   The process of creating a preliminary version of a document or plan.

easement   A right to use the land of another for a specific purpose.

EEOC   Abbreviation for *Equal Employment Opportunity Commission*. A federal agency whose purpose is to prevent and remedy discrimination based on race, color, religion, national origin, age, or sex with respect to most aspects of employment, including hiring, firing, promotion, and wages.

entrepreneur   A person who starts his or her own business, organizing, operating, and assuming the risk for the business venture.

escrow   A written instrument, money, or other property deposited by the grantor with a third party until the performance of a condition or the happening of a certain event, upon the occurrence of which the property is to be delivered to the grantee.

estate   The property left by a decedent.

expert   A person who has special skill or knowledge in a given field.

express warranty   A warranty created by the seller in a contract for sale of goods, in which the seller, orally or in writing, makes representations regarding the quality or condition of the goods.

FCC   Abbreviation for *Federal Communications Commission*. The federal regulatory agency for radio and television, telegraph, telephone, cable television, and satellite communication.

flood certificates   Certificates which provide proof of insurance, which protects the insured against loss of or damage to property caused by flood.

freelance   A person who sells his or her services to employers without a long-term commitment to any one of them.

freelance paralegal   A self-employed paralegal who contracts his or her services to attorneys.

full-time employee (FTE)   An employee who is fully employed (customarily 40 hours per week) on a regular basis.

garnishment   A proceeding by a creditor to obtain satisfaction of a debt from money or property of the debtor which is in the possession of a third person or is owed by such person to the debtor.

HMO   Abbreviation for *health maintenance organization*. A network of healthcare providers who provide medical services under a group insurance plan which requires that an insured be treated only by providers within the HMO.

home-rule, charter-based government   The right of a city, town, or county to self-government with respect to purely local matters. A state's constitution may or may not confer such a right upon its cities or towns.

implied warranty   In the sale of personal property, a warranty by the seller, inferred by law, as to the quality or condition of the goods sold.

infringement   A violation of a right or privilege.

in-house billing   The system by which legal departments within companies or other organizations track the amount of time spent on specific matters, and any expenses paid out, for time and cost management purposes.

instrument   Any formal legal document evidencing an agreement or the granting of a right.

INTA   Abbreviation for *International Trademark Association*.

intellectual property   Property (e.g., copyrights, patents, trade secrets) that is the physical or tangible result of original thought.

Lawyer's WillWriter   A computer software program that automatically produces wills.

lease   A contract for the possession of real estate in consideration of payment of rent, ordinarily for a term of years or months.

legal assistant   A term used interchangeably with *paralegal*.

legal department   The department in a corporation, business, school, or some other entity which employs attorneys, paralegals, and staff and which provides legal representation of the entity.

legal ethics   The code of conduct which governs the moral and professional duties of attorneys toward each other, their clients, and the courts.

legal issue   A question arising in a case with respect to the law to be applied or the meaning of the law.

lemon law   A state statute providing that a purchaser of a new car may return it within a specified period of time and be entitled to receive a refund or a comparable replacement if the car is substantially defective and if reasonable efforts to repair it have failed.

LEXIS   A computerized system for legal research. Its database includes almost all reported cases from state and federal courts, all federal statutes, the statutes of many states, federal regulations, and law review articles.

lien   A claim or charge on, or right against, personal property, or an encumbrance on real property, for the payment of a debt.

limited licensure   A proposed system under which paralegals could obtain a license to provide services directly to the public in a limited area of law.

litigation   A legal action; a lawsuit.

litigator   An attorney who practices in the area of litigation.

Lotus 1-2-3   A computer software program for spreadsheets.

malpractice   The failure of a professional person to act with reasonable care; misconduct by a professional person in the course of engaging in his or her profession.

materialmen's lien   A lien provided by law, often under a mechanic's lien statute, for the protection of a person who supplies materials for use in the construction of a building or other improvement.

mediator   An impartial person trained to assist parties in resolving their disputes amicably.

merger   The combining of one of anything with another or others.

minutes   The record of the business transacted at a meeting of the stockholders or directors of a corporation, or a record of the proceedings of any group.

National Association of Legal Assistants (NALA)   A national organization of legal assistants and paralegals whose purpose is to enhance professionalism and the interests of those in the profession, as well as to advance the administration of justice.

National Federation of Paralegal Associations (NFPA)   An organization of paralegal and legal assistant organizations nationwide whose purpose is to enhance professionalism and the interests of those in the profession, as well as to advance the administration of justice.

National Labor Relations Board (NLRB)   A federal administrative agency created by the National Labor Relations Act for the purpose of enforcing the act.

network   To informally share information and services with individuals and groups who have a common interest, so as to advance one's career.

non-profit   Not done for profit.

non-profit organization   An association, corporation or organization organized for purposes other than making a profit, usually educational, fraternal, or charitable.

non-traditional career   A career in which the person is employed outside of the traditional places of employment—for example, a paralegal employed outside a law firm.

OJT Abbreviation for *on-the-job training*. Training or experience learned or gained while working at a job, under supervision.

Pagemaker A desktop publishing computer software program.

paralegal A person who, although not an attorney, performs many of the functions of an attorney under an attorney's supervision.

paralegal certificate A certificate awarded by a school upon the completion of a paralegal education program.

paralegal placement company A company whose business is finding and placing paralegals in full-time or part-time positions in law firms, corporations, etc.

placement department The department of a school which finds and places graduates in jobs.

plaintiff A person who brings a lawsuit.

pleadings Formal statements by parties to an action setting forth their claims or defenses.

power of attorney A written instrument by which a person appoints another as his or her agent or attorney in fact and confers upon him or her the authority to perform certain acts.

probate The legal process wherein the estate of a decedent is administered, including collecting assets, liquidating liabilities, paying taxes, and distributing the estate.

pro bono Work that is done free of charge for the public good.

process The means of compelling a defendant to appear in court in a civil case.

product liability The liability of a manufacturer or seller of an article for an injury suffered by a person or property caused by a defect in the article sold.

professional liability insurance Another term for *malpractice insurance*. A type of liability insurance that protects professional persons from liability for negligence and other forms of malpractice.

profit sharing An arrangement or plan under which the employees participate in the profits of the company that employs them.

proprietary schools A school which is owned by a private individual or corporation and which makes a profit for its owner(s).

registry of deeds A list, book, or office for the registration or recording of deeds and other documents as required by law.

regulatory agency An administrative agency empowered to promulgate and enforce regulations.

respondent The party against whom an appeal is taken to a higher court; that is, the successful party in the lower court.

SBA Abbreviation for *Small Business Administration*. A federal agency whose purpose is to make loans to small businesses to provide them with working capital and to help them finance construction and the purchase of equipment.

scheduling The practice of listing all times and dates when certain events will occur or deadlines must be met.

SEC Abbreviation for *Securities and Exchange Commission*. The agency that administers and enforces federal statutes relating to securities.

Secretary of State In many states, a public official whose duties include supervising and certifying the results of elections, monitoring compliance by corporations with certain legal requirements imposed upon them by the state, and accepting the filing of financial statements that give notice of the existence of a security interest.

service mark A mark, design, title, or motto used in the sale or advertising of services to identify the services and distinguish them from the services of others. A service mark is the property of its owner and, when registered under the Trademark Act, is reserved for the exclusive use of its owner.

settlement agreement The agreement by which a lawsuit is ended outside of court.

sole proprietorship Sole ownership, as opposed to ownership by more than one person, ownership by a corporation, or ownership by a partnership.

specialty programs Paralegal programs in schools which focus on a specialized area of law, such as estate planning and probate.

statutes Laws enacted by a legislature.

subpoena A command in the form of written process requiring a witness to come to court to testify.

summons In a civil case, the process by which an action is commenced and the defendant is brought within the jurisdiction of the court.

SuperCalc A computer software program for spreadsheets.

tax levies Government-imposed and -collected taxes.

Timeslips A computer software program that automatically does timekeeping and billing.

torts   Wrongs involving a breach of duty and resulting in an injury to the person or property of another. A tort is distinguished from a breach of contract in that a tort is a violation of duty established by law, whereas a breach of contract results from a failure to meet an obligation created by the agreement of the parties.

trademark   A mark, design, title, logo, or motto used in the sale or advertising of a product to identify that product and distinguish it from the products of others. A trademark is the property of its owner and, when registered under the Trademark Act, is reserved for the exclusive use of its owner.

trial   A hearing or determination by a court of the issues existing between the parties to an action.

trial notebook   A notebook used during trial of case containing everything needed to prosecute or defend a case.

tuition refund program   A benefit of employment whereby an employer reimburses an employee for all or a portion of the costs of the employee's school tuition.

venue   The county or judicial district in which a case is to be tried. In civil cases, venue may be based on where the events giving rise to the cause of action took place or where the parties live or work.

Verdict   A computer software program used for timekeeping and billing.

wage garnishment   A proceeding by a creditor to obtain satisfaction of a debt by having all or part of the debtor's wages paid directly to the creditor by the debtor's employer.

water rights   An easement for the use of water or for the right to use another's premises to transport water over or through.

WESTLAW   A computerized system for legal research.

will   An instrument by which a person makes a disposition of his or her property, to take effect after his or her death.

zoning   The creation and application of structure, size, and use restrictions imposed upon the owners of real estate within districts or zones in accordance with zoning regulations or ordinances.

ZyINDEX   A computer software program for litigation support.

INDEX

EMPLOYMENT AGENCIES

Consult your local telephone directory. List here the agencies,
addresses, and telephone numbers. Contact for specialization
(Do they place paralegals?) and fees (Who pays? If you, how
much?). Do not forget temporary agencies.

PARALEGAL & BAR ASSOCIATIONS

Consult your local telephone directory, NALA/NFPA, and the ABA. List key information here. Obtain membership information (how to become one and the number of members) and a list of officers (with employment affiliations).

CORPORATIONS & BUSINESSES

Consult your local telephone directory or local business newspaper. Which would you enjoy working for as a paralegal? List here the names, addresses, and telephone numbers. Obtain information on positions and key decision-makers.

GOVERNMENT OFFICES

Consult your local telephone directory for local, state, and federal government offices. List here the ones you would enjoy working for as a paralegal. Contact for hiring potential and key decision-makers.

NONPROFIT ORGANIZATIONS

Consult your local telephone directory. Do not forget hospitals, libraries, unions, political associations, religious institutions, schools, clubs, etc. List here the names, addresses, and telephone numbers. Obtain information on hiring opportunities and key decision-makers.

LAW FIRMS

Consult your local telephone directory. Generally law firms and attorneys are classified by specialization. Choose those that are of interest to you. List here their names, addresses, and telephone numbers. Contact for hiring potential and key decision-makers.

NETWORKING

List here the names of everyone who may be able to provide you with employment leads. Include family, friends, association/club members, coworkers, local elected officials, neighbors, clergy, instructors (past and present), professional acquaintances (doctor, dentist, plumber, car mechanic). Contact all for leads. Ask each for additional leads, and so on.

(RESUME)

Draft here your resume as you see yourself today. Include employment objectives, background, skills, and accomplish-ments.

GOALS

Draft here a set of goals (five easy, five moderate, five difficult) you would like to attain for yourself in five years. Include a plan on how to achieve them.

INTERVIEW RESEARCH

Before going to a job interview, it is advisable to learn as much as possible about the potential employer and position. List here all the key issues you would want to know about every employer. Include number of employees, number of paralegals, and history and focus of the employer.

(INTERVIEWING)

List here your five greatest strengths and weaknesses and explain. List 10-15 very specific skills you can bring to an employer (i.e., provide them with reasons why they should hire you). Build in the information you have researched about the employer when listing these skills.